CW01018264

WOMEN'S WRITING AND THE CIRCULATION OF IDEAS

Until recently it was widely believed that women in Renaissance and early modern England either did not write, or did not publish their work. It is now becoming clear that instead of using the emerging technology of print, many women writers circulated their works by hand, with friends copying and recopying poems, plays, and novels from each other or with the help of professional scribes. Through manuscript publication, women's writing reached wide audiences and was collected and admired by both men and women. *Women's Writing and the Circulation of Ideas* contributes to the discovery and reevaluation of women writers by examining the writing and manuscript publication of key authors from 1550 to 1800. The collection's analysis of the range and meaning of women's writing and its circulation during the rise of the modern print industry alters our understanding of the history of the book and early modern British literature alike.

GEORGE L. JUSTICE is Assistant Professor of English at Marquette University, specializing in eighteenth-century British literature. He is the author of *The Manufacturers of Literature: Writing and the Literary Marketplace in Eighteenth-Century England* (2001). He has published reviews and articles in *Persuasions*, *The Age of Johnson*, *Eighteenth-Century Fiction*, *The Scriblerian*, and *The Year's Work in English Studies*.

NATHAN TINKER is completing his dissertation on Katherine Philips and seventeenth-century scribal culture, at Fordham University, New York; he has published on Philips and the print history of her work in *English Language Notes*.

WOMEN'S WRITING AND THE CIRCULATION OF IDEAS

Manuscript Publication in England, 1550–1800

EDITED BY

GEORGE L. JUSTICE AND NATHAN TINKER

CAMBRIDGE
UNIVERSITY PRESS

PUBLISHED BY THE PRESS SYNDICATE OF THE UNIVERSITY OF CAMBRIDGE
The Pitt Building, Trumpington Street, Cambridge, United Kingdom

CAMBRIDGE UNIVERSITY PRESS
The Edinburgh Building, Cambridge CB2 2RU, UK
40 West 20th Street, New York, NY 10011-4211, USA
477 Williamstown Road, Port Melbourne, VIC 3207, Australia
Ruiz de Alarcón 13, 28014 Madrid, Spain
Dock House, The Waterfront, Cape Town 8001, South Africa

http://www.cambridge.org

First published 2002

Printed in the United Kingdom at the University Press, Cambridge

Typeface Baskerville Monotype 11/12.5 pt.   *System* LaTeX 2ε [TB]

A catalogue record for this book is available from the British Library

Library of Congress Cataloging in Publication data
Women's writing and the circulation of ideas: manuscript publication in England,
1550–1880/edited by George Justice and Nathan Tinker.
p.   cm.
Includes bibliographical references and index.
ISBN 0 521 80856 1
1. English literature–Women authors–History and criticism.   2. Literature
publishing–England–History.   3. Women and literature–England–History.   4. Authors and
readers–England–History.   5. Books and reading–England–History.
6. Manuscripts–England–History.   7. Authorship–Sex differences.   8. Transmission of texts.
I. Justice, George.   II. Tinker, Nathan.
PR111 .W653   2002
820.9′9287′0903–dc21
2001037827

ISBN 0 521 80856 1 hardback

Contents

Illustrations

Contributors

VICTORIA BURKE is Assistant Professor of English at Ottawa University. She is the coeditor of *The Centuries of Julia Palmer: Devotional Poetry 1671 – 1673* and the author of articles on women and seventeenth-century manuscript culture, Ann Bowyer's commonplace book, Elizabeth Richardson's mother's advice writing, and the compilation of religious manuscripts.

MICHAEL G. BRENNAN is a Reader in Renaissance Studies at the University of Leeds. His publications on the Sidneys and Lady Mary Wroth include *Literary Patronage in the English Renaissance: the Pembroke Family*; the first complete edition of Lady Mary Wroth's *Loves' Victory: the Penshurst Manuscript*; and *The Collected Works of Mary Sidney Herbert, Countess of Pembroke* with Margaret P. Hannay and Noel J. Kinnamon, 2 vols.

LEIGH EICKE is Assistant Professor of English at Grand Valley State University. She earned her Ph.D. from the University of Maryland, writing her dissertation on women and Jacobitism in British literary culture.

MARGARET J. M. EZELL is the John Paul Abbott Professor of Liberal Arts at Texas A&M University. She is the author of *The Patriarch's Wife: Literary Evidence and the History of the Family*, *Writing Women's Literary History*, and *Social Authorship and the Advent of Print*. She is currently working on Volume V of the forthcoming Oxford English Literary History series.

ISOBEL GRUNDY is Henry Marshall Tory Professor in the Department of English at the University of Alberta. She holds a D.Phil. from Oxford University, where she was a member of St. Anne's College. She taught at Queen Mary College (now Queen Mary and Westfield College), London University, from 1971 to 1990. She is author of *Samuel Johnson and the Scale of Greatness*, *Lady Mary Wortley Montagu, Comet of the*

Enlightenment, and *The Feminist Companion to Literature in English: Women Writers from the Middle Ages to the Present* with Virginia Blain and Patricia Clements. She is a coinvestigator on the Orlando Project, which is producing, in the form of an electronic textbase and printed volumes, the history of Women's writing in the British Isles. She is a Fellow of the Royal Society of Canada.

MARGARET P. HANNAY, Professor of English Literature at Siena College, has edited *The Collected Works of Mary Sidney Herbert, Countess of Pembroke* with Noel J. Kinnamon and Michael G. Brennan. She is the author of *Philip's Phoenix: Mary Sidney, Countess of Pembroke* and editor of *Silent but for the Word: Tudor Women as Patrons, Translators and Writers of Religious Works.* She has also edited, with Susanne Woods, *Teaching Tudor and Stuart Women Writers* and is currently working on a modernized edition of *Antonius and Selected Works of Mary Sidney Herbert, Countess of Pembroke* with Noel J. Kinnamon and Michael G. Brennan.

GEORGE JUSTICE is Assistant Professor of English at Marquette University. He holds degrees from Wesleyan University and the University of Pennsylvania and is the author of *The Manufacturers of Literature: Writing and the Literary Marketplace in Eighteenth-Century England.*

KATHRYN KING, Professor of English at Montevallo University, is the author of *Jane Barker, Exile: A Literary Career, 1675–1725* and numerous articles on eighteenth-century women authors.

NOEL KINNAMON, Professor of English, Mars Hill College, North Carolina has written articles on manuscript studies in *English Manuscript Studies, Notes and Queries, Sidney Journal, English Literary Renaissance,* and other journals. He is the coeditor with Margaret Hannay and Michael Brennan of *The Collected Works of Mary Sidney Herbert, Countess of Pembroke.* He is currently working on an edition of the letters of Robert Sidney, Earl of Leicester, with Margaret Hannay and Michael Brennan.

DEBRA RIENSTRA, Assistant Professor of English at Calvin College, is the author, most recently, of an essay in *Discovering and (Re)Covering the Seventeenth Century Religious Lyric,* edited by Eugene R. Cunnar and Jeffrey Johnson. She received her Ph.D. in English Literature from Rutgers University.

Acknowledgments

The editors wish to thank Margaret Ezell, who was instrumental in the conception and the compilation of this volume. John Pollack of Special Collections at the University of Pennsylvania libraries went above and beyond the call of duty in helping us obtain the cover image. We would also like to thank Linda Bree and Rachel de Wachter of Cambridge University Press for encouraging the project and shepherding it through to publication. Lesley Atkin, the Press's copyeditor, did heroic work; any remaining errors are our sole responsibility. And thank you to Joseph Black, editor of the *Sidney Journal*, for permission to reprint essays by Margaret Hannay, Debra Rienstra and Noel Kinnamon and Michael G. Brennan.

CHAPTER I

Introduction

George Justice

Recent scholarly interest in manuscript publication in England has taken place against a backdrop of the computer revolution. Pen, ink, and paper would seem to be far removed from a world in which information technology has digitized most forms of symbolic communication. The text is no longer a material object, made by people in ways that can be seen and described by its creators. This new interest in the old – perhaps anachronistic – form of publication in our current state of flux is not merely coincidental. Looking back at the period 1550–1800 seems more like peering in a looking glass rather than examining a fossil through a microscope – optical or otherwise. Just as we are now extremely self-conscious about the forms of publication and its channels of distribution, writers in Renaissance and eighteenth-century England faced unavoidable social and technological choices in the production and dissemination of their works. Margaret J. M. Ezell (one of the contributors to this volume) has been one of the most far-reaching scholars of manuscript cultures in the seventeenth and eighteenth centuries. Ezell has pushed other scholars to reconsider not only what we see in our research – the object of study – but the ways in which we look. Her work fulfills the promise of the endeavor to make the theory and practice of literary scholarship feed each other. Her most recent book, *Social Authorship and the Advent of Print*, consists of six chapters dedicated to a rigorous historical analysis of authorship, challenging the widely held belief – now almost a truism – that an expansion of printing in seventeenth-century England led directly to the association of the category "literature" with the mechanisms of print production and distribution. Each chapter comes at the history of authorship from a different direction; taken together, they argue for a broader conception of the practice of authorship, including various modes of collaborative writing and methods of publication that operate outside of the publishing industry centered in London.

In her Postscript, Ezell asks,

> What can we learn from early culture of authorship that is relevant to our current situation? Are we returning to the early modern model of manuscript text and social authorship, or are we positioned to invent yet another story to add to this tale?[1]

My answer to Ezell's question, informed by the work of the scholars included in this volume and by an analysis of contemporary information technologies, is "both." Clearly, we are not returning to manuscript circulation if by the word "manuscript" we mean the material product of a hand applying ink, or another marking substance, to paper or other writing surfaces. But, as the first part of Ezell's question implies, there are aspects of the exchange of digital information that seem to point back to the world of social authorship that coexisted with the beginning centuries of print culture.

Contemporary information cultures include both professional writing and other forms of written communication that reject – or merely bypass – the version of literary authorship common over the past three centuries. Professional authorship has become increasingly corporate, and dominant profit-making entities like Disney are attempting to alter fundamentally the legal and cultural basis of copyright hammered out over the course of the very long eighteenth century. Mark Rose's *Authors and Owners* (1993) demonstrates that the almost accidental history of copyright in the eighteenth century created the individual, printing author as a proprietor of "intellectual property." In rejecting the book-sellers' claim that a "perpetual copyright" existed in common law, the House of Lords in the Donaldson v. Becket ruling of 1774 asserted public interest in information that has been "published." Rose points out that the legal doctrine of copyright coincides in the eighteenth century with developing notions of the "author" – usually an individual human being, whose creation of a *work* from the bare stuff of immaterial language renders him, like Chaucer, like Shakespeare, like Milton, like Samuel Richardson, a creative genius. In his celebrated essay "What is an Author?" Michel Foucault noted that "texts, books, and discourses really began to have authors . . . to the extent that authors became subject to punishment, that is, to the extent that discourses could be transgressive."[2] By the end of the period under consideration, though, the author was more like Milton's God than Milton's Satan: authors were celebrated for their creative self-sufficiency rather than punished for violating the established order. The publishing industry and its machinery, comprising reviews, libraries, reading clubs, schools, and other elements, seemed to change its structures in response to (and in promotion of) the new cultural prominence of the author.

Hypertext and its machinery of publication, primarily the World Wide Web accessible through the Internet, would seem to pose an obvious challenge to the ideology of the creative author. Challenges to the publishing author predate the existence of the category, of course. The theatre has always been in English culture a collaborative enterprise, the best example being the imposition of "Shakespeare" on the plays he wrote in the centuries following his death. Film and television were the dominant cultural forms of the second half of the twentieth century, and even if individual directors and producers are lionized as *auteurs*, films and television shows remain essentially corporate undertakings. However, publication via the World Wide Web poses a more fundamental threat to the cult(ure) of authorship in that successful designs, containing content, operate from the anticipation of a user's interaction with a site. No longer does the information provider bring us the product of inspiration; instead, so the argument goes, the user controls the dynamic exchange, picking and choosing at will among a variety of options. The web provides a crude literalization of Barthes's poetic essay, "The Death of the Author": content providers must fight for the eyes and ears of a mass public in what Michael H. Goldhaber has called "an economy of attention."[3]

In this way, non-professional forms of writing may come to seem more important than the paid work of writers providing content for the electronic outlets of multinational corporations. The cultural meanings as well as practices of publishing will change as the new technology suffuses people's lives. The Internet has already given rise to a number of methods through which "private publication" occurs. Email correspondence, including listserv mailing lists, Usenet, web-based news boards, and text-based chat rooms, create structures of communication that break down the paradigms set up by print culture. Publication through the Internet is not always promiscuous: various networks (or various sites) create voluntary interest groups, many of which are technically public but which function with semi-permeable boundaries. The relevant definition from the Oxford English Dictionary for "publication" dates from 1576: "The issuing, or offering to the public, of a book, map, engraving, photograph, piece of music, or other work of which copies are multiplied by writing, printing, or any other process; also, the work or business of producing and issuing copies of such work."[4] It is clear that such a definition for publication must change when digital technologies come to dominate

the process of publication. The notion of what a "public" is has already
come into question. As I discuss below, and as the contents of this volume
imply, when "writing" was the technology of publication, the form and
meaning of the "public" addressed had not yet been fixed as the bourgeois structure identified by Jürgen Habermas.

Not surprisingly, those profiting from information technology laud
the future and predict the demise of now-outdated technologies. Jakob
Nielsen, for example, a leading expert on contemporary information
technologies, boldly proclaims the demise of print in his book, *Designing
Web Usability*: "Most current media formats will die and be replaced
with an integrated Web medium in five to ten years. Legacy media
cannot survive because the current media landscape is an artifact of
the underlying hardware technology. Whenever the user experience is
dictated by hardware limitations, it is a sure bet that something better will
come along once these limitations are lifted."[5] Early in his book, Nielsen
preempts attacks on his own use of the soon-to-be-outdated mode of
print by acknowledging the current superiority of books to the web in a
number of different ways, including poor screen resolution (a hardware
problem), poor web browsing user interfaces (a software problem), and
readers' inexperience at dealing with hypertext documents (a cultural
problem).[6] He sets the date of 2007 for the demise of books and says
"legacy publishers be warned: This *will* happen."[7] Nielsen posits a world
in which communication is shaped directly by technology, and in which a
better technology "wins." It is a version of economic determinism with an
interesting consumer-oriented twist. The fittest technology will survive
a bitter struggle with other "legacy" technologies, but it will survive
not because it meets the demands of an impersonal "history." Rather,
Nielsen argues, consumers will adopt web communications from free
choice because the new technologies are more useful. Nielsen's book is
directed at the supplier in a capitalist communications world of supply
and demand, but his book is a warning rather than a celebration. To be
useful, communications technologies must be "usable."

Thus we are, to use Ezell's phrasing both, "returning to the early modern model of manuscript text and social authorship" *and* "positioned to
invent yet another story to add to this tale." The "official" culture of
web-based distribution of information exhibits a tension between corporate entities – including universities, traditional media industries, and
newcomers like Yahoo! and America Online – and individual authors.
On the one hand, even if these "publishers" often empower individuals to create their own sites, posting family photos of a trip out west or

their ungrammatical assessment of current political and cultural trends, it is the provider, the corporation, whose logo adorns the "pages" and whose advertising creates profits. On the other hand, there has been a genuine explosion of cultural production operating not only without central control, but without the need or even existence of a "center," as users manipulate technologies that have remained stubbornly resistant to state – or corporate – control. The shape of communications remains to be determined by the advance of technology and the instruments of social control. For every advocate of "filters" placed on Internet browsers in schools and public libraries there are many users of potentially revolutionary technologies like data encryption and the copyright-busting Napster file-sharing system. Information cultures are being made by users engaging in struggles in the world. Neither "the system," nor "the technology," nor even "history" is determining the world of communications.

Women's Writing and the Circulation of Ideas: Manuscript Publication in England, 1550–1800, operates from a similar presupposition about the relationship between culture – here, particularly literature – and the technologies that allow for communication beyond the face-to-face. The writers discussed in the various essays all used manuscript rather than print for the circulation of their various works. Although the essays included here are heterogeneous in subject matter and approach, they all operate from the working premise that the decision to use manuscript rather than print publication resulted from a set of choices, made in positive terms for the most part. "Scribal publication"– a term that can limit the range of manuscript practices and that does not describe all the literary cultures discussed in this volume – turns out to be more "usable" for the writers and readers it connects. The variety in these essays therefore should be seen as a necessary laying of the groundwork for further study that would build upon research into actual practices rather than proceeding inductively from abstract social theories. Writers used manuscripts (or print technology, for that matter) because it suited their needs.

The particular focus of the essays in this volume is the use of manuscript circulation by women writers in England in the Renaissance and eighteenth century. Many previous studies of women writers – including self-consciously feminist interpretations – have assumed that women published their writings in manuscript rather than print as a direct and simple result of social prohibitions placed upon women writers. Women, it has been argued, faced even more than male courtiers what J. W. Saunders influentially labeled "the stigma of print."[8] For example,

Mary Ellen Lamb's important *Gender and Authorship in the Sidney Circle* operates from the principle that print publication should be considered the
norm in the Renaissance: women were therefore relegated to an inferior
mode of distribution of their writing by prohibitive social codes. The bias
toward print as a norm is suggested by her thesis – that women writers
represent female authorship as powerless in their writings – and betrayed
by language that probably would have passed unnoticed when the book
was published in 1990. Lamb writes, for example, that "unfortunately,
many writings by women . . . have undoubtedly been lost, for relatively
few works by women *achieved* publication" (emphasis added).[9]

In contrast, the essays in this volume take varied approaches toward
the problems (and opportunities) confronting women writers in historical
circumstances that made manuscript circulation a necessity, or an option,
for the distribution of their works. Not only do these essays reject a notion
of essential womanhood across historical periods, but they refuse as well
to see "women" as a monolithic category within the time periods covered
by their breadth. The essays focus in different ways upon women's active
agency within the overarching constraints placed upon them by cultures
structured upon rigid hierarchies of gender and social class. Following
the lead of critics like Lamb and Ezell, the authors of these essays focus
on the biographical and literary particularities of the subjects of their
study. In doing so they question some of the presuppositions of earlier
writers on the circulation of ideas in early modern England.

The history of publication in recent years has been dominated by an
interest in the material circumstances of script and print that has extended beyond the specialized fields of paleography and bibliography
into British literary history and literary criticism more broadly. Interest
in "print culture" led the way, inspired by Lucien Febvre and Henri-Jean
Martin's *L'Apparition du livre* (1950 – translated as *The Coming of the Book* in
1976). McLuhan's controversial *The Gutenberg Galaxy: the Making of Typo-
graphic Man* (1962) and Elizabeth Eisenstein's *The Printing Press as an Agent
of Change* (1979) were large-scale attempts to see the "history of the book"
as crucial to the course of western history. The historical and socio-
logical approaches taken in these works dovetailed with trends in literary
theory, which moved from establishing either the author's intention, or,
in the New Criticism, the structural unity of the "text," to exploration
of the social meaning and uses of literature. "Reception" and "reader-
response" theories located the meaning of literature in the interaction
between work and audience. This critical move allowed for a more accurate hermeneutic (when the audience's "horizon of expectation," to use

Hans Robert Jauss's term, is used to delineate possible responses) and simultaneously to open up interpretation through acknowledging the wide range of uses that could be and were in fact made of literary texts. Texts could be liberating acts of communication (as argued, for example, in Jürgen Habermas's *Strukturwandel der Öffentlicheit* [1962 – translated as *The Structural Transformation of the Public Sphere* in 1989]) or oppressive carriers of power (in popular Anglo-American interpretations of Foucault's *Les Mots et les choses* [1966 – translated as *The Order of Things*, 1970]). In either case, literary critics and literary historians required an understanding of the material structures of communication – writing, publishing, distribution, reading – to make their broad claims even slightly plausible.

And so the most grandly (or most absurdly) ambitious scholars and critics turned to paleographers and bibliographers for their expertise in the history and meaning of the physical objects of manuscripts and books. Until then, the focus of these specialists had for the most part been on reconstructing their micro-histories and determining authoritative texts. Scholars of publishing history were, in many cases, more interested in the workings of printing houses than in the interplay between publishing (whether via the press or through script) and literature. Works like Philip Gaskell's *New Introduction to Bibliography* (1972) and the many essays and books by D. F. McKenzie have narrowed the gap between bibliography and literary criticism from the "book history" side of the relationship, providing critics, teachers, and students with a framework for applying material history to understanding of literary art. The result has been a common acceptance that the "meaning" of a literary work can no longer be fixed in bare rhetorical structures, untainted by the circumstances of composition and dissemination. The material history of a book and its meaning as a work of the imagination can now be understood as inextricably linked. Books make and are made in history by women and men who use, and delight in, the possibilities of writing.

Adrian Johns's *The Nature of the Book: Print and Knowledge in the Making* (1998) is the best recent account of the convergence of book history, literary theory, and the history of knowledge. In this lengthy tome, Johns questions some of the central assumptions made by McLuhan, Eisenstein, and their various followers about the cultural characteristics determined by the technology of the printing press. Johns looks closely at (and doubts) the heretofore widely accepted triumvirate of print culture's "standardization, dissemination, and fixity" established by Eisenstein, taking the last particularly to task and refuting the notion that fixity (and the perception of fixity) engendered trustworthiness. Johns argues that the phrase "print culture" should express the effect rather than the cause of the "cultural construction of print" in early modern London.[10] He therefore focuses on the actions of a number of important agents who create the uses and understanding of print by actions taken in precise historical and geographical times and spaces. A literary history emerging from an application of Johns's stunning work must calibrate the realms of print publication and manuscript circulation in new ways. We should no longer see the conventions and properties of manuscript circulation as peripheral to a simple set of procedures established by a dominant world of print publication. Instead, it is necessary to look at manuscript culture as a persisting set of procedures with its own history and customs as well as balancing manuscript and print as unfinished, in-process cultures with strong cross-fertilization. The essays in this volume take up Johns's challenge to the history of the book by locating manuscripts in ecclesiastical and political history; in the technological history of the production and dissemination of information; and in the history of imaginative writing.

Women's Writing and the Circulation of Ideas: Manuscript Publication in England, 1550–1800 points to the notion that women writers created a number of "manuscript cultures." Women responded to the medium's particular advantages and opportunities, even if their adoption of manuscript circulation was influenced by external social and political conditions. The work in this volume builds on scholarship on manuscript culture undertaken in the past decades, particularly the prescient work of a few literary critics such as J. W. Saunders. Saunders had called for the integration of literary criticism, book history, and sociology before the impact of flashy arguments like McLuhan's could be made known. In "The Stigma of Print" (1951) Saunders argued that "if literary history is to be history in anything more than name . . . criticism must be supplemented by sociology."[11] His article breaks ground in differentiating among possible meanings of literature in courtier and professional (manuscript and print) literary cultures. While the contributors to the present volume may dispute the existence or the valences of the "stigma of print," they nearly uniformly trace their own critical lineage to Saunders's exploration of the meaning of Tudor court verse in a manuscript culture understood through the scholarly recovery of actual practices.

The past two decades have witnessed an increased knowledge of the circumstances of scribal publication in the early modern period. Peter Beal's *Index of English Literary Manuscripts* covering the years 1450–1700 (published 1980–93) has enabled research into the forms and meanings of literary works published either solely or additionally in scribal form.

Harold Love's *Scribal Publication in Seventeenth-Century England* (1993) follows up his essay from 1987 and presents a compelling account of the mechanics and meaning of scribal publication primarily in the seventeenth century. Studies by Arthur F. Marotti, Mary Hobbs, and Steven W. May, among many others, have situated sixteenth- and seventeenth-century writing in the context of "manuscript cultures." In these cultures, literary works are enmeshed in a complex world comprising personal situation, political power, and the technologies of script and print. Central to the essays in this volume is the work of Margaret Ezell. Her three books, *The Patriarch's Wife* (1987), *Writing Women's Literary History* (1993), and *Social Authorship and the Advent of Print* (1999), establish the phenomenon and explore the meaning of women's participation in networks of publication that have, until recently, remained invisible to literary scholars. Women, Ezell demonstrates, published widely through the formal and informal exchange of manuscripts. Ezell hopes to recover for our time writing that has been lost and, as well, wishes to reconfigure the shape of literary history to take into more accurate account the amount and importance of women's writing. The essays in this volume build upon the work of the line of scholars of manuscript culture from Saunders to Ezell, moving back and forth between theoretical models and the difficult to recover (and sometimes stubbornly resistant to theorizing) traces of what was a thriving world of literary manuscripts.

The essays in this volume hope to alter our broader understanding of the relationship of technology to literary history. Instead of working according to a "decline and rise" model of competing technologies, in which a "legacy" technology dies out to be replaced by a more efficient, more powerful competitor, the overlap between various literary cultures of print and manuscript suggest that a "growth into" model more accurately describes the relationship of technologies in periods of change. Mary Hobbs and H. R. Woudhuysen both describe, for example, an explosion of interest in literary manuscripts in the third decade of the seventeenth century. They account for this odd blip in a number of ways, including the dire political situation faced by the social class most accustomed to writing and reading poetry. Another explanation might be that the increased availability of written language through the medium of print fueled all sorts of poetic culture, even when those engaged in literature did not, for various reasons, wish to use the printing press. The phenomenon addressed by Hobbs and Woudhuysen may be related to the development of print technology, but it neither signals the "triumph" of print nor the demise of manuscripts as means for producing

and distributing literary writing. Because writers and publishers working with print were fully aware of manuscripts – and vice-versa – the two
modes should be seen in relation in this period. Further study of miscellaneous collections of verse might concentrate on the interpenetration of
manuscript with print across a range of manuscript and printed sources –
even within particular miscellanies, either printed or written. The various
cultures of manuscript and print may have aided each other rather than
locking in battle in a Darwinian struggle to the death.

Again, we might turn to the contemporary situation to understand
better what was happening in the period 1550–1800, and then reap-
ply scholarship on the older period to our understanding of the uses of
information technology more generally. The mid-1990s witnessed the
dream of the "paperless office," an efficient and money-saving use of
information technology to replace the consumption of paper in ordinary
settings of communication. Companies were promised that an invest-
ment in computers hooked into networks would save time and material
resources, since most routine communications could be made through
email and most databases of information placed online in easily revisable
form. The typewriter was dead, and the computer printer was merely
a transitional technology. Manufacturers like Hewlett-Packard scram-
bled to move into other areas of information technology. As it turns out,
though, printers have become even more integral to the actual use of
information networks. Users take advantage of printing technology in
new (and mostly unforeseen) ways that foster a hybrid between "purely"
electronic information and old-fashioned uses of typewriters and the
printing press. This is bad news for trees, but it points out that the historical model argued for by Eisenstein and her followers too easily assumes
the "replacement" of an "outdated" technology by a new technology.
Instead, we see a burst of activity in the "legacy" technology even with
the rapid growth of the new "superior" technology. Near the end of
his book, Jakob Nielsen admits that his own predictions for the future
of information technology will almost certainly turn out to have been
wrong. A continued integration of "legacy" technologies with the Internet might very well be one of his errors, if this volume's analysis of
manuscript publication in the period of "the rise of print" can establish
new ways of thinking about the history of the production and dissemination of knowledge.

Women's Writing and the Circulation of Ideas overturns simplified miscon-
ceptions about book history and literary history that have plagued many
discussions of early modern women's writings. Individually its essays

challenge traditional literary histories of the Renaissance, the Restoration, and the eighteenth century in Britain. Collectively they begin to offer a new, more inclusive vision of literary history, most importantly in understanding the quantity, quality, and importance of women's writing in the literary history of the period. Not only do the essays bear witness to the continuing importance of scribal publication as a positive option for writers, but they also demonstrate the inadequacy of interpretations of manuscript circulation as the "safe choice" for women. The women writers and editors described in these pages are active agents who choose, as far as they can, among media that offer different cultural, economic, literary, religious, and personal advantages. Instead of understanding scribal publication as a restriction upon women writers, many of the essays in this volume analyze the opportunities provided for different kinds of writing across a range of possibilities for publication. Women writers (and editors) geared publication toward a wide array of possible results: remuneration, social prestige, aesthetics, religion, and family among them. The varied strategies pursued by women writers in the wide field of writing help present a more clear understanding of the world of publication for women *and* men during the period. In this way, the end aimed at by this volume as a whole involves the recognition of the ways that literature was integrated into the whole fabric of social life, whether for aristocrats or commoners, men or women. *Women's Writing and the Circulation of Ideas* does not offer the last word on the role of scribal publication in the literary life of the period, nor on the importance and extent of women's writings. Instead the writers of the essays herein hope that their work will spur further study as well as ask and answer questions about a number of increasingly important writers.

The essays in this volume approach a variety of cases with different methodologies and goals. Some contributors use traditional techniques of literary history to uncover the actual circumstances behind instances of print publication. These essays demonstrate how paleography and bibliography remain essential to the accurate (and imaginative) interpretation of literary texts. Others use existing data to interrogate assumptions about literary culture that have stood unchallenged for years. Each essay is an original contribution to the scholarship on increasingly important figures such as Mary Sidney Herbert, the Countess of Pembroke; Lady Mary Wroth; Lady Mary Wortley Montagu; and Frances Burney. Taken together, these essays create a complex portrait of a world of writing in which the spheres of manuscript and print publication interpenetrate in diverse and unpredictable ways.

When Sir Philip Sidney's sister printed his works, she neglected to publish the *Psalmes* that he had begun and she finished. In "The Countess of Pembroke's Agency in Print and Scribal Culture," Margaret Hannay tries to account for the Countess of Pembroke's reluctance to print her translation of the Psalms and to turn instead to scribal publication. None of the conventional explanations seems to hold water. Hannay quotes John Davies of Hereford, who in 1619 gives four possible reasons that women should disdain print: modesty; the conflation of publication and unchastity that was so commonly used against women writers; the "stigma of print"; and what he sees as the declining popularity of verse, that "Fame for Versing, now, is held but Shame." These standards have commonly been held as true since the seventeenth century. In her close analysis of the Countess of Pembroke's decisions, however, Hannay demonstrates that social class was a much more powerful influence than prohibitions associated with gender. Hannay discusses the Countess of Pembroke's "liminal" position between print and scribal publication as an editor who published her brother's works in print but reserved their *Psalmes* for scribal publication.

Debra Rienstra and Noel Kinnamon's "Circulating the Sidney–Pembroke Psalter" follows up on Hannay's essay by examining the theological ramifications of the Countess of Pembroke's decision to circulate her and Sidney's *Psalmes* in manuscript only. Their essay provides close analysis of the literary/theological virtues of the *Psalmes* and places their translation into the context of Reformation notions of language and religion. Rienstra and Kinnamon examine different manuscript versions of the *Psalmes* in order to show that the Countess of Pembroke's revisions move towards potentially controversial presentations of scripture. The Countess of Pembroke "strains" accepted theology by presenting the psalms in increasingly vivid imaginative language. Scribal publication, the writers suggest, was better suited to the claims the *Psalmes* implicitly make about religion and literature.

In "Creating Female Authorship in the Early Seventeenth Century: Ben Jonson and Lady Mary Wroth" Michael G. Brennan discusses the poetic relationship between Ben Jonson and Lady Mary Wroth. Brennan breaks ground by speculating about the influence of Jonson's printed works on Lady Mary's transition from a private to a public figure in the second decade of the seventeenth century. Brennan argues that a small coterie who had access to her writings in manuscript helped lay the groundwork for Lady Mary's entry into the public world of literature. Brennan's essay reveals as much about Ben Jonson as it does about Lady Mary Wroth, suggesting that lines of politics, patronage, and literature extend between the genders (and between social positions) in complex ways that resist simple oppositions.

Victoria Burke's "Medium and Meaning in the Manuscripts of Anne, Lady Southwell" examines the history and meaning of Lady Southwell's poetic oeuvre in manuscript. Although Lady Southwell proclaimed in her verse that she wrote for none but herself, Burke's analysis of the two extant manuscripts reveals that the poems were written to be read. The essay encompasses bibliography as well as textual analysis, with a focus on the specifically scribal form of publication shedding light on the meaning of Southwell's verse. In particular, Burke looks at Southwell's verse in the context of criticism of the court. Burke's essay reveals some of the political implications of women's verse and the means of literary production chosen by women for its publication.

Margaret Ezell looks at the interesting and not widely discussed practice of posthumous scribal publication in "The Posthumous Publication of Women's Manuscripts and the History of Authorship." Ezell points to four varieties of the posthumous publication of women's verse: first, publication for commercial gain; second, the fulfillment of a woman author's wishes, when her manuscript had been carefully prepared for publication; third, the decision by a family or friends to publish a collection of a deceased author's writings as a public tribute – a monument – to the memory of the writer; and fourth, the posthumous publication of a woman writer's verse in collections not necessarily devoted only to their writing. Ezell's essay ranges broadly over a wide variety of examples of these phenomena in the seventeenth and eighteenth centuries. Ezell explicitly places her essay in the context of her earlier (and forthcoming) work that attempts to recover the nature of social literary culture in a more accurate (and more generous) way than has been possible without an understanding of the persistence of manuscript culture in the seventeenth and eighteenth centuries.

In "Jane Barker's Jacobite Writings," Leigh A. Eicke examines the strange tactical uses Barker makes of scribal conventions in her print publications. Eicke demonstrates that Barker overcomes the "stigma of print" through associating the form of manuscript exchange with works such as *A Patch-Work Screen for the Ladies* (1723) and its sequel, *The Lining of the Patch-Work Screen* (1726). These works are somehow excused – and their Jacobite politics insinuated into the public sphere – by their presentation as compendia of manuscripts, complete with Barker's own manuscript poems. Eicke's essay, like Brennan's, Ezell's, King's, and my own, demonstrates that even when many women's writings are prepared and circulated in print (or performed on stage), the practices of manuscript culture implicitly, or in Barker's case even explicitly, carry over into the exploitation of the newer technology. Eicke's Barker is far from a reticent, modest writer shunning print as dangerous; rather, she is an active agent who exploits the tradition of scribal publication for political and literary purposes.

Kathryn King's essay, "Elizabeth Singer Rowe's Tactical Use of Print and Manuscript," charts the move from manuscript to print, and back to manuscript taken in the fascinating and unusual career of Rowe (1674–1737), best known for her popular *Friendship in Death in Twenty Letters from the Dead to the Living*, published in 1728 and often reprinted throughout the century. Rowe had been present in the 1690s at the commercial revolution in print, assisting John Dunton with his groundbreaking periodical *The Athenian Mercury*. She was dubbed the "Pindarical Lady," contributing poems and becoming one of the periodical's most popular sub-celebrities. Soon Rowe turned away from Dunton and print and circulated her works in manuscript. Conventional interpretations have tied this "retreat" from print to an increasingly restrictive ideal of femininity, but King suggests that it would be more accurate to see Rowe as using an established manuscript culture to her own benefit: "Her turn to manuscript as her preferred medium of transmission . . . would seem to reflect less the rise of the domestic ideal than an elevation in her social position." King then examines Rowe's re-entry into the world of print with *Friendship in Death* and *Letters Moral and Entertaining* (Part 1, 1729). In effect, Rowe resorts to print for the vastly superior cultural reach it provides for her religious fervor. In the final section of her essay, King uses Elizabeth Singer Rowe's manipulations of the advantages presented by each system of publication to argue for a more subtle interpretation of the varieties of publication in the eighteenth century: gender, class, religion, region, family, and other local influences provide a range of "strategies" of publication available to writers.

Isobel Grundy takes a close look at the manuscript books of Lady Mary Wortley Montagu (1689–1762) and the circle of writers and readers including her daughter and niece. "Lady Mary Wortley Montagu and her Daughter: the Changing Use of Manuscripts" combines an acute literary critical approach with the expertise on Lady Mary's biography and book history that Grundy, Lady Mary's biographer, brings to bear. Grundy contrasts the writings of the two generations to describe the informal and private circles of reading and writing that all of these women participated in. The elder Lady Mary's manuscript book reveals her unique ambitions and talents as a writer; Grundy examines the younger generation's manuscripts not to denigrate their abilities or ambitions – in their own way, Grundy suggests, they are accomplished and individually talented writers – but to make broader arguments about their generation's understanding of itself through culture. Grundy discusses the creation of "teen-aged" culture in the eighteenth century in the difference between Lady Mary's juvenile manuscripts and those of her daughter and niece. In the public world of "expense and entertainment," Grundy argues, these young women begin to understand themselves as a distinct group a "counter-culture," bound (as always) by class, but also through their "far from literary" use of verse.

In the volume's final essay, I analyze the composition and content of Frances Burney's play, *The Witlings*, written after the popular success of her first novel, *Evelina* (1777). Burney was encouraged by leading theatrical figures of the day to try her hand at a comedy, but her father, the musicologist Charles Burney, quashed her hopes for theatrical production, perhaps on account of the play's satirical attack against the coterie of bluestockings led by Elizabeth Montagu. Dr. Burney claimed that it would be indecorous for Burney as a woman to have the play produced. Throughout her career Burney strove to meet expectations for proper femininity while pursuing a career as a professional author. *The Witlings*, like *Evelina* before it, presents the circulation of verse in manuscript as an anachronistic (and potentially damaging) relic of oppressive aristocratic culture that must be engaged – and rejected. Frances Burney's professional orientation required that in her career and in her literary works she reject scribal publication as closed and private in favor of print and performance for the "public" her preface to *Evelina* claimed to serve.

The narrative that the essays create follows the "ambiguous triumph of print," as Love has termed the growing domination of print as a means of public communication. Scribal publication remains, at the end of the eighteenth century, an alternative mode of publication, as print loses most of its "stigma" and women enter the literary marketplace for print on their own terms as readers, writers, editors, and publishers. Even without scribal publication as a viable option for the widespread dissemination of literary writing, manuscript cultures continue to thrive. It is not only that we need to "recover" a practice that has been "lost." It is perhaps even more important to change the lenses through which we understand literature in history. Manuscript cultures always existed, but we have needed to learn how to look for them and rethink what it means when we find them. Women – and men – have continued since the eighteenth century to circulate manuscripts for pleasure, power, and social advancement.

I have insisted in this Introduction on making comparisons between the period covered by this volume's contents and the present situation in which I am writing and in which my writing will be published. We are entering now a world of nearly unlimited communication in which information can be tailored to the particular needs of any recipient. Uniformity and persistence – two of the qualities often (if somewhat inaccurately) attributed to print – may no longer be the most important factors in written exchange. The informal – if not exactly "private" – networks of electronic communication that the editors used to bring these scholars together, to work with a press, and to prepare the "manuscript" to be printed have a social function that differs from that of the formal publication of the work. Recovering the complex and various networks of manuscript cultures in the period 1550–1800 might help us see differently literary works that have never left our minds.

NOTES

1 Margaret J. M. Ezell, *Social Authorship and the Advent of Print* (Baltimore: Johns Hopkins University Press, 1999), 142.
2 Michel Foucault, "What is an Author?" in *The Foucault Reader*, ed. Paul Rabinow (New York: Pantheon Books, 1984), 108.
3 Michael H. Goldhaber, "Attention Shoppers!" *Wired*, December 1997, 182–90.
4 *The Compact Oxford English Dictionary*, 2nd edn. (Oxford: Clarendon Press, 1991), "publication."
5 Jakob Nielsen, *Designing Web Usability* (Indianapolis: New Riders, 2000), 372.
6 Ibid., 4.
7 Ibid., 5.
8 J. W. Saunders, "The Stigma of Print: a Note on the Social Bases of Tudor Poetry," *Essays in Criticism* 1 (1951), 139–64.
9 Mary Ellen Lamb, *Gender and Authorship in the Sidney Circle* (Madison: University of Wisconsin Press, 1990), 10.
10 Adrian Johns, *The Nature of the Book: Print and Knowledge in the Making* (Chicago: University of Chicago Press, 1998), 56.
11 Saunders, "Stigma of Print," 164.

CHAPTER 2

The Countess of Pembroke's agency in print and scribal culture

Margaret P. Hannay

Dedicating *The Countess of Pembrokes Arcadia* to his sister, Philip Sidney entrusts her with his manuscript, saying that its "chiefe safety, shall bee the not walking abroad" and its "chiefe protection the bearing the livery of your name." With decorous modesty he refers to "this idle worke of mine" that he says he wrote simply because "you desired me to doe it, and your desire, to my heart is an absolute commaundement." Now she is asked to "keepe it to your selfe, or to such friends, who will weigh errors in the ballance of goodwill."[1] Sidney obviously anticipates limited scribal publication within her coterie.[2] What actually happened, of course, is that four years after his death the *Arcadia* was printed under the direction of Fulke Greville (1590), followed the next year by an unauthorized edition of Sidney's *Astrophil and Stella* (1591). Printing Sidney's works meant that what was written "for the eyes of just a few, now became available to all."[3] The Countess of Pembroke then intervened in the printing of Sidney's works, culminating in the handsome 1598 folio edition of the *Arcadia* that was almost a Collected Works of Sir Philip Sidney, along the lines of the Petrarchan *Rerum vulgarium fragmenta*, as Roger Kuin suggests.[4]

The 1598 *Arcadia*, however, did not include Sidney's metric paraphrases of Psalms 1–43 nor Pembroke's 128 poems completing that work. Reserving this work for scribal publication, Pembroke uses the same metaphor of court livery in her presentation of the Sidneian *Psalmes* to Queen Elizabeth:

> but hee did warpe, I weav'd this webb to end;
> the stuffe not ours, our worke no curious thing...
> And I the Cloth in both our names present,
> A liverie robe to bee bestowed by thee[.][5]

That is, Philip Sidney began the *Psalmes* and Pembroke completed them; he laid out the warp threads that frame the work and she weaves the "stuff," or fabric, that becomes the livery robe.[6] Intending to present the finished manuscript to Elizabeth, Pembroke writes to encourage the queen to bestow it on other appropriate readers by permitting them to make copies. In this presentation manuscript she would thus be engaging in what Harold Love calls "the apparently paradoxical notion of publication through a single copy," anticipating that the queen will initiate wider scribal publication.[7]

In a subsequent metaphor, she makes the queen herself the site of poetic inspiration. When she says that the queen's breast is "the Cabinet, thy seat the shrine" of the Muses, she continues this idea that the queen is responsible for the arts, for "What English is, by many names is thine." Who else could be "so meet a Patrones / for Authors state or writings argument?" She develops the comparison between Elizabeth and David to say that the queen is the most fit recipient for the *Psalmes* because of the parallels in their lives, "For ev'n thy Rule is painted in his Raigne." The tradition of presenting Psalters to monarchs was longstanding, but Elizabeth did seem a particularly appropriate recipient to others who presented her their renditions of the Psalms, including Esther Inglis in this same year, 1599.[8]

The Countess of Pembroke herself thus stands in a liminal position between scribal publication and print. On the one hand, her name was used to legitimize print for works by her famous brother Philip, herself, and others; on the other hand, she actively participated in the manuscript culture, and her fame as a writer derived primarily not from her works circulated in print, but from a work she reserved for scribal publication, the Sidneian *Psalmes*.

Why did she refuse to print the *Psalmes*, despite repeated entreaties? Or, as Margaret Ezell suggests rephrasing such questions to avoid privileging print, what was she attempting to do?[9] The simplest explanation would be that she was deterred from printing her most significant work by cultural strictures against female speech, but we must be wary of making facile assumptions about the operation of gender restrictions. In this case class prestige seems a more important factor than gender, although John Davies of Hereford, who transcribed the authoritative Penshurst manuscript of the Sidneian *Psalmes*, suggests the frequent existence of a gender motivation for women writers' reluctance to publish. In his triple dedication of *The Muses Sacrifice* (1612) to three aristocratic women writers (Pembroke; Lucy, Countess of Bedford; and Elizabeth, Lady Cary, the author of *Mariam*) he gives four possible reasons for disdaining print: modesty; the conflation of publication and unchastity that was so commonly used against women writers; the "stigma of print"; and what he sees as the declining popularity of verse, that "Fame for Versing, now, is held but Shame."[10] In the remainder of the poem he champions poetry, by which he means primarily verse rather than imaginative literature more broadly defined. Since Davies is overly pessimistic about the reception of verse, particularly on sacred subjects, that argument is not relevant here. Of his other suggested reasons, the first two may appear the most compelling for women writers, and may in fact have influenced other women, but, as we shall see, they do not fit the circumstances of Pembroke's own life and work.

In his opening praise of "Pembroke, (A Paragon of Princely Parts)," Davies's first suggested motivation for scribal publication is modesty: "And didst thou thirst for *Fame* (as al *Men* doe) / thou would'st, by all meanes, let it come to light."[11] A shy, retiring modesty, however, was unlikely to be her motivation for scribal publication, for she was justifiably proud of her *Psalmes*. Her pride in her poetry is portrayed by her niece Lady Mary Wroth, who "shadows" her in the Queen of Naples. She is "as perfect in Poetry and all other Princely vertues as any woman that ever liv'd, to bee esteemed excellent in any one, [but] shee was stor'd with all, and so the more admirable."[12] Wroth also mentions Pembroke on the title page of *The Countess of Montgomerys Urania* (1620), identifying herself as "Daughter to the right Noble Robert Earle of Leicester. And Neece to the ever famous, and renowned Sir Phillips Sidney knight. And to the most Excellent Lady Mary Countesse of Pembroke late deceased." In so doing, Wroth signals her rank and her membership in a literary dynasty, including a woman writer. (The name "Urania" itself had been associated with the Countess of Pembroke, notably in Spenser's praise of her as "Urania, sister unto Astrofell" in *Colin Clouts Come Home Again* [1595], and in Nathaniel Baxter's poem dedicated to her, *Sir Philip Sydneys Ouránia*.)[13] The title of the romance was obviously modeled on *The Countess of Pembrokes Arcadia* and may well have been intended as a compliment to Pembroke as well as to Wroth's friend and Pembroke's daughter-in-law Susan de Vere Herbert, Countess of Montgomery.

Urania includes "Verses framed by the most incomparable Queene, or Lady of her time, a Nightingale most sweetly singing, upon which she grounded her subject."[14] Wroth dramatizes the coterie dissemination of this spontaneous verse. After the queen recites the poem, Perissus exclaims "that he never had heard any like them, and in so saying, he did right to them, and her who knew when she did well, and would be unwilling to lose the due unto her selfe, which he gave her, swering he never heard any thing finelier worded, nor wittilier written on the sudden."[15] Wroth's depiction of Pembroke as someone "who knew when she did well, and would be unwilling to lose the due unto her selfe" may be written with an affectionate smile. Certainly the Queen of Naples does not seem to be someone who modestly refrains from print publication; rather, Perissus's immediate and extravagant praise and Limena's request for a copy are the rewards she seeks.

Pembroke herself may present her poetry as inferior to that of her renowned brother Philip, as other poets did when praising Sidney, and she may demonstrate appropriate concern for the difficulties of translating sacred text, but there is nothing in the biographical records to suggest that she shyly hid her poetic works.[16] The modesty topos was extravagantly used by writers praising Sidney. No one was more effusive than John Dickenson, who apologizes to Edward Dyer for "tedious interrupting" of his "serious affaires," craves "pardon" for his "audacious enterprise," and then, if that were not humble enough, asks his "Gentlemen-Readers" to sympathize with his plight: "what pen can sufficiently expresse his praise which exceeds the praise of al pens, especially of mine, whose slender wit treating such an ample subject" is "overwhelmed." Nonetheless, he hopes they will not be offended that "my blushing Muse reverencing the steps wherein he traced, and hovering aloofe with awe-full dread, doth yet at last warily approach, and carefully observe the directions of so worthie a guide, and in part, glance at the unmatchable height of his heroique humor."[17] Spenser, Greville, and the authors represented in *Astrophel* and in the volumes of commemorative verses put out by Oxford, Cambridge and the University of Leiden all praise Sidney in terms so extravagant as to exceed human possibility.[18] Thus when Pembroke says that she is the "poorer" subject and her brother the "richer" ("Even now that Care," line 22), or calls herself a small stream in contrast to his "great sea" ("Angell Spirit," line 33) we should not exaggerate her self-abasement. As Beth Wynn Fisken notes, her poem "To the Angell Spirit" is "quietly subversive," and, in its praise of her brother, manages "to camouflage the assertiveness of her style with the self-abnegation of her subject matter."[19] Gavin Alexander similarly highlights the "aggressive humility" of "Even now that Care."[20]

Like Queen Elizabeth, Pembroke understood public relations. Like the queen, she crafted a self-image through her own writings and through her patronage. Part of that image is her position as Sidney's sister. As she says in the autograph postscript to a business letter written by her secretary: "it is the Sister of Sir Philip Sidney who yow ar to right and who will worthely deserve the same."[21] Far from abasing herself as merely Sidney's sister, she proudly claims both family connections and personal worth. A similar combined claim is made in the 1618 portrait engraved by Simon van de Passe. Dressed in the velvet, pearls, and ermine appropriate to her wealth, she is described by her rank (signified by the inscription in Latin and English and by the coronet), and by her Sidney heritage (signified in her name "Mary Sidney," rather than "Mary Herbert," and in the Sidney pheon above the portrait), yet she is most prominently signified as poet. The portrait is crowned with the poet's laurel wreath – above the pheon and above the coronet. The sides of the cartouche appear to be quill pens in ink wells, as Anne Prescott suggests.[22] Pembroke proudly holds out to the viewer her volume clearly labeled "Davids Psalmes." Her metrical Psalms are thus portrayed as her greatest achievement, as the French Psalms were portrayed as the greatest achievement of Théodore de Bèze in a contemporary portrait; he is shown working in his study, a copy of the *Psaumes* before him, with the title equally visible.[23] This presentation of Pembroke as a poet was echoed in contemporary poems as well. Michael Drayton, for example, who is depicted wearing the poet's laurel wreath in his own portrait, celebrates her as "learnings famous Queene," one who wears "the Lawrell crowne."[24] Nothing in Pembroke's own portrait denotes an inferiority based on gender nor a modest reluctance to hide her identity as an author. In fact, the van de Passe portrait of Pembroke would have been eminently suitable for a title page, had her works later been printed along the lines of Michael Drayton's *Poems . . . Collected into One Volume* (1619) or *The Whole Workes of Samuel Daniel* (1623).[25] Given the construction of Pembroke's role as a poet by herself and by others, including her beloved niece, modesty can probably be ruled out as a motive for refusing to print the *Psalmes*.

In his more general address to all three women, Davies gives two other reasons why Pembroke, Bedford, and Cary might "presse the *Presse* with little you have made," explaining why aristocrats such as they might disdain print:

> . . . the *Presse* so much is wrong'd,
> by abject *Rimers* that great Hearts doe scorne
> To have their *Measures* with such *Nombers* throng'd,
> as are so basely *got, conceiv'd*, and *borne*.[26]

In that final line, to the usual "stigma of print" (see below) that might deter the upper classes from printing poems, he adds a third possible motive, the conflation of publication and unchastity that was so commonly used against women writers, that "metaphorical equation . . . between an eagerness to appear in print and sexual immorality," as Harold Love observes.[27] Sixteenth-century lyric poetry was virtually synonymous with the Petrarchan tradition of amorous verse, a tradition that was flexible enough to be used to express subjectivity, or even to encode political discontent.[28] Ann Rosalind Jones notes the paradox that although the love lyric was "an ostensibly private discourse," and should thus be more open to women than the more public forms like epic and tragedy, "the ideological matrix that associated open speech with open sexuality in women" made the love lyric "an especially transgressive genre for them."[29] Though Continental women did write love poems, English women had more restrictions. Richard Lovelace, for example, satirizes a woman who "Powders a Sonnet as she does her hair, / Then prostitutes them both to publick Aire."[30]

Yet in the years when Pembroke was writing and circulating her works her learning and virtue were consistently praised. When she was criticized, it was for her actions as a woman with a degree of power – over texts and over the lives of some beneath her on the social scale. Aside from her disputes with Greville and John Florio over the publication of Sidney's works, and carping about patronage by Thomas Nashe, Nicholas Breton, and others, the only negative contemporary portrayals of her are muted references in bitterly fawning letters by those who opposed her in court cases.[31] Some fifteen years after the completion of the *Psalmes* she is more appealingly human than ideal in the letters of those cheerful gossips, John Chamberlain and Dudley Carleton, who note the Dowager Countess's concern with her fading beauty; discuss her amusements of taking tobacco, playing cards, dancing; speculate on an unlikely youthful indiscretion with Sir Walter Raleigh; and mention her flirtation with her handsome and learned physician, Sir Matthew Lister, a romance reflected in Lady Wroth's pastoral drama *Loves Victory*.[32] More serious sexual slander, of a type traditionally directed at prominent women, was not recorded until some sixty years after her death, when the Royalist John Aubrey wrote against her son Philip Herbert, whom he considered a traitor for switching to Parliament in the English civil war. Though some women were called unchaste because of their writing, Pembroke's *Psalmes* protected her reputation.[33] Even when Aubrey accuses her of incest ("there was so great love" between Sir Philip Sidney and "his faire sister that I have heard old Gentlemen say that they lay together, and it was thought the first Philip Earle of Pembroke was begot by him") he does not connect that alleged transgression with her writing but rather with producing Philip Herbert's supposed mental incapacity: "he inherited not the witt of either brother or sister."[34]

If Pembroke had boldly written more secular works, then her reputation might well have been soiled. But by choosing to write metric Psalms rather than secular verse, she was able to achieve contemporary renown for both godliness and poetic composition. Psalm paraphrase was seen as a devout activity for both men and women. In the fifteenth century, for example, Dame Eleanor Hull translated an Old French commentary on the Penitential Psalms, and Christine de Pisan composed allegorized French poems on the Penitential Psalms. Earlier in the sixteenth century the Earl of Surrey used Wyatt's Psalm paraphrases as evidence of his virtue, Anne Lock's twenty-six sonnets meditating on Psalm 51 were published with her translation of Calvin, Laura Battiferra composed metric Psalms in Italian to great acclaim, and Thomas Bentley's *Monument of Matrones* included Psalm versions and meditations by such "godly" women as Catherine Parr, Anne Askew, Elizabeth Tyrwhit, and Dorcas Martin, presented as models for private and public worship.[35] Like their works, Pembroke's *Psalmes* were consistently praised as a demonstration of her virtue and, like the authors in the *Monument*, she was held up as an ideal for other women to follow. Most famously, Sir Edward Denny, furious at her niece Mary Wroth for satirizing him in her *Urania*, used the obvious virtue of one who would translate "the holly psalmes of David" to castigate Wroth. Writing after Pembroke's death, he claims that she "now . . . sings in the quier of Heaven," implying quite a different fate for the "monster," the "hermaphrodite" who dared write original, secular works.[36] The bitter irony of his taunts would not have escaped Wroth, whose poetry was evidently encouraged by her famous aunt, and who, as we have seen, portrayed Pembroke as a secular poet in her *Urania*. Sir John Harington of Kelston uses Pembroke and her *Psalmes* more flatteringly as an example for another woman, sending "the devine, and trulie devine translation . . . Donne by that Excellent Countesse, and in Poesie the mirroir of our Age" to their kinswoman Lucy, Countess of Bedford, praising her similar "admirable guifts, of the mynde, that clothe Nobilitie with vertue."[37]

John Davies himself praises the *Psalmes* as "A Worke of Art and Grace," in a theological as well as poetic sense, in hyperbolic praise of his patron that says her Psalm lyrics will replace the Music of the Spheres:

> So sweet a *Descant* on so sacred *Ground*
> No *Time* shall cease to sing to Heav'nly *Lyres*:
> For, when the *Spheares* shall cease their gyring sound,
> The *Angels* then, shall chaunt it in their *Quires*.[38]

Her *Psalmes* were similarly praised by other contemporary writers, including John Donne, Aemilia Lanyer, and Henry Parry.[39] Samuel Daniel, in the most familiar celebration of the *Psalmes*, claims that not only all godly people but also God himself praises them:

> Those *Hymnes* that thou doost consecrate to heaven,
> Which *Israels* Singer to his God did frame:
> Unto thy voyce eternitie hath given,
> And makes thee deere to him from whence they came.
> In them must rest thy ever reverent name,
> So long as *Syons* God remained honoured.[40]

Emphasizing her own role in completing the *Psalmes*, and adapting the architectural metaphor that she herself had used in the dedicatory poems, he says "this is that which thou maist call thine owne," work that will endure even after "*Wilton* lyes low levell'd with the ground . . . This Monument cannot be over-throwne."[41]

Sir John Harington of Kelston also uses an architectural metaphor when he compares her translation to the godly work of building a college in his epigram "in prayse of two worthy Translations, made by two great Ladies" (Mary de Valence, Countess of Pembroke, and Mary Sidney, Countess of Pembroke), praising their contribution to "sacred lore":

> Two *Maryes* that translate with divers arte
> Two subjects rude and ruinous before . . .
> Both works advance the love of sacred lore,
> Both helpe the soules of sinners to converte.
> Their learned payn I prayse, her costly almes;
> A Colledge this translates, the tother *Psalmes*.[42]

That is, Pembroke's *Psalmes* were said to make a contribution to learning parallel to establishing a college for divines (by definition male), as Mary de Valence, Countess of Pembroke, did in founding Pembroke College, Cambridge in 1347.[43] It is an astonishing claim, but hardly more so than saying her works "helpe the soules of sinners to converte." With such a torrent of praise for her virtue in translating the Psalms, it is most unlikely that Pembroke would have been dissuaded from printing them by fear of being called unchaste.

The evidence thus indicates that Pembroke was not deterred from print by feminine modesty nor by the insidious conflation of publication and unchastity that was so commonly used against women writers. That leaves the aristocratic disdain of "abject Rimers" who have wronged the press, so that "great Hearts doe scorne / To have their *Measures* with such *Nombers* throng'd." In this poem printed in 1612, Davies has to negotiate carefully his own participation in print, which he explains in terms of class:

> ... did my Fortunes not expose me to
> contempt of Greatnesse, with so meane I am,
> I should, with Greatnesse, greatly scorne it too,
> sith Fame for Versing, now, is held but Shame.[44]

That is, he would scorn to print his poetry if he could afford to do so, but needing money, he must submit to print. Finances play a somewhat different role in John Donne's decision to print poems, since he must establish that he can afford to print them at his own expense. He tells Sir Henry Goodyer in 1614 that he was forced to print his verses and dedicate them to the Lord Chamberlain, but did so "not for much publique view, but at mine owne cost, a few Copies."[45] That is, printing the verses will seem more acceptable if their circulation is still limited and, most importantly, if printing them is costly rather than profitable.

This is the "stigma of print," in the familiar words of J. W. Saunders, which has been challenged by Steven May, who suggests that it was verse, not print, that was stigmatized.[46] Certainly in Pembroke's case the problem cannot be simply that print itself was suspect, as Davies indicated, for she had done much to legitimize print by issuing her brother's works and her own. Economic issues remained, however. Social circulation of manuscripts, allowing for controlled production and dissemination of a text, was widely practiced among educated men and women. Such circulation, controlled by the physical access to a manuscript, was the opposite of printed texts produced for financial profit. Pembroke would no doubt remember Philip Sidney's disdain of those who write for profit: "Base men with servile wits undertake [poetry], who think it enough if they can be rewarded of the printer" and so "by their own disgracefulness disgrace the most graceful poesy." As Davies must defend the printing of his poems, Sidney must defend his own role as poet. He justifies his work as spontaneous: "overmastered by some thoughts, I yielded an inky tribute unto them."[47] Such sprezzatura would fit the role of the courtier, who may have found poetry a means of advancement, but who would not wish to be seen as taking his poetic role too seriously.

Manuscript circulation had insured the cachet of Sidney's works during his lifetime. "To be left to read or to copy the poems in Sidney's own working collection, or to be given one or more by the author himself, must have been a rare and exciting privilege for his family, friends, and acquaintances . . . He may have allowed others a sight of his new work to reward them or to strengthen personal ties with a gift," as Henry Woudhuysen observes.[48] Pembroke herself was Sidney's original audience, at least for the romance. In dedicating the *Arcadia* to "My Deare Lady and Sister" Sidney says he wrote it because "you desired me to doe it, and your desire, to my heart is an absolute commaundement."[49] His working copy was given to her as it was written, "being done in loose sheetes of paper, most of it in your presence, the rest, by sheetes, sent unto you, as fast as they were done."[50] Such a method of composition using loose sheets was not unusual, as Michael Brennan demonstrates.[51] When Sidney sent her this copy, he thereby entrusted her with the preservation and circulation of the work, as we have seen. "Now, it is done onely for you, only to you: if you keepe it to your selfe, or to such friends, who will weigh errors in the ballance of goodwill." That is, Sidney entrusted the manuscript to her with the expectation that she would control its circulation to "such friends" as would read it sympathetically.

Because of Sidney's extensive revisions of the *Old Arcadia*, amounting to virtually a new work, on either the same set of papers or in separate manuscript(s), entrusted as Greville claims, only to him, or as the countess believed, only for her, the situation becomes fraught with conflict. Whatever the exact complexities of the manuscript circulation of the two versions of the *Arcadia*, variously outlined by William Ringler, Jean Robertson, Victor Skretkowicz, and Henry Woudhuysen, keeping the work in manuscript meant that the coterie quality of Sidney's writing was as strong as that of Donne's poetry, demonstrated by the addresses to "faire ladies" in the *Old Arcadia*, and by the later search for the "key" to the printed *New Arcadia*, so that the seventeenth-century reader might become one of the cognoscenti.[52] *Astrophil and Stella* was originally even more restricted; Sonnet 37, with its transparent references to Penelope Devereux Rich, was omitted from the poems that were allowed to circulate outside the family circle and was withheld until Pembroke herself included it in the 1598 edition.[53] Resentment against such restricted circulation by the Countess of Pembroke and her aristocratic circle is, as Helen Vincent reminds us, reflected in Henry Olney's preface to his edition of Sidney's *Apology for Poetry*: "Those great ones, who in themselves have interr'd this blessed innocent, wil with Aesculapius condemne me as a detractor from their Deities."[54] Similar resentment against those family members who sought to restrain print publication of Sidney's work is seen in Thomas Newman's dedication of the 1591 *Astrophel and Stella* to

Frauncis Flower, in which he casts himself as a hero rescuing the text from the corruption of manuscript circulation: "I have beene very carefull in the Printing of it, and whereas being spred abroade in written Coppies, it had gathered much corruption by ill Writers: I have used their helpe and advice in correcting it and restoring it to his first dignitie, that I knowe were of skill and experience in those matters." He printed the text, he claims, only "because I thought it pittie anie thing proceeding from so rare a man, shoulde bee obscured, or that his fame should not still be nourisht in his works."[55] Josuah Sylvester, deprecating his "unlearned" translation of Du Bartas in contrast to Sidney's "heavenly Labour," justifies publishing his own translation, because Sidney's is a "Holy-RELIQUE" that is "shrin'd / In som High-Place, close lockt from common light."[56] He thereby combines praise of the heavenly Sidney with criticism of the family that is unwilling to share his relics. Presumably family opposition is why the poem was never printed, even though William Ponsonby had entered it for publication on 23 August 1588, along with the *Arcadia*. Unfortunately, the manuscript(s) no longer survive. As William Ringler reminds us, the loss is tragic, for if Sidney did translate the entire first *Semaine*, as Florio and Greville say, then "we have lost a body of his verse equal in bulk to more than half of that which survives."[57]

Not anticipating such a loss, the family no doubt would have preferred to maintain control of the circulation of Sidney's works after his death. In "The Dolefull Lay" the speaker shows herself part of a close community that heard Sidney's poems read aloud:

> Ne ever sing the love-layes which he made,
> Who ever made such layes of love as hee?
> Ne ever read the riddles, which he sayd
> Unto your selves, to make you mery glee.
> Your mery glee is now laid all abed,
> Your mery maker now alasse is dead.[58]

The coterie would know the meaning of these "riddles" that Sidney "sayd / Unto your selves," not to the world at large. The mourning here consists in *not* repeating Sidney's poems, for the "mery maker" is himself gone; the only comfort is knowing that he is in eternal bliss. Nowhere is there the suggestion that he would live through his poems, that circulating them more widely would enhance his memory.

Yet that is exactly the sense given in Pembroke's dedicatory poem to the *Psalmes* manuscript, "To the Angell Spirit of the most excellent, Sir Philip Sidney." She claims that she completed the *Psalmes* only to

honor him: "sithe it hath no further scope to goe, / nor other purpose
but to honor thee." She describes the state of his work using the same
architectural metaphor that later appears in praise of her own *Psalmes*:

> As goodly buildings to some glorious ende
>   cut off by fate, before the Graces hadde
>   each wondrous part in all their beauties cladde,
> Yet so much done, as Art could not amende;
>   So thy rare workes to which no witt can adde,
>   in all mens eies, which are not blindely madde,
> Beyonde compare above all praise, extende.[59]

All reasonable people praise Sidney's writings, which are "Beyonde com-
pare above all praise" even if he left them incomplete. That is, the speaker
here anticipates a much wider readership. Qualified readers have access
to those writings – and so do those who are "blindely madde." She may
allude here to the *Arcadia*, as well as to the *Psalmes* themselves. In a continuation of the architectural metaphor the works themselves become

> Immortall Monuments of thy faire fame,
>   though not compleat, nor in the reach of thought,
>   howe on that passing peece time would have wrought
> Had Heav'n so spar'd the life of life to frame
>   the rest? But ah! such losse hath this world ought
>   can equall it? or which like greevance brought?
> Yet there will live thy ever praised name.   (lines 71–77)

In this parallel to Hugh Sanford's observation that "Sir Philip Sidneies
writings" could not be "perfected without Sir Philip Sidney," Pembroke
claims that no one can imagine how his works would have been
completed.[60] Yet despite their unfinished state Sidney's literary works
now have become his monument, in them his name will live. What has
happened between the time the first poem was written, probably close
to Sidney's death in October 1586, and the second poem, dated 1599 in
the one extant copy, is the print circulation of his works.

Sidney's relationship to print began inauspiciously. His death, like that
of Diana, Princess of Wales, or John F. Kennedy, Jr., presented a mer-
chandizing opportunity. From Thomas Lant's engravings of the funeral
procession, used as a toy by young John Aubrey, to broadsides describing
the manner of his death and pirated editions of his works, the publishing world sought to cash in on his reputation. Fulke Greville's 1586
letter to Walsingham, alerting him to the planned unauthorized printing

of the *Old Arcadia*, expresses his distress at mercenary motivations for attempting to print both that work and Arthur Golding's "completion" of Sidney's translation of Mornay's *De la Verité de la religion chrétienne.*[61] The rush to print Sidney's work evidently surprised the family who had, in their grief, made no effort to disseminate his writings. What is particularly notable here, as Woudhuysen says, is Greville's belief that he has a right to stay publication of the *Old Arcadia* and to publish instead the *New Arcadia*, along with Sidney's Psalms 1–43 and his translation of Du Bartas's *Semaine.*[62] Greville's struggle to control Sidney's reputation continues in his important and lengthy "Dedication," but takes a bizarre twist – almost grave robbing – in the joint tomb he planned, some thirty years after Sidney's death, to put in St. Paul's for himself and Sidney.[63] Evidently he never gave up trying to wrest control of Sidney's corpus, and even his corpse, from his family.

This rivalry may paradoxically explain both Pembroke's effort to print Sidney's secular works and her efforts to restrict the *Psalmes* to manuscript circulation. Not satisfied with Greville's 1590 edition of the *Arcadia*, the countess took it upon herself to stabilize his works in print. Hugh Sanford opens the preface to the 1593 edition with disparagement of Greville's editorial work: "The disfigured face, gentle Reader, wherewith this worke not long since appeared to the common view, moved that noble Lady, to whose honour consecrated, to whose protection it was committed, to take in hand the wiping away those spottes wherewith the beauties therof were unworthely blemished."[64] Though he evidently did much of the more detailed work himself, he attributes to Pembroke the oversight of this revised edition, which was "most by her doing, all by her directing," so that "it is now by more then one interest *The Countesse of Pembrokes Arcadia*; done, as it was, for her: as it is, by her." Sanford reiterates Pembroke's right to control the presentation and circulation of the work when he calls her "that noble Lady, to whose honour consecrated, to whose protection it was committed." His preface thus provides an "uneasy explanation for why the text has been printed despite the explicit desires of the author," Wendy Wall observes, as Sanford "twists the language of coterie manuscript circulation to accommodate the literary marketplace." Printing that letter of dedication just before Sanford's preface "To the Reader" means that "Sidney's dedication of his trivial amateur labors to his sister is thus recast as her dedication to him of the published monumental folio."[65] The title page of the 1593 *Arcadia*, reprinted in 1598, attempts to retain the social status of a manuscript even in print, by including the Sidney porcupine, the Dudley bear, and the Pembroke lion.[66] Pembroke herself evidently stabilized the text of *Astrophil and Stella*. Those who had copied manuscript poems into their own commonplace books selected poems and chose their own order of presentation. The unauthorized 1591 edition continues this fluid presentation, including poems by Daniel and running poems together on the page, whereas the 1598 edition supervised by Pembroke assigns numerals to each poem and numbers pages sequentially, thereby fixing their order.[67]

Pembroke obviously took seriously her brother's request that she offer the work her "protection." As Sanford concludes: "Neither shall these pains be the last (if no unexpected accident cut off her determination) which the everlasting love of her excellent brother, will make her consecrate to his memory."[68] In this effort she worked closely with William Ponsonby, who first alerted Greville to the impending, unauthorized publication of the *Arcadia*, as Brennan has shown, and with the printer John Windet, as Mark Bland established.[69] Ponsonby was the first to put her name into print with *The Countess of Pembrokes Arcadia* (1590, 1593, and 1598), followed by Abraham Fraunce's *The Countesse of Pembrokes Emmanuel* (1591), *The Countesse of Pembrokes Ivychurch* (1591), and *The Third Part of the Countesse of Pembrokes Ivychurch* (1592). (Others wrote works using her names as well, including "The Countess of Pembrokes Pastoral by Shep. Tonie" (Antony Munday) in *Englands Helicon*, and Nicholas Breton's "The Countesse of Penbrookes love" and "The Countess of Pembrokes Passion.")[70] As Gavin Alexander observes, believing that he could gain a monopoly on publications of Sidney's works by gaining Pembroke's favor, Ponsonby "bombarded" her with works dedicated to her in the early 1590s.[71] Between 1590 and 1600, he also published Sidney's *Defence* (1595); other works associated directly with the countess include Thomas Watson's *Amintae gaudia* (1592) and several of Spenser's works with addresses to her, including *The Faerie Queene* (1590), *Complaints* (1591), *Colin Clout*, and *Astrophel* (1595). Ponsonby also published Pembroke's *Antonius* (1592 and 1595) and *A Discourse of Life and Death* (1592 and 1600); the works were issued with her own name on the title page and without any apology either for her gender or for her appearance in print.[72] Steven May surmises that she authorized the publication of *Antonius* because it fit the "precepts of dramatic tragedy outlined in the *Defence*."[73] Sidney was thus, in a sense, authorizing that work, even as her translation of Philippe de Mornay's *Discours de la vie et de la mort* was authorized by Sidney's own translation of Mornay's *De la Verité de la réligion Chrétienne*.

Only one secular translation by an English woman preceded her into print, Margaret Tyler's translation of a Spanish romance, *The first part of the Mirrour of Princely Deedes and Knighthood* (1578), which includes a preface attempting to justify translating a "storye profane, and a matter more manlike then becometh my sexe." To justify the romance genre, Tyler uses the same argument that Sidney will later use in his *Defence of Poetry*, that it gives examples of virtuous behavior; to justify a woman's translation of such a work, she notes that men dedicate romances to women, and "it is all one for a woman to pen a storie, as for a man to addresse his storie to a woman." When Tyler observes that her critics would "enforce me necessarily either not to write or to write of divinitie," she points to a commonplace.[74] Women's religious writing, particularly translation, was often considered less transgressive of gender restrictions than secular writing, since it could be framed as religious instruction for those who were younger or less educated. Yet even previous religious translations by English women were likely to be anonymous, as Margaret More Roper's translation of Erasmus's *Devout Treatise Upon the Pater Noster* (1526?); or just published under initials, as Anne Lock's translation of John Calvin's *Sermons of John Calvin, upon the Songe that Ezechias made after he had bene sicke and afflicted by the hand of God* (1560). Anne Lock's second printed translation, of Jean Taffin's *Of the Markes of the Children of God, and of their Comforts in Afflictions*, published under her own name (by then Anne Prowse) in 1590, perhaps inspired Pembroke to be equally forthcoming two years later with her own translations.

During the period when Pembroke was "directing" the printing of Sidney's works, two more of her own works appeared in print, "The Dolefull Lay of Clorinda" in Spenser's *Astrophel* (1595), and "Astrea" in Francis Davison's *A Poetical Rapsody* (1602). "Astrea" certainly seems to have been published with the countess's permission, since no effort to recall it has been found, nor is there any record of dismay that the volume was dedicated to William Herbert, who had recently become Earl of Pembroke. A celebration of Elizabeth that had been intended for presentation on the queen's (canceled) progress to Wilton, it therefore parallels Sidney's "The Lady of May" presented to Elizabeth at Wanstead, included by Pembroke in the 1598 *Arcadia*.

The *Astrophel* elegies were probably printed in collaboration with Spenser and Lodowick Bryskett and may therefore also have been produced with Pembroke's cooperation. In her 1594 letter to Sir Edward Wotton we may catch a glimpse of the transmutation of her work from manuscript to print. Like Donne, she had to ask for her poem back, having sent a friend the only extant copy.[75] The letter attempts to establish her control of her own work: she asks that she "maie redeeme a certain

Idle passion which loonge since I left in your hands onlie beinge desyrous
to review what the Image could be of those sadd tymes, I very well know
unworthy of the humour that then possest me and suche as I knowe no
reason ~~whie~~ yow should yeld me any account of." She asks, "yf your care
of these follies of suche a toy have chanced to keepe that which my self
have lost, my earnest desire is that I maie againe see it," adding the in-
centive that she will give him "other things better worth your keepinge,"
presumably works by her brother.[76] Her self-deprecating dismissal of the
work as "a toy" echoes the sprezzatura of her brother's description of
the *Arcadia* as "this idle work of mine . . . being but a trifle" in his dedicatory letter and need not indicate any particular dissatisfaction with
her own work. The letter to Wotton does vividly show, however, why so
much poetry by the Sidneys and their contemporaries has been lost. She
evidently sent one copy of this elegy to a friend and then misplaced the
original, probably "The Dolefull Lay of Clorinda," which she needed
for inclusion in *Astrophel*, printed the following year. Such lost (and occasionally retrieved) poems were not uncommon among socially circulated
texts.

Another work that was almost lost was her translation of Petrarch's
"The Triumph of Death," which happened to be preserved in a transcription of a letter Harington sent to Lucy, Countess of Bedford, along
with a miscellaneous collection juxtaposing three of Pembroke's *Psalmes*
(Psalms 51, 104, and 137) with secular works, including Thomas Nashe's
notorious "The choice of Valentines." In fact, we have no real proof that
she did not complete the rest of the *Trionfi*, since the preservation of this
one "Triumph" was so haphazard, and since her physician, Thomas
Moffet, seems to refer to a longer work when he tells her to take some
time off from poetic composition: "Let *Petrarke* sleep, give rest to *Sacred
Writte*."[77] Her "Triumph of Death" may have had some manuscript circulation, although no other copies are extant. Aemilia Lanyer, Michael
Drayton, and Gabriel Harvey, for example, may allude to this work.[78]
Mentioning such a work indicated some access to a literary coterie,
although knowing of a work did not necessarily mean reading it.

Printed miscellanies attempted to reproduce the sense of belonging
to such a coterie, so that readers could imagine themselves looking over
the shoulder of the Countess of Bedford, say. They could not buy either
Pembroke's "Triumph" or her *Psalmes*, but they could buy selections from
her printed work adapted in John Bodenham's printed verse miscellany
Bel-vedére (1600). Bodenham's method is to reduce the quotations to brief
sententiae under headings like "Of Pride" and "Of Courage."[79] *Antonius*, a

Senecan drama replete with *sententiae*, is particularly suited to his purpose, although he also includes lines from "The Dolefull Lay." Among the authors cited is "Mary, Countesse of Pembrooke," listed just before her brother Philip Sidney, both of whom help to confirm the aristocratic status of the collection. As Wendy Wall has demonstrated, a printed volume might be set up to give a sense of privacy, of entering "an enclosed or secret sphere."[80] Bodenham literalizes the metaphor as he tantalizes the reader with admittance into "the Muses Garden, (a place that may beseeme the presence of the greatest Prince in the world.) Imagine then thy height of happinesse, in being admitted to so celestiall a Paradise." He frames his work as a variation of the private commonplace book, adapted from court speeches and performances, songs, from some printed works, and from the "privat Poems, Sonnets, Ditties, and other wittie conceits, given to [the queen's] Honorable Ladies; and vertuous Maids of Honour; according as they could be obtained by sight, or favour of copying."[81] Readers, even those who must be warned not to "trample . . . rudely" on these poetic flowers, thus have (belated) access to works circulated in the aristocratic coterie.

This is all known to have appeared in print during Pembroke's life, but she circulated other works in manuscript, at least among a small circle of friends. Edward Wotton had the only copy of an early elegy, as we have seen; Edmund Spenser said in "The Ruines of Time" (1590) that he had read her work and in *Astrophel* (1595) that he was printing her poem; Samuel Daniel's papers included an early version of "To the Angell Spirit."[82] Her printed letters to Tobie Matthew, if authentic, indicate that Matthew had been circulating works (since lost) that she had entrusted to him; they would also indicate that John Donne, the younger, had access to her private correspondence. She sent Rowland Whyte, Robert Sidney's agent, an autograph copy of a letter written to the Lord Treasurer urging Robert Sidney's leave from his duties in Flushing: "The copies of her letter she did vouchsafe to send unto me of her own hand writing. I never reade any thing that could express an earnest desire like unto this."[83] Her ability as a letter writer was evidently well known, for Francis Osborne also says that he has read some "incomparable *Letters* of hers" that he had seen.[84] Her correspondence with her brothers and additional literary works and translations were probably lost to the fires at her primary residences of Wilton, Baynards Castle, and Ramsbury; or they may have been discarded by the recipients or subsequent generations; or, the most intriguing possibility, some may be extant and, to date, not correctly attributed.

Sir Edward Denny tantalizes us with the possibility that additional sacred translations have been lost, when he says that she had "translated so many godly books."[85] The *Psalmes*, however, are the work that Pembroke took most care to preserve. Her presentation of the *Psalmes* in 1599 may parallel her presentation of Sidney's works in the 1598 edition of the *Arcadia*, which elegantly preserved his secular works. She stabilized the text of three works originally printed without her authorization (the *New Arcadia*, *Defence of Poetry*, and *Astrophil and Stella*), to which she added "Certain Sonnets never before printed" and "The Lady of May," as well as *Astrophil* 37. She may have initially viewed this publication as a regrettable necessity, undertaken to right Sidney's reputation, to establish him as a writer, and to establish her own right to control his literary remains. The care taken in this folio volume indicates, however, a significant effort to monumentalize Sidney.

With the Sidneian *Psalmes* she was more successful in retaining control of their circulation, so that none of them were printed during her lifetime.[86] Sir John Harington, who had seen his own work through print in the 1590s, was particularly eager to see the Sidneian *Psalmes* printed. In his "Treatise on Play" he alluded to Samuel Daniel's famous statement (quoted above), "seeing it is allredy prophecied those precious leaves (those hims that she doth consecrate to Heaven) shall owtlast Wilton walls, meethinke it is pitty they are unpublyshed, but lye still inclosed within those walls lyke prisoners, though many have made great suyt for theyr liberty."[87] He thus transmutes Bodenham's metaphor of the enclosed garden to a prison; potential readers, barred from entry, attempt to free the *Psalmes* from captivity. Since so many other metric Psalms were in print by the end of the sixteenth century, "Neither the 'stigma of print' nor the Sternhold–Hopkins stranglehold [on printed Psalters] provides a complete explanation" for why the Sidneian *Psalmes* were not printed in Pembroke's life, as Alexander argues.[88] Frequently the authors of metric Psalters, like Matthew Parker, said that they printed the work reluctantly, only after friends who had read the manuscript urged them to circulate the work in print, and that was a justification that Pembroke could truthfully have made if she had so desired.[89]

Certainly others sought to print them, beginning with Sidney's paraphrases of Psalms 1–43, perhaps as early as 1587. Greville seems to have planned a second volume of Sidney's "religious works," including his now lost translation of Du Bartas's *Semaine*, his translation of Mornay, and his Psalms 1–43. That second volume may have been prevented by "later disputes between Greville and the Countess of Pembroke over the text of the *Arcadia*," as Woudhuysen suggests. Pembroke may have not wanted to trust Greville with the religious works, because of his treatment of the *Arcadia*, or "she may have felt that Greville's version of her brother's literary career did not match her own." Her 1598 edition presented not "his sacred translations, but . . . his profane writings."[90] Pembroke, following her brother's arguments in his *Defence of Poetry*, may well have thought that the *Psalmes* were a special case, as Rienstra and Kinnamon argue.[91] Of his three types of poets "The chief, both in antiquity and excellency, were they that did imitate the unconceivable excellencies of God," and the Psalms are themselves "a divine poem."[92]

Pembroke's decision to restrict the circulation of the *Psalmes* must have been deliberate, as Brennan observes, because she had better access to the stationers than any other aristocratic woman, and they would have sold briskly.[93] One motivation for restricted scribal publication was "the very real danger that a text in uncontrolled circulation would sooner or later be piratically propelled into print," exactly what had happened with Philip Sidney's secular works. The pleas in printed works that the author feared publication from an unauthorized or corrupt manuscript were not "coy attempts to disarm criticism," Love argues, but "a real and pressing dilemma for scribally publishing authors."[94] George Wither, for example, complained that if a bookseller "gett any written Coppy into his powre, likely to be vendible; whether the Author be willing or no, he will publish it" with whatever title and corruptions the bookseller chooses.[95] Printing the work could be a preemptive move, as may have happened when Pembroke gave her translations of *Antonius* and the *Discourse* to William Ponsonby for printing. Ponsonby would have been eager to print the *Psalmes* as well, but perhaps she did not need to print the *Psalmes* simply because she was successful in preventing a copy from reaching an unauthorized printer. Francis Davison certainly tried to print them. His list of "Manuscripts to gett" includes the "*Psalmes* by the Countes of Pembroke. Qre. If they shall not bee printed."[96] He may mean by this simply that he needed to check whether they had been printed or registered already, as Roger Kuin suggests.[97] By listing the *Psalmes* as Pembroke's, rather than Sidney's, Davison implicitly recognizes her authorship of most of the work and perhaps even her desire to control its circulation. She may have given him permission to print her "Astrea," but she presumably refused him permission to print the *Psalmes*.

An examination of her agency in the print and manuscript circulation of both her brother Philip's work and her own indicates a preference for scribal publication, which provided both more prestige and more control over their circulation. The Sidneian *Psalmes* were first presented in the form of author publication, when "the production and distribution of copies takes place under the author's personal direction," as Love explains.[98] The authorial autograph is what Samuel Woodforde claimed to be saving when he transcribed what was left of a manuscript that his brother was using to put up coffee powder. In reference to all the corrections to Psalm 49 he says: "The very manner of this *Psalms* being crossd and alterd almost in every line and in many words thrice makes me believe this was an originall book that is[,] the book before me was so for none but an author could or would so amend any Copy."[99] Woodforde seems to have discarded the original, erroneously believing that his own fair copy was preferable to the authors' foul papers.

Two elegant transcriptions were evidently completed under Pembroke's direction. The Tixall manuscript, with its unique copy of the dedicatory poems, may have been the presentation copy for Queen Elizabeth, copied from the Penshurst manuscript (which is missing the opening leaves). The Penshurst manuscript is transcribed in the best Italian style by John Davies, a professional calligrapher and author of *The Writing Schoolemaster or the Anatomie of Faire Writing*.[100] As Davies himself declares, "My Hand once sought that glorious WORKE to grace; / and writ, in Gold, what thou, in Incke, hadst writ."[101] (He flatters her by saying, "But Gold and highest Art are both too base / to Character the glory of thy Wit!") In other words, he took her working papers and made them into a work of visual art, highlighted with gold ink in capital letters and in the loops of letters such as *l* or *p*. Such a copy was far more prestigious than any printed book could be.

When Pembroke describes her own work on the *Psalmes* in "To the Angell Spirit," she uses the traditional clothing metaphor to depict translation, desiring "That Israels King may daigne his owne transform'd / In substance no, but superficiall tire" (lines 8–9). This metaphor, although it ostensibly refers to translation, may also point to the manuscript itself. As Love argues, "the dress of texts, in the sense of appearance as well as style, might offer grounds for positing a published status."[102] Not only the words but also the appearance is important. When Pembroke presents the Sidneian *Psalmes* to Elizabeth as a livery cloth, she notes that the Psalms have often "worse, without repining worne" ("Even now that Care," line 32). That is, others had dressed them in humbler garb. William Hunnis acknowledges as much when he apologizes for the quality and presentation of his own metric versions of the penitential psalms set to music. He defensively claims that the Psalms are

"More rich . . . in threedbare cote, / than some in silken gowne." Class
consciousness is evident in his contention that, since they come originally
from a king, they are worthy despite the poor attire he has given them. Yet
perhaps, he says, "some woorthie wight / will shape thee rich araie, / And
set thee foorth as thou deserv'st / with costlie jewels gai."[103] This is exactly what Pembroke did, both metaphorically in the quality of her verse
and literally in the manuscripts themselves. She spared no expense in
her presentation of the Sidneian *Psalmes*. Dressed in the elegant calligra-
phy of Sir John Davies, adorned with gold ink, they presented the King
David's songs in both content and appearance with "better grace" than
"what the vulgar form'd," her description of the ubiquitous, and often
hastily printed, Psalters such as the editions of Sternhold and Hopkins.[104]

These three manuscripts include the markers Love suggests for
authorial publication, such as a dedication, corrections in the hand
of the author or a "known amanuensis," and an accurate text. Love
notes two other types of scribal publication, entrepreneurial and user.[105]
Pembroke seems to have successfully prevented entrepreneurial publication even in manuscript, but there was substantial user publication.
Those who obtained copies of *Psalmes* often felt free to shape them to
their own purposes. Sir John Harington of Kelston, for example, adapted
the *Psalmes* for a variety of uses. A Sidney relative and a close friend of
Robert Sidney, he was invited by Pembroke to visit Wilton. He exchanged
verses with Robert Sidney, transcribed some of the *Astrophil* sonnets from
manuscript, and owned two manuscripts of the *Psalmes* that he shaped
to his own ends (MSS I and K, BL MSS Additional 12047 and 46372);
both have been rubricated for morning and evening prayer like the *Book
of Common Prayer* and like the Psalms and prayers by Elizabeth Tyrwhit
framed for private and public devotional use in Thomas Bentley's *The
Monument of Matrones* (1582). That is, Pembroke's paraphrase of the Psalms
was also seen as sacred text, suitable for use in worship by men and
women. Seven psalms found in Harington's papers were eventually
printed in *Nugae Antiquae*. He sent three Psalms to Lucy, Countess of
Bedford, as we have seen, and quotes from the *Psalmes* in the *Metamorphosis
of Ajax* and the *Aeneid*.[106]

Several other of her *Psalmes* seem to have circulated independently
and to have been enclosed in correspondence, including a manuscript
copy of Psalm 137 now at the University of Nottingham (MS Cl Lm 50)
and copies of Psalms 51, 105, and 137 in a manuscript at All Souls College,
Oxford (MS 155).[107] Additionally, two penitential Psalms (51 and 130)
were set for treble voice and lute in BL Additional MS 15117, a music

miscellany that may reflect a woman's own musical taste, as Linda Austern argues.[108] The alternate versions of Psalms 120–27 in manuscripts G and M also seem to have been intended for singing, since Pembroke's typical scholarship, metric complexity, and word play in those quantitative poems were replaced by simple rhymed paraphrases of the *Book of Common Prayer*, probably by someone other than the author. Psalm 124 in that simplified version, for example, fits the familiar tune of the Doxology.[109] The first print publication of her *Psalmes* was also intended for singing, since part of her Psalm 97 (ll. 10, 15, 32, 38) was adapted in *All the French Psalm Tunes with English Words* (1632).[110]

The eighteen extant *Psalmes* manuscripts indicate considerable circulation. By comparison, there were possibly as many as eighteen manuscripts of the *Old Arcadia* when Greville dismissed it as "so common," as Woudhuysen has shown.[111] Among her contemporaries who read Pembroke's work in manuscript, or claimed to, are Samuel Daniel, John Donne, John Donne the younger, Francis Davison, Michael Drayton, Sir John Harington of Kelston, George Herbert, Aemilia Lanyer, Tobie Matthew, Thomas Moffet, and Edmund Spenser. Her brother Robert sent her his autograph copy of his poems, and he undoubtedly read her work in return. Wroth, who was so often at Wilton when Pembroke was involved in the publishing of Philip Sidney's works and in her own writing, knew her work as well and, as we have seen, portrays her as reading her poetry aloud to friends and circulating copies among a coterie.

The very restriction of a manuscript's circulation increased its desirability. The process is demonstrated by Jonson's "An epigram to my muse, the Lady Digby, on her husband, Sir Kenelme Digby" which demonstrates how a copy could be given to a friend "on the explicit understanding that he or she would bring it to wider attention." Jonson says, "what copies shall be had, / What transcripts begg'd?" Thus "being sent to one, they will be read of all."[112] Drayton, who printed his works, complains that other poets' "Verses are wholly deduc't to Chambers, and nothing esteem'd . . . but what is kept in Cabinets, and must onely pass by Transcription."[113] Asking for a manuscript copy was beneficial for both the writer, who controlled her own work and also bestowed a favor, and for the recipient, who thereby demonstrated membership in an elite coterie. When Pembroke refers to Elizabeth's breast as "the Cabinet" of the Muses, she is thus emphasizing the exclusivity of manuscripts kept by the queen.

As Michael Brennan suggests, her dedication of the manuscript to Queen Elizabeth "granted a kind of ownership to the patron."[114] While her more conventional praise of Elizabeth in "Astrea" might circulate in print, her poem of admonitory flattery was not permitted even manuscript circulation. If Pembroke wanted to tell the queen to give additional support to the Protestant cause, as I have argued elsewhere, then her advice was for the queen only.[115] The presentation copy, dated 1599, was evidently prepared in the same year that she addressed the queen in "Astrea." Those literary tributes were followed by an appropriately obsequious letter seeking a position for her young son William at court, and may well have been timed to influence the queen to favor him.

By presenting the *Psalmes* as her own work, as well as that of her famous brother, and by presenting them to a queen, Pembroke addresses gender obliquely. She describes Elizabeth as the equal of the biblical King David and lists a series of paradoxes embodied in her reign, from a woman's rule, to her imperial role in New World exploration, to gender reversal, to Elizabeth as the *primum mobile*:

> Kings on a Queene enforst their states to lay;
> Main-lands for Empire waiting on an Ile;
> Men drawne by worth a woman to obay;
> one moving all, herselfe unmov'd the while.
> ("Even now that Care," lines 81–84)

Pembroke never apologizes for or even mentions her own role as a woman writer, thereby making her most powerful statement on gender. Women rule, women write, and women are leaders in the godly kingdom. There is no hint here that women would refrain from print publication.

Pembroke's choice of scribal rather than print publication for the *Psalmes* thus does not seem to be a decision based on cultural restrictions on women's speech. As Philip Sidney claimed that he wrote "onely for you, only to you" when he presented *The Countess of Pembrokes Arcadia* to her, so Pembroke claimed that she wrote only for Elizabeth when she presented the *Psalmes* to her: "A King should onely to a Queene be sent" ("Even now that Care," line 53). Her effort to control circulation of her brother's work and her own may be reflected in Sanford's attempts to construct a defense against unworthy readers: "the wortheles Reader can never worthely esteeme of so worthye a writing: and as true, that the noble, the wise, the vertuous, the curteous, as many as have had any acquaintaunce with true learning and knowledge, will with all love

and dearenesse entertaine it."[116] Such a preface is a rear guard action,
taken to protect a work already open to general criticism; printing the
Psalmes would have exposed them to the same readership. Pembroke no
doubt believed that she was more successful in offering the *Psalmes* the
"protection" that her brother had sought than she was for the *Arcadia*,
perhaps because she entreated the aid of Elizabeth. As Sidney had said
that the *Arcadia*'s "chiefe protection" would be "bearing the livery of
your name," so Pembroke presents the *Psalmes* to the queen as "holy
garments" that become Elizabeth's "liverie robe." Saying that they are
"to bee bestowed by thee" asks the queen to perform the same function in the distribution of the *Psalmes* that she herself had been asked to
undertake for the *Arcadia*. Pembroke's agency in print and scribal publication thus suggests neither feminine modesty, nor fear at being thought
unchaste, but rather a determined effort to present the works of her
brother Philip and herself in the most elegant form possible to informed
and sympathetic readers.

NOTES

1 "To my Deare Ladie and Sister, the Countesse of Pembroke," *The Countesse
   of Pembrokes Arcadia. Written by Sir Philip Sidney Knight. Now since the first edition
   augmented and ended* (London: William Ponsonby, 1593), sig. A3. See also
   Wendy Wall, *The Imprint of Gender: Authorship and Publication in the English
   Renaissance* (Ithaca: Cornell University Press, 1993), 154. On the modesty
   topos, see Ana Kothe, "Displaying the Muse: Print, Prologue, Poetics, and
   Early Modern Women Writers Published in England and Spain," Ph.D.
   thesis, University of Maryland (1996).
2 Sidney entrusts this manuscript to his sister as John Donne entrusts
   Biathanatos to two friends who would "(a) preserve it, and (b) decide for him
   who should see it and who not," Peter Beal, *In Praise of Scribes: Manuscripts and
   their Makers in Seventeenth-Century England* (Oxford: Clarendon Press, 1998), 35.
3 H. R. Woudhuysen, *Sir Philip Sidney and the Circulation of Manuscripts
   1558–1640* (Oxford: Clarendon Press, 1996), 384.
4 Roger Kuin, "The Genesis of *Astrophil and Stella*," paper read at Medieval
   Congress, Kalamazoo, Michigan, May 2000.
5 "Even now that Care," lines 27–34, *The Collected Works of Mary Sidney Herbert,
   Countess of Pembroke*, eds. Margaret Hannay, Noel Kinnamon, and Michael
   Brennan (Oxford: Clarendon Press, 1998), 1:102–03.
6 Lisa Klein emphasizes that Pembroke presents her poems as cloth, referring
   to her "handmaids taske" and thereby "alluding to the works of her hand
   as well as to her own subservient position before God and her queen." Like
   other handmade gifts, such as Esther Inglis's book or Arbella Stuart's gloves,
   the *Psalmes* "had a unique capacity to evoke the giver, her hands occupied in

painstaking and loving labor and outstretched in an attitude of presentation, devotion or supplication," "Your Humble Handmaid: Elizabethan Gifts of Needlework," *Renaissance Quarterly* 50 (1997), 476. See also Jane Donawerth, "Women's Poetry and the Tudor–Stuart System of Gift Exchange," *Women, Writing, and the Reproduction of Culture in Tudor and Stuart Britain*, eds. Mary E. Burke, Jane Donawerth, Linda L. Dove, and Karen Nelson (Syracuse: Syracuse University Press, 2000), 3–18.

7 Harold Love, *Scribal Publication in Seventeenth-Century England* (Oxford: Clarendon Press, 1993), 70.

8 Georgianna Ziegler, "Jewels for the Soul: the Psalm Books of Esther Inglis," paper read at the 1998 annual meeting of the Renaissance Society of America, University of Maryland, March 1998. On other Psalters presented to Elizabeth, see "'Even now that Care': Literary Context," *Collected Works of Mary Sidney* 1:92–101.

9 Margaret J. M. Ezell, *Social Authorship and the Advent of Print* (Baltimore: Johns Hopkins University Press, 1999), 23.

10 John Davies of Hereford, "To the most noble, and no lesse deservedly-renowned Ladyes, as well Darlings, as Patronesses, of the *Muses*; Lucy, Countesse of Bedford; Mary, Countesse-Dowager of Pembrooke; and, Elizabeth, Lady Cary, (Wife of Sr. Henry Cary:) Glories of Women," *The Muses Sacrifice, or Divine Meditations* (London: George Norton, 1612), sig. A1v.

11 Ibid., sig. ***3.

12 *The First Part of The Countess of Montgomery's Urania by Lady Mary Wroth*, ed. Josephine A. Roberts (Binghamton: MRTS/RETS, 1995), 371.

13 Graham Parry, "Lady Mary Wroth's *Urania*," *Proceedings of the Leeds Philosophical and Literary Society* 21.4 (1975), 54; Wroth, *Urania*, 715.

14 Josephine Roberts and I discussed this poem, concluding that there is a slight possibility that it was written by, or in conjunction with, Pembroke, thus paralleling the poem by William Herbert attributed to Amphilanthus (*The Poems of Lady Mary Wroth*, ed. Josephine A. Roberts, Baton Rouge: University of Louisiana Press, 1983, 217). In the Folger manuscript of Wroth's poems, the nightingale poem is inserted between numbers 3 and 4 in a sequence, but is not itself numbered (MS V.a.104, fol. 49v). This version varies in wording from that printed in the *Urania*.

15 Wroth, *Urania*, 490.

16 Debra Rienstra and Noel Kinnamon, "Circulating the Sidney–Pembroke Psalter," in this volume.

17 John Dickenson, *Arisbas, Euphues amidst his Slumbers: Or Cupids Journey to Hell* (London, 1594), sigs. A3, A4. See also Gavin Alexander, "Five Responses to Sir Philip Sidney 1586–1628," Ph.D. thesis, University of Cambridge (1996), 113.

18 Marjon Poort, "The Desired and Destined Successor," *Sir Philip Sidney: 1586 and the Creation of a Legend*, eds. Jan Van Dorsten, Dominic Baker-Smith, and Arthur F. Kinney (Leiden: J. J. Brill and Leiden University Press, 1986), 34; and Dominic Baker-Smith, "'Great Expectation': Sidney's Death and

the Poets," *Sir Philip Sidney: 1586 and the Creation of a Legend*, eds., Jan Van Dorsten, Dominic Baker-Smith, and Arthur F. Kinney (Leiden: J. J. Brill and Leiden University Press, 1986), 89. *Epitaphia in Mortem Nobilissimi et Fortissimi Viri D. Philippi Sidneii Equitis*, ed. Georgius Benedicti (Werteloo) (Leiden and Louvain: J. Paedts, 1587); *Academiae Cantabrigiensis Lacrymae Tumulo Nobilissimi Equitis, D. Philippi Sidneii Sacratae*, ed. Alexander Neville (1587); *Peplus, Illustrissimi viri D. Philippi Sidnaei Supremis Honoribus Dicatus*, ed. John Lloyd of New College, Oxford (Oxford, 1587); *Exequiae Illustrissimi Equitis, D. Philippi Sidnaei, Gratissimae Memoriae ac Nomini Impensae*, ed. William Gager (Oxford, 1587).

19 Beth Wynne Fisken, "'To the Angell spirit . . .': Mary Sidney's Entry into the 'World of Words,'" *The Renaissance Englishwoman in Print: Counterbalancing the Canon*, eds. Anne M. Haselkorn and Betty S. Travitsky (Amherst: University of Massachusetts Press, 1990), 265–66.

20 Alexander, "Five Responses to Sir Philip Sidney 1586–1628," 33. See also Suzanne Trill, "Spectres and Sisters: Mary Sidney and the 'Perennial Puzzle' of Renaissance Women's Writing," *Renaissance Configurations: Voices/ Bodies/Spaces, 1580–1690*, ed. Gordon McMullan (London: Macmillan, 1998), 202–05.

21 Correspondence XII, *Collected Works of Mary Sidney*, 1:295.

22 Anne Prescott, discussion at the meeting of the Society for the Study of Women in the Renaissance, CUNY, 20 April 1998. I am also grateful to Betty Travitsky, Richard McCoy, and other members of the Society for the Study of Women in the Renaissance who participated in the discussion of an earlier version of this paper.

Quill pens and/or laurel wreaths figure prominently in many portraits of writers, but there is nothing quite like this design in Arthur M. Hind, *Engraving in England in the Sixteenth and Seventeenth Centuries*, 3 vols. (Cambridge: Cambridge University Press, 1952) or in Jonathan Goldberg, *Writing Matter: from the Hands of the English Renaissance* (Stanford: Stanford University Press, 1990).

Esther Inglis portrays herself at a table with a quill pen and uses a device of crossed golden quills derived from a prize given to calligraphers, as Georgianna Ziegler informed me, private correspondence. See Anthony R. A. Croiset Van Uchelen, "Dutch Writing-Masters and the 'Prix de la Plume Couronée,'" *Quaerendo* 6 (1976).

23 The portrait of Théodore de Bèze, at the Bibliothèque Nationale, is reproduced in George A. Rothrock, *The Huguenots: a Biography of a Minority* (Chicago: Nelson Hall, 1979).

24 Michael Drayton, "The sixth Eglog," *Idea: the Shepheards Garland*; rpt. *The Works of Michael Drayton*, ed. J. William Hebel. Introductions, notes and variant readings, eds. Kathleen Tillotson and Bernard Newdigate (Oxford: Basil Blackwell, 1931) 1:74, 76.

25 On the evolution of Drayton's and Daniel's title pages, see Wall, *Imprint of Gender*, 75–86. As Arthur Marotti notes, such collected works were

acceptable only as posthumous publication; Ben Jonson was ridiculed for issuing his own volume, *The Workes of Benjamin Jonson* (1616). *Manuscript, Print, and the English Renaissance Lyric* (Ithaca: Cornell University Press, 1995), 243–44.

26 Davies, *Muses Sacrifice*, sig. A1v.

27 Love, *Scribal Publication*, 54–55. On the sexual connotations of "press" see Wall, *Imprint of Gender*, 15–16, 279–81.

28 Roland Greene, *Post-Petrarchism: Origins and Innovations of the Western Lyric Sequence* (Princeton: Princeton University Press, 1991); Heather Dubrow, *Echoes of Desire: English Petrarchism and its Counterdiscourses* (Ithaca: Cornell University Press, 1995); Mary Thomas Crane, *Framing Authority: Sayings, Self, and Society in Sixteenth-Century England* (Princeton: Princeton University Press, 1993), 136–96; Roger Kuin, *Chamber Music: Elizabethan Sonnet Sequences and the Pleasure of Criticism* (University of Toronto Press, 1997).

29 Ann Rosalind Jones, *The Currency of Eros: Women's Love Lyric in Europe, 1540–1620* (Bloomington: Indiana University Press, 1990), 7. But note the interesting reversal that Marguerite de Navarre, who was warned to stay out of religion and politics by her brother François I, turned to secular poems. Valerie Forman, "Contested Narratives: Historical Writing and the Genealogy of 'Women' in Marguerite de Navarre's *The Heptameron*," paper presented at the Shakespeare Association of America conference, Cleveland, March 1998. See also *Women Poets of the Italian Renaissance: Courtly Ladies and Courtesans*, ed. Laura Anna Stortoni. Translated by Laura Anna Stortoni and Mary Prentice Lillie (New York: Italic Press, 1997).

30 *The Poems of Richard Lovelace*, ed. C. H. Wilkinson (Oxford: Clarendon, 1953), 200; Love, *Scribal Publication*, 55.

31 On the conflicts inherent in Pembroke's patronage, see Mary Ellen Lamb, *Gender and Authorship in the Sidney Circle* (Madison: University of Wisconsin Press, 1990), 28–71; on court cases involving Edmund Mathew and Peter Samyn see Margaret Hannay, *Philip's Phoenix: Mary Sidney, Countess of Pembroke* (New York: Oxford University Press, 1990), 173–84, 203.

32 Sir Dudley Carleton to John Chamberlain, 2 August 1616, *Dudley Carleton to John Chamberlain 1603–1624: Jacobean Letters*, ed. Maurice Lee (New Brunswick: Rutgers University Press, 1972), 209; *Lady Mary Wroth's "Love's Victory": the Penshurst Manuscript*, ed. Michael G. Brennan (London: The Roxburge Club, 1988). The identification of Lissius with Lister was first made by Josephine Roberts, "The Huntington Library Manuscript of Lady Mary Wroth's Play, *Loves Victorie*," *HLQ* 46 (1983), 156–74. See also *Aubrey's Brief Lives*, ed. Oliver Lawson Dick (London: Secker and Warburg, 1949), 139, 378.

33 Cf. Lamb, *Gender and Authorship*, 31.

34 *Aubrey's Brief Lives*, 139. On the political context of Aubrey's statement and similar slanders against Philip Herbert's widow, Anne Clifford, see Margaret P. Hannay, "'O Daughter Heare': Reconstructing the Lives of Aristocratic Englishwomen," *Attending to Women in the Renaissance*, eds. Betty

Travitsky and Adele Seeff (Newark: University of Delaware Press, 1997), 44–46.

35 "A Tribute to Wyatts Psalms," *The Poems of Henry Howard, Earl of Surrey*, ed. Frederick Morgan Padelford (Seattle: University of Washington Press, 1928), 97; Rivkah Zim, *English Metrical Psalms: Poetry as Praise and Prayer, 1535–1601* (Cambridge: Cambridge University Press, 1987), 183; Thomas Moffet, *Nobilis or a View of the Life and Death of a Sidney and Lessus Lugubris*, eds. Virgil B. Heltzel and Hoyt H. Hudson (San Marino: Huntington Library, 1940), 74. See Suzanne Trill, "'Speaking to God in His Phrase and Word': Women's Use of the Psalms in Early Modern England," *The Nature of Religious Language: a Colloquium*, Roehampton Institute London Papers (Sheffield: Sheffield Academic Press, 1996), 269–83; and Margaret P. Hannay, "'So may I with the *Psalmist* truly say': Early Modern English-women's Psalm Discourse," *Write or Be Written: Early Modern Women Poets and Cultural Constraints*, eds. Barbara Smith and Ursula Appelt (Ashgate Press, 2001), 105–34. Victoria Kirkham is working on the secular poems and Psalm paraphrases of Laura Battiferra.

36 Sir Edward Denny, "To Pamphilia from the father-in-law of Seralius," and Sir Edward Denny to Lady Mary Wroth, 26 February 1621/22, cited in *The Poems of Lady Mary Wroth*, ed. Josephine A. Roberts (Baton Rouge: Louisiana State University Press, 1983), 32, 239.

37 Sir John Harington of Kelston to Lucy, Countess of Bedford, 19 December 1600, Inner Temple Petyt MS 538.43.14, fol. 303v. He probably wrote the epigram in praise of Pembroke's works, No. 398 in *The Letters and Epigrams of Sir John Harington*, ed. Norman Egbert McClure (Philadelphia: University of Pennsylvania Press, 1930), 310. See also Alexander, "Five Responses to Sir Philip Sidney 1586–1628," 29.

38 Davies, *Muses Sacrifice*, sig. ***3.

39 *The Poems of Aemilia Lanyer: Salve Deus Rex Judaeorum*, ed. Susanne Woods (New York: Oxford University Press, 1993), 27–29; Lanyer was seeking a poetic model – or even to displace Pembroke, as Kari Boyd McBride argues, "Remembering Orpheus in the Poems of Aemilia Lanyer," *SEL* 38 (1998), 87–108; Thomas Moffet, *The Silkewormes and their Flies: Lively Described in Verse, by T.M. a Countrie Farmar, and an apprentice in Physicke* (London: 1599), sig. G1; Henry Parry, *Victoria Christiana* (1594), sig. A3v–A4. Michael G. Brennan, "The Date of the Countess of Pembroke's Translation of the Psalms," *RES* 33 (1982), 434–36.

40 Samuel Daniel, *Delia and Rosamond Augmented*. Cleopatra (London: 1594), sig. H6. Cf. Elaine Beilin, *Redeeming Eve: Women Writers of the English Renaissance* (Princeton: Princeton University Press, 1987), 126.

41 Daniel, *Delia*, sig. H6v.

42 Harington, *Letters and Epigrams of Sir John Harington*, 310; Franklin Williams, "Sir John Harington," *TLS*, 4 September 1930, 697.

43 On her scholarship in the *Psalmes*, see *Collected Works of Mary Sidney* 2: 3–32.

44 Davies, *Muses Sacrifice*, sig. A1v.

45 John Donne to Sir Henry Goodyer, 1614, quoted in Arthur F. Marotti, *John Donne: Courtier Poet* (Madison: University of Wisconsin Press, 1986), ix.

46 J. W. Saunders, "The Stigma of Print: a Note on the Social Bases of Tudor Poetry," *Essays in Criticism* 1 (1951), 139–64 and "From Manuscript to Print: a Note on the Circulation of Poetic MSS. in the Sixteenth Century," *Proceedings of the Leeds Philosophical and Literary Society* 6 (1951), 507–28. Steven May, "Tudor Aristocrats and the Mythical 'Stigma of Print,'" *Renaissance Papers* 10 (1980), 1–18 and *The Elizabethan Courtier Poets: the Poems and their Contexts* (Asheville: Pegasus Press, 1999).

47 Sidney, *Defence of Poetry, Miscellaneous Prose of Sir Philip Sidney*, eds. Katherine Duncan-Jones and Jan Van Dorsten (Oxford: Clarendon Press, 1973), 111. On social production of texts, see Ezell, *Social Authorship*, 21–44.

48 Woudhuysen, *Sir Philip Sidney and the Circulation of Manuscripts*, 297.

49 See Saunders on women assigning poetic tasks, "From Manuscript to Print," 513.

50 "To my Deare Ladie and Sister, the Countesse of Pembroke," Sidney, *Arcadia*, sig. A3v. George Carleton says that it was composed at Wilton in his elegy "*D. Philippus Sidnaenus. Silva,*" *Exequiae*, sig. L1v–L2.

51 Michael G. Brennan, "The Badminton Manuscript of Sir Richard Barckley's *A Discourse of the Felicitie of Man* (1598)," *EMS* 6 (1996), 80–81.

52 On the complex textual history of the *Old* and *New Arcadia* see particularly *The Poems of Sir Philip Sidney*, ed. William A. Ringler, Jr. (Oxford: Clarendon Press, 1962), 373–74; *The Countess of Pembrokes Arcadia [The Old Arcadia]*, ed. Jean Robertson (Oxford: Clarendon Press, 1973), lxiv; *The Countess of Pembrokes Arcadia [The New Arcadia]*, ed. Victor Skretkowicz (Oxford: Clarendon Press, 1987), lxxviii; Woudhuysen, *Sir Philip Sidney and the Circulation of Manuscripts*, 299–355. On Pembroke's editorial responsibility for the *Arcadia*, see also the sources listed in Hannay, *Philip's Phoenix*, 237, note 71. On Sidney's female audience and the addresses to "faire ladies" see Lamb, *Gender and Authority*, 72–114.

53 On the editions of *Astrophil and Stella* as a struggle over patronage, see Marotti, *Manuscript, Print, and the English Renaissance Lyric*, 312–14.

54 "To the Reader," *An Apologie for Poetrie. Written by the Right Noble, Vertuous and Learned, Sir Philip Sidney, Knight* (London: Henry Olney, 1595); Helen Vincent, "'Divine *Sir Philip*'?: Henry Constable's Dedicatory Sonnets and Henry Olney's edition of the *Apologie for Poetrie*," paper read at the Sixteenth-Century Studies Conference, St. Louis, October 1999.

55 Thomas Newman, "To the worshipfull and his very good Freende, Ma. Fraucis Flower," *Syr P. S. His Astrophel and Stella* (London: Thomas Newman, 1591), sig. A2v. See Germaine Warkentin, "Patrons and Profiteers: Thomas Newman and the 'Violent Enlargement' of *Astrophil and Stella*," *Book Collector* 34 (1985), 461–87.

56 Josuah Sylvester, trans. "Lectoribus," *Bartas: His Devine Weekes and Workes* (London: Humfrey Lownes, 1605), sig. B2. Sylvester's comments on Sidney's translation are cleverly shaped as a Sidney pheon. John Florio implies

that it is Sidney's daughter Elizabeth, Countess of Rutland, who holds the Du Bartas manuscript, or at least that she would be able to put it into print, "To the Right Honorable and all praise-worthie Ladies, Elizabeth Countesse of Rutland, and Ladie Penelope Riche," *The Essayes or Morall, Politike and Millitarie Discourses of Michel de Montaigne* (London: Edward Blount, 1603), sig. R3. Cf. Josuah Sylvester, *The Divine Weeks and Works of Guillaume de Saluste Sieur du Bartas*, ed. Susan Snyder (Oxford: Clarendon Press, 1979) 1:70.

57 *Poems of Sir Philip Sidney*, 339. See also Anne Lake Prescott, *French Poets and the English Renaissance: Studies in Fame and Transformation* (New Haven: Yale University Press, 1978), 178–79.

58 "The Dolefull Lay," lines 43–48, *Collected Works of Mary Sidney*, 1:134. On the question of authorship see "'The Dolefull Lay of Clorinda': Literary Context," *Collected Works of Mary Sidney*, 1:119–32.

59 "To the Angell Spirit of the most excellent Sir Philip Sidney," lines 64–70, *Collected Works of Mary Sidney*, 1:112.

60 Sidney, *Arcadia* (1593), sig. A4v.

61 Sir Fulke Greville to Sir Francis Walsingham, November 1586, PRO SP 12/195/33. How much of the work was done by Sidney is unclear, but Mornay had a copy of the printed volume in his library, implying some authenticity for Golding's work. Roger Kuin, "Absent Presence: Sidney and Mornay's Library," paper read at Medieval Congress, Kalamazoo, Michigan, 8 May 1998.

62 Woudhuysen, *Sir Philip Sidney and the Circulation of Manuscripts*, 420.

63 Katherine Duncan-Jones, *Sir Philip Sidney: Courtier Poet* (New Haven: Yale University Press, 1991), 240. Joel Davis argues that Greville tried to fit Sidney into the Essex circle, but Mary Sidney placed Sidney in a Continental context, "Stoicism and Gender: the Conditions of the Literary Quarrel between Fulke Greville and the Countess of Pembroke," papers read at the Medieval Congress, Kalamazoo Michigan, Part 1 in 1999 and Part 2 in 2000.

64 Hugh Sanford, "To the Reader," *Arcadia* (1593), sig. A4.

65 Wall, *Imprint of Gender*, 155–56.

66 The Dudley and Sidney crests are noted by Wall, *Imprint of Gender*, 153 and Elizabeth Porges Watson, "Narrative Psychomachia: Rescue and Self-Mastery in *Arcadia*," *Sidney Journal* 15 (1997), 21–36. The lion had a dual value, serving as a Pembroke crest and also as a supporter for the Dudley, Sidney, and Pembroke crests. Such aristocratic symbols on the title page would help market the book. Cf. Paul J. Voss, "Books for Sale: Advertising and Patronage in Late Elizabethan England," *Sixteenth Century Journal* 29 (1998), 733–56.

67 Wall, *Imprint of Gender*, 70–71.

68 Sanford, "To the Reader," *Arcadia* (1593), sig. A4v.

69 Michael Brennan, "William Ponsonby: Elizabethan Stationer," *Analytical and Enumerative Bibliography* 7 (1983), 91–111. Alexander argues that it was

Ponsonby, not the countess herself, who controlled the editing and publication of Sidney's works, whereas Brennan says that it was the countess who "becomes the most important figure in the editing and publication of Sidney's compositions," *Literary Patronage in the English Renaissance: the Pembroke Family* (London: Routledge, 1988), 57. Mark Bland notes the importance of the printer, John Windet, "The Appearance of the Text in Early Modern England," *Text* 11 (1998), 14–17.

70 *Englands Helicon 1600*, ed. Hyder Edward Rollins (Cambridge: Harvard University Press, 1935), 1:167–70.

71 Alexander, "Five Responses to Sir Philip Sidney 1586–1628," 13.

72 *A Discourse of Life and Death. Written in French by Ph. Mornay. Antonius, A Tragedie written also in French by Ro.Garnier. Both done in English by the Countesse of Pembroke* (London: William Ponsonby, 1592).

73 Steven May, *The Elizabethan Courtier Poets: the Poems and their Contexts* (Asheville: Pegasus Press, 1999), 167.

74 Margaret Tyler, trans., *The First Part of the Mirrour of Princely Deeds and Knighthood...Nowe newly translated out of Spanish into our vulgar English Tongue, by M. T.* (London: Thomas East, 1580?), sig. A3, A4v.

75 Marotti, *John Donne: Courtier Poet*, x.

76 Correspondence III, *Collected Works of Mary Sidney* 1:286–87. Herbert Aston, for example, lost the original of one of his poems and requested a copy from his sister, Ezell, *Social Authorship*, 28.

77 Moffet, *Silkewormes*, sig. A2.

78 See "Origins, early reception, and influence," *Collected Works of Mary Sidney* 1:44–45.

79 John Bodenham, *Bel-vedére or the Garden of the Muses*, [ed.], A. M.[unday?] (1600), sig. A3v.

80 Wall, *Imprint of Gender*, 177.

81 Bodenham, *Bel-vedére*, sig. A3–sig. A4v.

82 Margaret Hannay, "The Countess of Pembroke as a Spenserian Poet," *Pilgrimage for Love: Festschrift for Josephine A. Roberts*, ed. Sigrid M. King (Tempe: RETS/MRTS, 1999), 41–62.

83 Rowland Whyte to Robert Sidney, 14 January 1598, De L'Isle and Dudley MS U1475 C12/121. De L'Isle and Dudley manuscripts quoted with the kind permission of the Viscount De L'Isle, MBE.

84 Francis Osborne, *Historical Memoires on the Reigns of Queen Elizabeth and King James* (London: 1683), sig. Gg2.

85 Sir Edward Denny to Lady Mary Wroth, 26 February 1621/22, cited in Wroth, *Poems*, 239.

86 Approximately 20 years after her death the Trinity College, Cambridge, MS R.3.16 (MS G) was licensed for printing by John Langley, but no such edition is extant, Michael G. Brennan, "Licensing the Sidney Psalms for the Press in the 1640s," *N&Q* 31 (1984), 304–05.

87 John Harington, "Treatise on play," *Nugae antiquae: being a Miscellaneous Collection of Original Papers in Prose and Verse; Written in the Reigns of Henry VIII, Queen*

Mary, Elizabeth, King James, &c. A New, Corrected, and Enlarged Edition, in 3 vols. ed. Henry Harington (London: Printed for J. Dodsley and T. Shrimpton, 1779) 2:158–59. On Harington's connections with the Sidneys, see Michael G. Brennan, "Sir Robert Sidney and Sir John Harington of Kelston," *N&Q* 34 (1987), 232–37.

88 Alexander, "Five Responses to Sir Philip Sidney 1586–1628," 28.

89 Matthew Parker, *The Whole Psalter translated into English Metre, which Contayneth an Hundreth and Fifty Psalmes* (London: 1575), sig. B2v.

90 Woudhuysen, *Sir Philip Sidney and the Circulation of Manuscripts*, 226.

91 Rienstra and Kinnamon, "Circulating the Sidney–Pembroke Psalter," 53–77.

92 Sidney, *Defence of Poetry*, 77, 80.

93 Michael G. Brennan, private correspondence.

94 Love, *Scribal Publication*, 72.

95 George Wither, *The Schollers Purgatory* (London, 1624), 121.

96 BL Harleian MS 298, fol. 159v. Pembroke's Psalms are listed under the category "Poems of all sorts { Divine / Humane," along with Psalms by Josuah Sylvester and Sir John Harington, cited in Francis Davison's *Poetical Rapsody*, ed. A. H. Bullen (London: George Bell and Sons, 1890) 1:lii. John Donne had made a similar decision in refusing Davison access to his "Satires, Elegies, Epigrams, etc." which Davison also sought to print. Marotti, *John Donne: Coterie Poet*, xi.

97 I am grateful to Roger Kuin for his comments on this essay.

98 Love, *Scribal Publication*, 47.

99 Samuel Woodforde's note on Psalm 49, Bodleian, MS Rawl. poet. 25.

100 John Davies, *The Writing Schoolemaster or the Anatomie of Faire Writing.* 1636 (Amsterdam: Walter J. Johnson, 1976).

101 Davies, *Muses Sacrifice*, sig. ***3.

102 Love, *Scribal Publication*, 42.

103 William Hunnis, Dedication to Frances, Countess of Sussex, *Seven Sobs of a Sorrowfull Soule for Sinne: Comprehending those seven Psalmes of the Princelie Prophet DAVID, commonlie called Poenitentiall* (London, 1589), sig. A3v.

104 "To the Angell Spirit: Variant," line 11, *Collected Works of Mary Sidney* 1:113.

105 Love, *Scribal Publication*, 65–83.

106 Harington, *Nugae Antiquae* 1:277–96; Brennan, "Sir Robert Sidney," 232–37; May, *Elizabethan Courtier Poets*, 205, 211; Alexander, "Five Responses to Sir Philip Sidney 1586–1628," 29–30; Marotti, *Manuscript, Print, and the English Renaissance Lyric*, 63; Woudhuysen, *Sir Philip Sidney and the Circulation of Manuscripts*, 106.

107 See "Manuscripts of the *Psalmes*," *Collected Works of Mary Sidney* 2:308–36.

108 Linda Austern, "'For Music is the Handmaid of the Lord': the Psalm Tradition and Women's Musical Performance in Late Renaissance England," paper read at the annual meeting of the Renaissance Society of America, University of Maryland, March 1998.

109 Margaret Hannay, "'My lute awake': Music and Pembroke's *Psalmes*," paper read at the annual meeting of the Renaissance Society of America,

University of Maryland, March 1998. I am grateful to all those who so
bravely sang the revised Psalm 124.
110 Jim Doelman, "A Seventeenth-Century Publication of Three of Sir
Philip Sidney's Psalms," *N&Q* 38 (1991), 162–63. William Drummond of
Hawthornden mentions this edition of "some psalms of David" composed
"to the french Tunes, in Meter" by Philip Sidney and others, printed by John
Standish. National Library of Scotland MS 2060, fol. 150, cited in Ringler,
ed. *Poems of Sir Philip Sidney*, 500. See also Alexander, "Five Responses to Sir
Philip Sidney 1586–1628," 28–29.
111 Woudhuysen, *Sir Philip Sidney and the Circulation of Manuscripts*, 310. For
a description of the newly recovered eighteenth manuscript, see Gavin
Alexander, "A New Manuscript of the Sidney Psalms: a Preliminary
Report," *Sidney Journal* 18 (2000): 43–56.
112 Love, *Scribal Publication*, 41.
113 Drayton, Preface to *Poly-Olbion*, *Works* 4:v; Marotti, *John Donne: Coterie
Poet*, 4.
114 Brennan, private correspondence.
115 Hannay, *Philip's Phoenix*, 86–105.
116 Sanford, "To the Reader," *Arcadia* (1593), sig. A4v.

CHAPTER 3

Circulating the Sidney–Pembroke Psalter

Debra Rienstra and Noel Kinnamon

It seems to me that the biblical faith and life expressed in the psalms and in the Reformed tradition is authentic personal faith and life only by membership in the covenant community, which is antecedent to the individual, and in which only does the individual find real meaning and hope. Touched on here is a basic problem now in church and world: atomism and anomie. Related thereto is the tension between the prophetic and the aesthetic. Do you suppose we would be better off if we, like our forebears, sang in our corporate worship only the psalms and other texts of biblical revelation in the most accurate, if not literal, renderings possible and made use of other, individual, human, artistic compositions on other occasions?

The paragraph above was written in 1994, but it might well have been written in 1594. The author voices dismay over the tendency among religious folk, Protestants in particular, to embrace so readily the validity of individual expression that an essential function of the community – accountability to the text and tradition – is lightened or lost. This temptation lurks with special deceptiveness, according to this author, when people attempt to fiddle with Scripture, translating freely or rearranging material according to an individual's style or purpose, and then presenting the result to the community as something useful, perhaps even with a measure of authority. What might appear useful and pious can be dangerous, a problem the author responds to with the hierarchical binaries in that final sentence: literal is better than aesthetic, public worship is more important than personal piety.

To assume a discernible division between literal and artistic, and to assume further that when it comes to Scripture, the aesthetic response pulls on the loose string of the literal and threatens to unravel it, may seem a peculiarly finicky response for a modern person, even a pious one. But this contemporary voice stands in a long tradition of anxiety about the proper uses of Scripture, a problem that arose the moment the translated texts became widely available in the wake of the Reformation. As Protestant devotional literature bloomed and burgeoned in response to prose translations and commentaries, writers and readers enjoyed a new familiarity and freedom with the Scriptures; at the same time, they pressed upon one another the importance of preserving the integrity of the inspired text they were admonished to meditate upon, study, return to, and apply to themselves in every detail. One way to negotiate that tension between faithful transmission of the text and freedom with it – then and today – is to posit personal devotional practices and public worship practices as two different realms, the former permitting more freedom than the latter.[1] The above voice insists on this division, in fact, in reference to a late sixteenth-century work that seems to collapse it: the Sidney–Pembroke Psalter. The paragraph is taken from a letter of response to an article on the psalter that appeared in *Perspectives: a Journal of Reformed Thought*. The author of the letter complained that, in expressing admiration for what Sir Philip Sidney and the Countess of Pembroke had achieved in their metrical versions of the Psalms, the article had given "undue weight" to "individual interpretation of the Scriptures and to individual piety."[2]

The Sidney–Pembroke Psalter is a peculiar work – a translation, a paraphrase, a scholarly meditation, an artist's sketchbook of poetic forms, an intensely personal devotional exercise – and it slips frustratingly in and out of familiar categories. By circulating the completed psalter not through print but via scribal publication, Mary Sidney, Countess of Pembroke, may have been navigating cleverly between conceptions of public and private religious practice, staving off potential suspicion among her contemporaries of the kind of impiety referred to above, that of "undue weight." As Margaret Hannay demonstrates in her essay in this volume, Pembroke's decision against print for her *Psalmes* cannot be attributed straightforwardly to either class or gender. During the period in which she was working on the *Psalmes*, she defied typical assumptions that print was only for the vulgar by publishing authorized editions of her brother's works, doing so in order to preserve and heighten his honor and fame. Nor did she seem to consider publishing improper for a woman, as she published several of her own works, both religious and non. She thereby "did much to legitimize print," as Margaret Hannay argues.[3] But there are reasons other than class or gender for maintaining careful control over a

manuscript. In the case of the *Psalmes*, Pembroke's reasons for choosing scribal publication appear to have been motivated by a sense that
the theological implications of her artistic method would not be widely
appreciated.

Pembroke's revision process, as evidenced by comparing early versions
of certain psalms to their more final version, demonstrates a deliberate
methodology of moving from the straightforward, literal rendering of
the prose text to the more vivid, particular, even idiosyncratic. Her completed psalter therefore strained conventional understandings of what
it was appropriate to do with Scripture by affirming individual assertion before the Divine through poetry. The psalter declares the validity of recreating the scriptural source to reflect the particular cultural
context, aesthetic values, even individual experience of the artist. In circulating the psalter at all, Pembroke was countering the aesthetic of
plainness, of transparent mediation, with another Reformation notion:
the idea that the individual is free to, even obligated to, particularize
the text to his or her own experience.[4] Although her approach is de-
fensible from the premises of certain Reformation notions, such as the
priesthood of all believers,[5] she may still have suspected that allowing
this particularizing process to leave the confines of the private meditative mind and spill out onto a presented page with elaborate artistry
might be misunderstood by a wider public.[6] So by keeping her work
in the realm of scribal publication, she could push the limits of what
was considered acceptable when mediating Scripture, for she appeared
to assert nothing about its public use. That Pembroke was wise in her
endeavor to control access to her aesthetic approach to Scripture is interestingly demonstrated, as will be described below, by the complete
replacement of some of her most rarefied psalms in two late manuscripts
by an editor who exhibited a preference for plainer, more literal
versions.

IN SUBSTANCE NO

Pembroke's dedicatory poem attached to manuscript *J*, "To the Angell
spirit of the most excellent Sir Philip Sidney," is an elegy to her brother,
but also, as the editors of *Collected Works* observe, "a meditation on her
own role as a writer."[7] And while Pembroke neglects to express self-
abnegation for being an audacious writing *woman* – the absence of which
gesture is remarkable in this period – she does express humility and
caution about her role as a mediator of sacred texts. She writes that she

combined her muse with Sidney's,

> That heaven's King may daigne his owne transform'd
> in substance no, but superficiall tire
> by thee put on; to praise, not to aspire
> To, those high Tons, so in themselves adorn'd,
> which Angells sing in their celestiall Quire.
>
> (lines 8–12)

Her care to disclaim substantial alteration of or rivalry with the inspired Psalm originals is a response to the English metrical psalm tradition out of which her work arises. Translators and metrical psalmists of the period who published their work typically acknowledged in one way or another that they were about a dangerous business. Thomas Norton wrote about his work in translating Calvin's *Institutes*:

If I should leave the course of wordes, and graunt my selfe liberty after the naturall maner of my owne tonge, to say that in English which I conceaved to be his meaning in Latine, I plainely perceiued howe hardely perilous it was to erre.[8]

But if translations, even of commentaries, were a perilous business, composing metrical psalms was in a sense even more so. One would not wish to eclipse the text's power to speak with too thick a patina of "inventions fine," nor would one wish to distort the text to the point of leading a reader into error. But the demands of a verse form augment the temptation to alter, however slightly, for reasons of art rather than truth – to choose a word because it is vivid or completes a rhyme and not because it carries the nuance the original demands. Thus George Wither writes of his endeavor to "keepe a decent meane" between a literal and a literate metrical translation:

And because I know that whosoeuer followes the sense ouer-securely, without great heed ro [sic] the words, may sometime make a sense of his owne: and seeing he who addicts himselfe wholly to the words, without much care of the sense, may often times make *Non-sense*; Therefore I haue euer-more carryed an indifferent regard, both to the *Sense* and the *Words*: which middle way euery man ought to keepe.[9]

Wither, writing in 1619, voices issues that persisted as of the utmost concern to seventeenth-century Puritans. But these issues were laid out first among the Elizabethan metrical psalmists of various sympathies. While confident that versifying psalms was appropriate and edifying for poet and public alike, metrical psalmists typically register this anxiety to stay close to the Text.

One strategy for relieving anxiety among metrical psalmists over manipulating the sacred text was to offer more or less articulated justifications of their endeavors. They defend the propriety of versifying the psalms on generic grounds (after all, the originals are poems, too), they offer metrical psalms as strategic cultural weapons against vulgar love lyrics – in ways that remind us of those who advocated baptized versions of pop music idioms in late twentieth-century American evangelical churches – and they present their volumes of psalms as teaching resources, complete with headnotes and glosses. But it was also important for early metrical psalmists to defend their poetic methodology: to deny any aspiration on their part to interpretation or artistry, relinquishing authority to weave explication or decoration into the text. Sixteenth-century metrical psalmists attempted to alter as little as they could while satisfying the requirements of the meter, positioning themselves as middle men between scholars and common people. In some cases, their alterations did attempt to soften or explain passages that seemed to contradict Protestant doctrine, but these were indulged, cautiously, to keep readers new to the Scriptures from the danger of "misunderstanding." Francis Seager, who published *Certayne Psalmes Select out of the Psalter of David and Drawen into Englyshe Metre* in 1553, explains that when he came upon a difficult passage, he deferred to other authorities:

> But where the text, in some places
> Was doubtfull and obscure:
>   I haue sought helpe, of learned books
>   Because I woulde be sure.[10]

Seager himself claims no authority to interpret, merely to consult.

The persistent choice of ballad meter especially was a way of effacing the poet before the text, as it is supposed to make the artistic aspect of the result as unobtrusive as possible. Ballad meter, being wholly predictable, assists in memorization but otherwise draws very little attention to itself as meters go, and therefore seems to allow the words themselves to carry the meaning. William Hunnis, a servant to William Herbert who later became Queen Elizabeth's Master of the Chapel, published in 1550 six metrical psalms in ballad meter under the title *Certayne Psalmes Chosen out of the Psalter of David, and Drawen Furth into Englysh Meter*.[11] His preface exemplifies the common move of denying his artistry as a gesture of humility before the text:

And this enterpryse I haue taken in hande not intendynge therby anye praises or glorye shulde redounde unto me but cheifly for thys purpose that those, whiche in psalmes and pleasaunt songes hathe delyte, myghte hereof receiue some pleasure or profyt...And although that in som places they be not so eloquentlye turned as paraduenture the matter of them requireth, yet for the exceding profit that doth procede of them, reiecte them not.

To apologize for his lack of artistic ability was to foreground the excellency of the "matter," an appropriately pious deference. It was also an indisputable defense against criticism, since the author's presentation was intended to be transparent to the unquestionable value of the Psalms for the reader's edification. Matthew Parker, whose 1567 psalter includes a small variety of metrical forms with melodies composed by Thomas Tallis, reminds his readers that, attentive to their edification, he attempted to retain the old words, rather than introducing new ones:

> Conceyve in hart: no griefe to sore,
>   wordes olde so ofte to vewe:
> Thy gayne therby: is wrought the more,
>   though wordes be never newe.

Concerned that readers might consider the melodies a further frivolous innovation, Parker defends that modest artistic addition with the story of David dancing before the ark. He associates "carping" readers with David's wife Michal, who was punished for criticizing David's unfettered celebration:

> If some will carpe: so light a warke,
>   grave Psalmes in rythmes displayde:
> Let Michol heare: before the arke,
>   how David daunced and playde.[12]

In his second volume of psalm translations, published in 1583 and titled, with melodramatic alliteration, *Seven Sobs of a Sorrowfull Soule for Sinne*, Hunnis meditates on each of the seven penitential psalms in long, ballad-meter poems into which he has intertwined the actual words of the text, slightly altered to fit the meter. This time, Hunnis does not apologize for his lack of skill (perhaps he felt he had improved), but he still images his work as an appropriately plain, humble garment meant to set off the inherent glories of the Psalms. In "The Authour to his *Booke*," Hunnis addresses the Psalms:

> More rich thou art in thred-bare cote,
>   than some in silken gowne.[13]

We see in these examples, then, that metrical psalmists perceived the meter itself as having theological implications, as it embodies the author's assumptions about her or his relationship to the authoritative text.

Mid-century metrical psalms can be seen as early, very cautious experiments with Protestant meditative literature sparked by the new availability of English-language Bibles and the mandate to read them. During this period, the danger of leading worshipers and readers "astray" was best avoided by steering as close as possible in a plain style to prose sources reliable in their studious adherence to Hebrew originals. But toward the end of the sixteenth century, Protestant principles were beginning to validate the individual's faith-filled response to Scripture. Versifiers from about the 1580s were willing to exercise more interpretive freedom with the text, claiming the text as a resource that they were free to adapt in edifying ways, not only for their own use but also for distribution to others. This, then, is the tradition out of which Sidney and Pembroke began their metrical psalms, but it is a tradition they clearly meant to surpass. As the editors of *Collected Works* note, Sidney and Pembroke took as their artistic model not English predecessors, but the French Marot–Bèze psalter, in all its metrical variety.[14] In fact, Pembroke makes reference in an early version of her dedicatory poem to Queen Elizabeth that she hoped to improve upon an English tradition she considered "by the vulgar form'd."[15] So unlike metrical psalmists before them, who render the Psalms as literally as possible within the square strictures of ballad meter, or who, at most, experiment rather modestly with other forms, the Sidneys present a metrical showcase, sparkling with rhetorical flourishes and stuffed with extensive study of translations and commentaries. Pembroke's 107 psalms especially, though they stay within the genre of metrical psalm, and are even termed "translations" on the title page of one manuscript, stretch the generic boundaries rather far. Her psalms rearrange material, create rhetorical structures to fill in the loose handshakes of Hebrew conjunctions, intensify imagery, and add details or images reflective of her own study and experience – all to a much greater extent than Sidney, and all while advancing the pattern Sidney established of rendering each psalm in a unique metrical form.[16] Rather than announcing a deferral of authority to commentators where a passage is doubtful, as Seager did, Pembroke presents the *Psalmes* as her own and Sidney's. She did in fact make use of a whole bookshelf of commentators, sometimes ignoring them all and interpreting a passage her own way – but she does not bother to certify her psalms with borrowed authority. And rather than prefacing the *Psalmes* with denials of artistic intentions, the title page alluded to above (probably added by an editor) boasts that these psalms are "more rare & excellent for the method & varietie then ever yet hath bene don in English."[17] Pembroke may claim that in substance they are not altered, but neither are they dressed in a "thread-bare cote." Instead, they are, as Pembroke herself describes them to the Queen, "a liverie robe" suitable for royal presentation.[18]

"SUPERFICIALL" TIRE

The editors of *Collected Works* provide extensive notation of the hundreds of places in which Pembroke exhibits her carefully researched, yet boldly imaginative approach to meditating upon and re-presenting the psalms. Examples here will highlight a few of many remarkable moments and demonstrate the process by which she worked. Pembroke's beautiful reworking of Psalm 139 has been noted before, in Rathmell's 1963 edition of the psalter.[19] Her extension of verse 14 is especially skillful. Coverdale's Common Prayer version reads:

My bones are not hid from thee: though I be made secretly, and fashioned beneath in the earth.

Pembroke, working from a suggestion in Bèze's commentary, makes God into a carpenter of loving attention and then an embroiderer:

> Thou, how my back was beam-wise laid,
>   and raftring of my ribbs dost know:
>   know'st ev'ry point
>   of bone and joynt,
>   how to this whole these partes did grow,
> in brave embrodry faire araid,
>   though wrought in shopp both dark and low.
>   (50–56)

A less noted, but even more sensuous passage comes from Psalm 65, another of Pembroke's most successful efforts. This Psalm is one of praise for God's abundant care for Israel, for the speaker, and for the earth. Pembroke takes two brief and matter-of-fact references to rejoicing in the Psalm – as in the last verse, in which the pastures and valleys "showte for joye, and sing" (Geneva) – and builds a spirit of joy into the dancing meter and lush diction of her version. The Geneva renders verses 10 and 11:

10. Thou waterest abundantly the forrowes thereof: thou causest the raine to descend into the valleis thereof: thou makest it soft with showres, & blessest the bud thereof.
11. Thou crownest the yere with thy goodnes, and thy steps drop fatnes.

Pembroke, working not from commentators' suggestions this time but simply from poetic imagination, writes:

> Drunck is each ridg of thy cupp drincking;
>   each clodd relenteth at thy dressing:
> thy cloud-born waters inly sincking
>   faire spring sproutes foorth blest with thy blessing.
> the fertile yeare is with thy bounty crown'd:
> and where thou go'st, thy goings fatt the ground.
>
> (37–42)

The feminine rhymes, the vividness of the drunken soil yielding to God's drenching touch, the alliteration throughout, the polyptoton in lines 40 and 42, and the satisfaction of that final couplet all combine to create a richness beyond the literal; but it is a richness thoughtfully derived from study of the original psalm.

Psalm 51, one of the seven penitential psalms, is one of those most often rendered into meter, thus allowing a brief comparison of Pembroke's version not only to the prose translation but also to other metrical psalmists' versions. Verse 8 of the Psalm presents a particular challenge, both poetically and theologically:

8. Thou shalt make me heare of joy and gladnesse: that the bones which thou hast broken may rejoyce.

The image of the broken bones rejoicing carries the uncomfortable suggestion that God would deliberately break human bones (unpleasant whether taken literally or figuratively) and it asks the reader to picture bones rejoicing – something of a metaphorical puzzle. The Sternhold–Hopkins version replaces the image with a plain-speaking interpretation:

> 8 Therefore (O Lord) such joy me send,
>   that inwardly I may find grace:
> And that my strength may now amend,
>   which thou hast swaged for my trespasse.[20]

Seager draws out the implied when–then relationship between the two parts of the verse – a subtle touch – and then softens the bone imagery slightly with "some tymes" and "payne" rather than "hast broken":

> When thou wyth joye, shalt me indew
> And drawe to myrth agayne:
> Then wyll my bones, be voyde of woo
> Whych thou some tymes dydst payne.

Parker performs a similar operation, referring to "payne" and "shaken bones" without reference to a perpetrator. Pembroke, on the other hand, takes the opposite tack, strengthening rather than softening the image and its implications. She turns a difficulty into an opportunity. Imagining broken bones rejoicing may be puzzling, but turn their rejoicing – an emotional act – into dancing – a physical act – and the image comes alive:

> to eare and hart send soundes and thoughts of gladdnes,
> that brused bones maie daunce awaie their saddnes.
>
> (27–28)

This version is more carefully observant of the text and of human experience than the other metrical versions. It leaves the perpetration of the bruising uncertain by transforming that original subordinate clause into a past participle. It may have been God directly or just the suffering entailed by sin (God's work indirectly) – who can discern? The bones are bruised, rather than broken – a term that may seem gentler to modern readers but in this period still meant something more like "crush" or "mangle." The word "brused" seems a variation on injury chosen to continue the alliterative *d*- and *s*-sounds gathering in the lines. Most notably, Pembroke's version acknowledges that the text does not promise a cure of sin and sadness, merely a hope; the speaker shall "heare" of joy. So rather than rejoicing only after the sadness has been removed, as in some other versions, the bones in the Pembroke psalm respond to God's reassurance, in sounds and thoughts, by dancing *through* the pain. Pembroke's perception of the text's nuances here does not depend on any of her usual sources – neither Bèze, nor Calvin, nor the Geneva commentary suggest that any dancing ought to occur. In fact, Pembroke is here introducing a dance into the text against the precedent of her scholarly exemplars, who habitually *remove* references to dancing in the Psalms even where they clearly appear in the originals.[21]

Early versions of several of Pembroke's psalms provide evidence that such results arose from a deliberate method of composition.[22] Psalm 69, for example, seems based primarily on the Geneva text, but Pembroke's reworking of verses 8 to 10 illustrates how she moved from a more straight-forward metrical version to a version of greater immediacy and rhetorical complexity:

8. I am become a stranger unto my brethren, even an aliant unto my mothers sonnes.
9. For the zeale of thine house hathe eaten me, and the rebukes of them that rebuked thee, are fallen upon me.
10. I wept and my soule fasted, but that was to my reprofe. (Geneva)

From this, Pembroke creates first a rhymed version that follows the text fairly closely in its diction and word order:

> My Brethren me did for a stranger hold
> My mothers children so did me behold
>   As one they did not know
> Zeale of Thy house my Soule did eate and burn
>   What shame on Thee was layd
> Transferrd on me to my reproach did turn
> I wept, I fasted, yet for doing so
>   How did they me upbraid?   (25–32)

The awkward inversions here primarily assist the rhyme scheme, and the final rhetorical question is the most notable alteration. In the final version, however, the improved inversions assist not only rhyme but tone: here the speaker's indignation comes to life, with the added words "quite," "very," and "most" to protest the insult of the situation. The material of verse 9 becomes a parallel construction, and the suffering of the speaker is vivified with the metaphors of scourging and piercing:

> To my kynn a stranger quite,
>   quite an alian am I grown:
> in my very bretherens sight
>   most uncar'd for, most unknow'n.
>   with thy temples zeale out-eaten,
>   with thy slanders scourges beaten,
> while the shott of piercing spight
> bent at thee, on me doth light.   (25–32)

In this version, Pembroke preserves the weeping and fasting for the next stanza, where she combines material from verse 10 with the next two verses, a more logical grouping than in the first version.

Another brief example of this process of revising away from straight versifying toward greater immediacy, vividness, and interpretive specificity comes from Psalm 119s. In this case, Pembroke's revision process leads not to an expanded version, but to a more compressed version created through combining grammatical structures and suggestive diction. What ends up as eight intense lines in the final version begins as four distinct verses in the Geneva text:

137. Righteous art thou, o Lord, and juste are thy judgements.
138. Thou hast commanded justice by thy testimonies and trueth especially.
139. My zeale hathe even consumed me, because mine enemies have forgotten thy wordes.
140. Thy worde is proved moste pure, and thy servant loveth it.

Pembroke's first draft offers a nicely direct opening which she retains for the final version as well: "Sure lord Thy Self art just / And sure Thy lawes be right." The next four lines cover verse 138, and the subsequent stanza follows the contours of verses 139 and 140:

> How neare my heart it goes
> And pains me to endure
> Thy Words forgotten by Thy foes!
> Whose pureness doth excell
> What is of all most pure
> By me Thy Servant loved well.
>   (7–12)

Here Pembroke begins the compression process by placing verse 140 material into a subordinate clause, creating a connection between the thoughts not explicit in the prose version. Her finished version goes back to "zeale" from the Geneva text, combining it with "inflame," a word taken from Bèze's commentary. Through further grammatical compression, the passage is reduced from 12 to 8 lines:

> Sure, lord, thy self art just,
>   thy lawes as rightfull be:
> what rightly bid thou dost,
>   is firmly bound by thee.
> I flame with zeale to see
>   my foes thy word forgett:
> pure wordes, whereon by me:
>   a servantes love is sett. (1–8)

This passage demonstrates that Pembroke was not after elaboration or expansion per se; instead, she strove for a kind of muscularity that set in motion the skeleton of the original.

One of the most striking reworkings in her corpus is that of Psalm 58, a psalm full of pitfalls for translators because of its embarrassingly imprecatory content. Bèze, attempting to cope with the viciousness of the imprecations, explains in his commentary that David

> doth pronounce the sentence against [his enemies] in the name of God himselfe, not as a private man, but as a Prophet, and as a king alreadie allowed of God: and he useth similitudes moste agreeable to the covetousnesse and ambition of such maner of men.

The word "zeal," which happens to appear in both of the forementioned examples of Pembroke's psalms, could well describe Pembroke's approach to this psalm, in which she does not attempt to cloak the speaker's call for violent vengeance under a prophetic mantle, but rather puts the force of a zealous and eloquent poetic voice behind it. The Psalm is worth examining in full detail, but we will present only three excerpts. Pembroke's opening takes its cue from the rhetorical opening of the Common Prayer text:

> Are your mindes set upon righteousnesse, O yee congregation: and do ye judge the thing that is right, O ye sonnes of men?

Pembroke's first draft introduces immediately the idea, closely linked with her Psalm 82, that this psalm is addressed to those in power, and she also expands on the "sonnes of men" by reaching back to Genesis to name the first sinful man:

> You that in judgment sitt
> Is this to speake what is in judgment fitt
> Is this aright to sentence wronged case
> O you but earthly Adams race
> Though higher sett in honourd place?
>
> (1–5)

In her final version, Pembroke revises the parallel structure by creating two parallel rhetorical questions, clarifies the definition of justice attempted in line 3 of the draft version, and begins the speaker's sentence *in medias res*. The wordy reference to the Genesis story in line 4 is revised to the pithy "sonnes of dust," a biting reminder to the arrogant addressees of exactly what they're made of.[23] The overall effect is to create an enraged and scornful voice, fully confident in its position of judgment on the judges:

> And call yee this to utter what is just,
>   you that of justice hold the sov'raign throne?
> and call yee this to yeld, O sonnes of dust,
>   to wronged brethren ev'ry man his own? (1–4)

Pembroke's revision of the serpent images in verses 4 and 5 is another striking example of the freedoms she takes, by steps, in recreating the text. The Common Prayer text offers a straight simile for the ungodly:

4. They are as venemous as the poyson of a serpent: even like the deafe Adder that stoppeth her eares.
5. Which refuseth to heare the voice of the charmer: charme he never so wisely.

In her first draft, Pembroke hits upon the idea that the ungodly are like the serpent in their poison and their hiss:

> Not only Serpents hisse
> But Serpents poyson in them lodged is.
> Poyson such as the Subtile Aspick beares
>   Whose talye ev'n then doth stop her eares
>   When shee the skilfull'st charmer heares.
>   (16–20)

In the final version, Pembroke has the speaker blustering in anger for just the right image, presenting but then rejecting the adder image as just not nasty enough:

> to shew the venim of their canc'red mynd
>   the Adders image scarcly can suffice.
>   nay scarce the Aspick may with them contend,
> on whom the charmer all in vaine applies
>   his skillful'st spells: ay missing of his end,
> while shee self-deaff, and unaffected lies.   (11–16)

The next line in the final version uses alliteration to enhance the violence of the speaker's wishes: "Lord crack their teeth, lord crush these lions jawes." Pembroke had already replaced "breake" and "smite" from the prose with "crack" and "crush," but her final version sets the words together in a single line for maximum effect. In the conclusion of the psalm, the psalmist justifies his vengeful ravings with the idea that if his wishes for his enemies' destruction come to pass, then all will see that

"Verely there is a reward for the righteous: doubtlesse there is a God that judgeth the earth." Pembroke's first six-line version of this concludes rather blandly with "There is a God whose justice never swerves / But good or ill to each man carves / As each mans good or ill deserves." Pembroke obviously noted that the word "carves" is the only interesting thing about this version, since she places the word prominently in her condensed, dramatic, revised version:

> while all shall say: the just rewarded be
> there is a god that carves to each his own.
>
> (31–32)

Here, God is no gentle judge; he acts with firm, even violent decisiveness in meting out both to righteous and wicked their deserved reward. These and many other instances demonstrate the kinds of interpretive and rhetorical freedoms Pembroke constantly and very consciously took with her material. The result is far from the safely "literal" renderings offered for public consumption through print; her psalms, rather, exhibit an individual's interpretive efforts, based on meditation and study, woven into the text through a process that values aesthetic considerations as well as doctrinal propriety.[24]

THOSE HIGH TONS

Psalms 120–27 and their variants provide an interesting illustration, both of Pembroke's willingness to bring artistry to bear on sacred texts and of anxiety in the period over how far one could go in particularizing the text. These psalms constitute perhaps the most idiosyncratic experiments in the finished psalter, reflecting the Sidney circle's involvement in the quantitative meter projects of the 1580s and 90s. They may also reflect the precedent of George Buchanan's Latin paraphrases of the psalms in quantitative meter, as these were widely read in England and as Buchanan was Sidney's friend. Buchanan's quantitative psalms, along with the *carmina* in Bèze's commentary and minute rhetorical analysis of the Psalms in the Tremellius-Junius Latin Bible, may have provided a justification for a highly rhetorical metrical psalm style that the English tradition did not.[25] In the *G* and *M* manuscripts, however, these quantitative psalms are completely replaced by more conventional rhymed versions. The editors of *Collected Works* have determined, based on stylistic study and on the relationship of these manuscripts to ones more assuredly prepared under Pembroke's guidance, that the alterations in these manuscripts, including the rhymed versions of 120–27, are non-authorial. Some later editor, perhaps working after 1611, made numerous emendations and saw fit to replace the quantitative psalms altogether.[26] An analysis of both the small changes and the replaced psalms indicates this later editor was not attempting to improve the poetic qualities of the verse, but rather to trim out at least some of the artistic flourish of Pembroke's psalms. About these changes, the editors write:

Often the motive was to eliminate the skilfully varied repetition that is a prominent feature of her paraphrases. At other times, her appropriation of unusual but, in context, evocative biblical thought and language is replaced by more conventional diction and phrasing. The overall effect is the opposite of what one notices in the revisions that seem to be her own.

Why would the later editor work backwards, as we might see it? The only convincing answer seems to be that these poems were a translation of *Scripture*. Their presentation as a whole psalter, moreover, suggested a claim to a certain authority as a devotional resource. After all, a few highly sophisticated psalm translations floating about in manuscript would have seemed a harmless exercise in personal piety – but a complete, beautifully presented psalter carried implications of speaking with more authority alongside the sacred text.[27] Such a work seems more an "aspiration" to "those high Tons" – exactly what Pembroke felt she had to disclaim. The *G/M* editor apparently had doubts about whether Pembroke's audaciously artistic, idiosyncratic approach was permissible in a work published even in the limited, scribal medium. Pembroke may have been a prominent cultural figure, the sister of Sidney, a prestigious patron respected for her intellect and piety – but would her readers have allowed that even all this gave her the authority to tamper with the text quite so boldly?

The section of *Collected Works* that considers the relationship of the various manuscripts offers numerous examples of places in which the *G/M* editor replaced an enhanced metaphor or rhetorical figure in Pembroke's version with a word or phrase closer to the Common Prayer prose text. In Pembroke's Psalm 51.33, for instance, the speaker cries "ah! cast me not from thee." In the *G* and *M* manuscripts, the editor makes the tiny alteration of "not from thee" to "not away" to echo the exact wording of the Prayer Book and the Geneva. In Psalm 45, where Pembroke's version has "On thie right side thie dearest queene doth stand," the *G/M* editor emends "side" to "hand." This follows the Common Prayer text, but creates an internal rhyme that is not repeated in corresponding places in other stanzas. It also reveals "ignorance of the probable source of the original word in Marot's paraphrase . . . '*a ton costé.*' "[28] For Psalms 120–27, however, such minor tinkering apparently was inadequate for the *G/M* editor's purposes. It may have been a matter of taste or fashion; the editor may simply have found quantitative meter unappealing. After all, as Derek Attridge's study of sixteenth-century English quantitative meter experiments suggests, the quantitative meter fashion had run its course by 1599.[29] Gary Waller proposes that the rhymed versions of Psalms 120–27 were created in response to unfavorable comments about quantitative meter in Samuel Daniel's 1603 *Defense of Rhyme.*[30] However, the nature of the minor alterations as well as the nature of the rhymed versions of Psalms 120–27 suggest that the *G/M* editor was troubled by the rarefied, artificial nature of quantitative meter as a medium for sacred texts.

There is at least one suggestion that quantitative meter may have represented to the *G/M* editor a certain class snobbery not appropriate for a biblical text. The Reformation principle of the priesthood of all believers, in other words, may have rendered quantitative meter, in the editor's mind, too undemocratic a medium for Scripture. Pembroke's Psalm 123.9–10 complains of "scorners" and "reprochers," then concludes with what could be mistaken for a courtly plea for favor:

> then frend us, favour us, lord then with mercy relive us,
>   whose scornfull misery greatly thy mercy needeth.

The *G/M* version, however, returns to the Prayer Book in identifying these enemies as the wealthy:

> Our *Soule*, with skorne o'reflowes
>   (For rich men us deride)
> And with despight of those
>   That swell in height of pride.
>   (17–20)

This version sets the speaker over against the rich, a contention the wealthy countess may have wished to suppress in her version. It would indeed seem strange for a poetic voice to complain about oppression by the rich in a poetic mode exclusive to the highly educated, leisured class.

Whether or not quantitative verse had certain class connotations for the *G/M* editor, it does not appear that the revisions are meant to improve poetic effectiveness. Pembroke's quantitative versions may at times seem, at least to our tastes, rather peculiar. The lyrical opening of Psalm 121, for example – "I will lift up mine eyes unto the hilles: from whence commeth my helpe" – is transformed in Pembroke's psalm into a stanza that depends for its effectiveness on an appreciation of its colloquially dramatic first line and its exact repetition of line 2's query as a confident statement in line 4:

> What? and doe I behold the lovely mountaines,
> whence comes all my reliefe, my aid, my comfort?
> ô there, ô there abides the worlds Creator,
> whence comes all my reliefe, my aid, my comfort.

While that passage might enjoy, from some readers, only a puzzled respect for its use of rhetorical amplification, Pembroke's quantitative versions do often achieve a lovely immediacy, even an eloquent melancholy. Even where this occurs, however, the rhymed versions make no attempt to preserve the vivid imagery or undulating rhythms. For instance, Pembroke's Psalm 125.9–20 has a dignity and beauty appropriate to this declaration of God's justice and favor to his people:

> Though Tirantes hard yoke with a heavy pressure
> wring the just shoulders: but a while it holdeth,
> lest the best minded by too hard abusing
>   bend to abuses.
>
> As the well-workers, soe the right beleevers;
> lord favour, further; but a vaine deceiver,
> whose wryed footing not aright directed
>   wandreth in error.
>
> Lord hym abjected set among the number
> whose doings lawles; study bent to mischiefe
> mischief expecteth: but upon thy chosen
>   peace be for ever.

The *G/M* version of the first stanza quoted above is enough to demonstrate what was lost by replacing the imagery and strong sound effects of Pembroke's poetry:

> The scourge ungodly men deserve
>   shall not the righteous portion be:
> Least they (too much afflicted) swerve
>   From *truth*, and unto falshood flee.
>   (9–12)

On other occasions, the *G/M* revisions lose not only imagery and beauty, but an interpretive gloss that Pembroke has worked into her lines. For instance, Pembroke follows Bèze in considering Psalm 122 a post-exilic psalm, one of rejoicing over the approach to a rebuilt temple. (Calvin disagreed, insisting that the psalm is "of David," as the Geneva heading maintains.) Thus, both of Pembroke's extant quantitative versions, the draft in manuscripts *B* and *I* and the final version in manuscript *A*, reflect Bèze's interpretation. The *A* version reads:

> O fame most joyfull! ô joy most livly delightfull!
> loe, I do heare godds temple, as erst, soe againe be
> > > frequented,
> and we within thy porches againe glad-wonted abiding,
> lovly Salem shall find: thou Citty rebuilt as a Citty.   (1–4)

The *G/M* version sounds much like the Prayer Book text, and loses the interpretive gloss completely:

> Right gladd was I in heart and minde
> > When thus I heard the people saye
> With one assent so well enclinde
> > To serve the Lord, and to him praie/
> > Unto Godes *Temple* let us goe
> > And there our service to him showe/
> > > (1–6)

Overall, the *G/M* versions display competent accentual poetry. Most of the metrical forms are not ballad meter; in fact, they follow the parameters set up by the Sidneys in using metrical forms not elsewhere appearing in the psalter. The variations here are, however, less imaginative than many of the Sidneys'. The *G/M* versions reflect a method of composition much closer to the mid-century metrical psalmists: an effort to follow the authoritative English translations with limited artistic intrusion and without offering obvious interpretive slants.

Even if the *G/M* editor simply found the quantitative meters unfashionable, he might have left them in the full manuscript of the *Psalmes* as a nostalgic reminder of a noble project now dead, or out of deference to Sidney's legacy and Pembroke's distinguished position as poet and patron. Or, the *G/M* editor might have included the rhymed versions in some kind of appendix, as an alternative for the squeamish. However, the fact that in these two manuscripts the quantitative versions are completely replaced suggests that the editor could not let them lie; the desire to have these sacred texts rendered appropriately was too strong. This person's discomfort with quantitative meter for Scripture appears to reflect the anxiety persisting throughout the period over the theological implications of metrical forms. Rendering the prose texts into meter was perceived as presenting poets with dual temptations: that of making unauthorized interpretive moves, and of using the text as a vehicle for the artistic aspiration of the poet rather than for the spiritual edification of poet and audience – of competing with the fully abundant beauty of the texts as they are. These are "temptations" that Sidney and especially Pembroke did not so much fall into as embrace.

Pembroke used clothing metaphors to describe the relationship of her psalms to their scriptural originals, but, as we have seen, her revision process indicates that she did more than re-dress the psalms. By freely employing her extensive study and the most sophisticated resources English poetry had to offer, she re-formed the psalmic material – or "re-revealed" it, as Donne later claimed. The boldness of her method is mirrored in the image of the devotional experience she creates: the eloquent "I" of her psalms confidently approaches the throne of God, demanding God's attention and favor and fully expecting that God will not only permit the artistry of the engagement, but even appreciate it. "With skillful song his praises sing" her speaker urges in Psalm 47. "At home, abroad most willingly I will / Bestow on god my praises uttmost skill," the speaker declares in the first lines of Psalm 111. The exuberance, sensuality, and passion of her speakers in her *Psalmes* suggest an unprecedented confidence in her poetically mediated relationship to the Divine and to the inspired text. Whether the weight her psalms give to individual artistry and interpretation is "undue" or not depends on how one calculates the value – artistic and spiritual – of the poetry of the early seventeenth century that clearly looks back to the Sidney–Pembroke Psalter as precedent. Pembroke's approach to metrical psalmody made legitimate the interiorization and adaptation of scriptural sources. Her strategy of scribal publication protected this rather audacious proposal from those who might find it the "too, too bold" assertion of the individual over the authoritative text. This strategy succeeded in presenting to a crucially exclusive circle of readers – including Donne and Herbert – a bold premise about what is possible and permissible in devotional poetry.

NOTES

1 For useful accounts of Protestant devotional literature of the period, see Barbara K. Lewalski, *Protestant Poetics* (Princeton: Princeton University Press, 1979), 147–78. Also Rivkah Zim, *English Metrical Psalms: Poetry as Praise and Prayer, 1535–1601* (Cambridge: Cambridge University Press, 1987), particularly the first chapter. Zim's account of the humanist notion of *imitatio*

helpfully describes the wide range of approaches to an original that fall under that heading. This article attempts to expand upon Zim's brief comments on how this range is complicated when the original in question is considered an inspired text.

2 Debra K. Rienstra, "Singing to the Lord a New Song: the Reformation and the English Religious Lyric," *Perspectives*, January 1994, 14–18. The letter of response, submitted by Richard W. Hudelson, appeared in the following issue, February 1994, 7.

3 See Margaret Hannay's essay in this volume, pp. 17–49. Hannay argues particularly against gender as a reason for Pembroke's scribal publication of her *Psalmes*. For an account of Pembroke's purposes in publishing Sidney's works, see Hannay, *Philip's Phoenix* (New York: Oxford University Press, 1990). Pembroke not only published her brother's works, but others of her own, including *Antonius* – her translation of Garnier – and *Discourse of Life and Death* – her translation of Philippe de Mornay.

4 For a useful survey of period writers who exhort readers to apply the Scriptures to themselves, see Lewalski, *Protestant Poetics*, 149–50.

5 For a more detailed explanation of how the idea of the priesthood of all believers may have impinged upon poets' methods, see Debra K. Rienstra, "Aspiring to Praise: the Sidney–Pembroke Psalter and the English Renaissance Lyric," Ph.D. thesis, Rutgers University (1995), 105–12.

6 Examples from published metrical psalm collections in this article, as well as other examples described in the sections of Zim and Lewalski already cited, demonstrate that published devotional works during this period were expected to be "safe." That is, writers took pains to provide assurances that their works were properly edifying for readers precisely because they provided a faithful transmission of Scripture.

7 *The Collected Works of Mary Sidney Herbert, Countess of Pembroke*, eds. Margaret P. Hannay, Noel J. Kinnamon, and Michael G. Brennan, 2 vols. (Oxford: Clarendon Press, 1998).

8 John Calvin, *The Institution of Christian Religion*, trans. Thomas North (London, 1578), STC 4418. Similarly, Arthur Golding, who translated Calvin's commentaries on the Psalms, explains in the dedication to his 1571 volume his efforts to translate "piththy [sic] and grounded matter" without the "rhetorical inlarging of painted sentences." See John Calvin, *The Psalmes of David and others. With J. Calvins Commentaries*, trans. Arthur Golding (London, 1571), STC 4395. See also Rivkah Zim, *English Metrical Psalms*, 5.

9 Of course, speaking as if there were an Absolute, Correct Sense may seem quaint to our poststructuralist sensibilities, but Wither himself knew it was something of a construction since he is among those who affirmed the multiplicity of translations. The underlying assumption for Wither (and others) was that the Sense exists, and can be approached, but is infinitely elusive. Nevertheless, the approach is worth the most assiduous effort. George Wither, *A Preparation to the Psalter* (London: 1619), STC 25914.

10 Francis Seager, *Certayne Psalmes Select out of the Psalter of David and Drawen into Englyshe Metre* (London, 1553), STC 2728.
11 William Hunnis, *Certayne Psalmes Chosen out of the Psalter of David, and Drawen Furth into Englysh Meter* (London, 1550), STC 2727.
12 Matthew Parker, *The Whole Psalter translated into English Metre* (London, 1567), STC 2729.
13 William Hunnis, *Seven Sobs of a Sorrowfull Soule for Sinne* (London, 1583), STC 13975.
14 The Marot–Bèze Psalter exhibits 110 metrical forms. In comparison, count-ing all metrical forms in all versions, the Sidney–Pembroke Psalter uses 167 different verse forms. Pembroke's psalms use 126 different forms. (However, these figures count the alternative versions in the *G* and *M* manuscripts. Assuming that the rhymed versions of Psalms 120–27 are not Pembroke's, the figures would be 159 total verse forms and 118 for Pembroke.)
15 See "Literary Context," 2:9. Donne likewise remarks on the dearth of artistry in English psalmody in his famous poem praising the Sidneys' psalter: "And shall our church, unto our spouse and king, / More hoarse, more harsh than any other, sing? / For that we pray, we praise thy name for this, / Which, by this Moses and this Miriam, is / Already done," John Donne, *The Complete English Poems*, ed. A. J. Smith (London: Penguin, 1971), 332.
16 Actually, there are a few repetitions. From *Collected Works*, 1:57: "Through-out the *Psalmes*, there are only four exact repetitions in metre and rhyme. Pembroke uses Sidney's form of Psalm 8 in Psalm 118, and his form for Psalm 32 in Psalm 71; in addition, she repeats her own stanzaic form in Psalms 60 and 119s, and uses *rhyme royal* in Psalms 51 (with feminine rhymes) and 63."
17 This title page is attached to manuscript *C*.
18 "Even now that Care," l. 34. The intense attention in the period to the beauty and rhetorical accomplishment of the Scriptures themselves was used to justify the use of the "grand style" in prose works expounding Scripture. See Debora K. Shuger, *Sacred Rhetoric: the Christian Grand Style in the English Renaissance* (Princeton: Princeton University Press, 1988). And, as mentioned above, the fact that the Psalms were poems was sometimes used to justify the appropriateness of rendering them into English meter. However, the in-herently poetic nature of the texts was considered the precise reason why further artistic embellishment was not only unnecessary but almost an af-front. For an account of contemporary analyses of scriptural beauties, see Part I of Lewalski, *Protestant Poetics*, and Zim, *English Metrical Psalms*, especially chapter 1.
19 *The Psalms of Sir Philip Sidney and the Countess of Pembroke*, J. C. A. Rathmell, ed. (New York: New York University Press, 1963), xx. Rathmell cites parallels in both Bèze's and Calvin's commentaries. The connection with the former is stronger, however: "Even when the joining of my bones was knowne unto thee, when I was formed in so secret a place, and was fashioned in the darke cave, as it were with needle worke," Théodore Bèze, *The Psalmes of David,*

Truly Opened and Explaned by Paraphrasis, trans. Anthony Gilby [London, 1581], STC 2034, sig. P7v.

20 Thomas Sternhold, John Hopkins, *et al., The whole Booke of Psalmes. Collected into English Meter, by Tho. Sternhold, Joh. Hopkins, and others* (London, 1569), STC 2440.

21 *Collected Works,* 2:27–29. For further examples of Pembroke introducing courtly imagery into her psalms, see Gary F. Waller, "'This Matching of Contraries': Calvinism and Courtly Philosophy in the Sidney Psalms," *English Studies* 55 (1974), 22–31, and Margaret P. Hannay, "'House-confinéd maids': the Presentation of Woman's Role in the *Psalmes* of the Countess of Pembroke," *English Literary Renaissance* 24 (1994), 20–35, as well as Hannay, "'When riches growes': Class Perspective in Pembroke's Psalmes," in *Women, Writing, and the Reproduction of Culture in Tudor and Stuart Britain,* eds. Mary E. Burke, Jane Donowerth, Linda L. Dove, and Karen Nelson (Syracuse: Syracuse University Press, 2000), 77–97.

22 For an explanation of the manuscripts and their relations, see *Collected Works,* 2:308–57.

23 Since the name "Adam" in the Hebrew text is a word play on "Adamah," or dust, Pembroke's usage here has been cited as one of several possible indications that she had access to a Hebrew text. See *Collected Works,* 2:17.

24 Pembroke does not always follow the Calvinist line in her psalms. For examples, see Waller, "This Matching of Contraries."

25 For an assessment of how Pembroke used Bèze's Latin edition of his commentary, see Noel J. Kinnamon, "God's 'Scholler': the Countess of Pembroke's *Psalmes* and Beza's *Psalmorum Davidis . . . Libri Quinque," N&Q,* March 1997, 85–88. For Pembroke's use of Buchanan's psalms and the Tremellius-Junius Bible, see *Collected Works,* 30–31.

26 For a brief consideration of the *G* and *M* manuscripts, see *Collected Works,* 2:352–57.

27 While Wyatt's and Surrey's psalm translations, especially Wyatt's, are often cited as early examples of free metrical versions of Psalms, we have not considered them directly here. Since neither sequence was presented in any way as a translation of the prose (Wyatt's was a translation of an Italian sequence in terza rima), and certainly not as a complete Psalter, they fall neatly into the safe category of miscellaneous personal meditations, suitable, if readers so choose, strictly for devotional use or aesthetic admiration.

28 *Collected Works,* 2:354.

29 Derek Attridge, *Well-Weighed Syllables: Elizabethan Verse in Classical Meters* (Cambridge: Cambridge University Press, 1974), 202.

30 Gary F. Waller, *Mary Sidney, Countess of Pembroke: a Critical Study of her Writings and Literary Milieu* (Salzburg: Institut für Anglistik und Amerikanistik, 1979), 176–77.

CHAPTER 4

Creating female authorship in the early seventeenth century: Ben Jonson and Lady Mary Wroth[1]

Michael G. Brennan

"SAFE IN YOUR JUDGMENT (WHICH IS A SIDNEYS)"[2]

By 1612 Lady Mary Wroth (1587–c.1653) may well already have been an enthusiastic versifier and perhaps even an experimenter in prose fiction.[3] (For all we know, she may have demonstrated her literary skills to family and close friends even earlier, although no evidence has survived to prove that this was so.) But the specific circumstances behind the sudden burgeoning of her public reputation as both an author and patron from about 1612 onwards, followed by what appears to have been a frenetic decade of writing culminating in the 1621 edition of her prose romance, *Urania*, and sonnet sequence, *Pamphilia to Amphilanthus*, remain something of a mystery. Was Lady Mary's determined espousal of the role of female author largely self-motivated or were there other directing influences behind her impressive literary output in the years leading up to 1621? While considerable critical attention has rightly been paid in recent years to the possible influences exerted over Lady Mary's literary creativity by her father (Sir Robert Sidney), her aunt (Mary Sidney Herbert, Countess of Pembroke), and her cousin (William Herbert, third Earl of Pembroke, who also fathered her two illegitimate children), rather less consideration has been given to ways in which her early reputation and compositions may have been stimulated (and perhaps even actively directed) by another individual no less committed to the preservation of the legend of Sir Philip Sidney – Ben Jonson. If this is so, then his warm dedication to her of *The Alchemist* (1612) – the only one of Jonson's plays to be addressed to a woman – may be interpreted as a key moment in Lady Mary's transition from private to public status as a patron and guardian of the literary reputation of her illustrious uncle.[4]

During the first half of King James's reign Jonson certainly seems to have wished to give the impression of holding Lady Mary Wroth's personal qualities and literary judgment in high regard. Given her success

73

in gaining early prominence at the new Stuart royal court, it is not hard to see why she attracted the attention of a patronage-hunter as sharp as Jonson. By the end of 1604 Lady Mary, the eldest daughter of Sir Robert Sidney and Lady Barbara Gamage, was already firmly ensconced in the personal circles of both the new king and queen. In 1603 her father had been appointed as Queen Anne's Lord Chamberlain and in September 1604 she married at Penshurst Sir Robert Wroth (1576–1614), a favored hunting companion of King James. As Lord Chamberlain, Robert Sidney exercised ultimate control over the queen's court entertainments and it was probably through her father's direct influence that Lady Mary first came to know Jonson as a performer in his masques.[5] Although it cannot be established exactly how the individual parts finally came to be allocated, following her marriage Lady Mary was almost immediately thrust into the theatrical limelight at court, as Josephine A. Roberts explains:

She gained one of the most coveted honors, a role in the first masque designed by Ben Jonson in collaboration with Inigo Jones, *The Masque of Blackness*, performed at Whitehall on 6 January 1605. She joined Queen Anne and eleven of her closest friends in disguising themselves as black Ethiopian nymphs. She also appeared with the queen in *The Masque of Beauty*, performed at Whitehall on 10 January 1608. She may have acted in other court masques for which the performance lists are incomplete, and it is likely that she attended masques such as *Hymenaei* (performed in 1606), *The Masque of Queens* (performed in 1609), and *Oberon* (performed in 1611). In the *Urania* she alluded to *Lord Hay's Masque* (performed in 1607) by Thomas Campion and probably to *Tethys' Festival* (performed in 1610) by Samuel Daniel. She also included descriptions of imaginary masques, complete with spectacular stage effects, in the second part of her romance.[6]

By the second decade of the seventeenth century Jonson's relationship with Lady Mary Wroth had apparently matured into an association of some importance to both sides. In particular, he seems to have considered it useful to promulgate her name as one of the most prominent female members of the Sidney/Herbert family network of patronage and influence. From a biographical perspective, it was perhaps in part the impact of family bereavements (for both Lady Mary and Jonson) that triggered Jonson's preoccupation with her dynastic and literary inheritance. Lady Mary's first cousin, Elizabeth Sidney Manners, Countess of Rutland, the only child of her uncle, Sir Philip Sidney, succumbed to the summer plague of 1612; and toward the end of that year Lady Mary's own brother, William Sidney, also died of the smallpox.[7] Partly as a consequence of these two bereavements, coupled with the fact that

Sir Philip's sister, Mary Sidney Herbert, Dowager Countess of Pembroke, no longer seemed to be much involved in either literary pursuits or court society, Lady Mary found herself bearing much of the responsibility for taking forward the Sidney family's still considerable public reputation for literary endeavor. By the end of 1612 she seems to have come to be viewed, in effect, as Sir Philip's direct literary heiress.[8] In retrospect, she carried out this "cross-gendered" inheritance during the next ten years with remarkable assiduity and skill, penning her voluminous prose romance *Urania*, her sonnet sequence *Pamphilia to Amphilanthus*, and her pastoral drama *Love's Victory*, thereby securing her place in literary history as the first Englishwoman to write a prose romance, a complete sonnet sequence, or a pastoral drama.

This essay will also examine how a small group of writers (several of whom possessed close links with Jonson and through him may well have enjoyed either first- or second-hand access to Lady Mary's manuscript compositions) assisted in the promulgation of her literary reputation long before any of her writings became more widely available in print. But before their role in the formulation of her literary reputation can be assessed, it is first necessary to define more specifically Jonson's own personal contacts with the Sidneys and Herberts during James's reign. As early as the 1590s Jonson had been associated with the acting company patronized by Mary Sidney Herbert's husband, Henry, second Earl of Pembroke. Whether Jonson maintained an unbroken intimacy with the Herberts from that time is not known. But when he was jailed for his part-authorship of *Eastward Ho* in 1605, one of those to whom he immediately turned for help was Henry Herbert's son, William, then third Earl of Pembroke.[9] Jonson's involvements in Queen Anne's court entertainments presumably served to consolidate his relationship with the Sidneys and Herberts; and when in 1611 he decided to dedicate the quarto edition of *Catiline* to William Herbert, he pointedly noted that it was "the first (of this race) that ever I dedicated to any person."[10] This potent public gesture of allegiance was rapidly followed up by an ode, written during a stay at Penshurst, to Sir Robert Sidney's eldest son, William, commemorating his twenty-first birthday in November 1611.[11] At about the same time Jonson probably composed "To Penshurst" (*The Forest* 2) celebrating the Sidneys' main residence and wholesome way of life; "To Sir Robert Wroth" (*The Forest* 3) in praise of Lady Mary's home at Durrance; and a significant group of epigrams addressed to various members of the Sidney and Herbert circle.[12] The culmination of this association came with his fulsome dedication to Lady Mary of the

1612 quarto edition of *The Alchemist*.[13] This implicit pairing in patronage of William Herbert and Lady Mary Wroth – as, respectively, the first male and female patrons of Jonson's quarto plays – seems, in retrospect, a prescient prefiguring of Herbert's and Wroth's central relationship to the more explicit statements on the efficacy and value of aristocratic patronage offered by the contents, ordering, and dedications of Jonson's 1616 folio.

What, then, might have Jonson hoped to get out of these personal contacts and literary tributes to the Sidney and Herbert circle between 1610 and 1612? On a political level, Jonson was undoubtedly attracted by their close dealings with the all-powerful Robert Cecil, Earl of Salisbury (whose favor he had also sought directly), and by their relative independence, in David Riggs's phrase, from "the fluid, anxiety-ridden world of court politics."[14] Another factor which may have encouraged Jonson to make a concerted attempt at this period to cultivate the (outwardly) resolutely Protestant Sidneys and Herberts was his decision in 1610 to distance himself from Rome by rejoining the Anglican Church.[15] Within a year of his conversion, as Riggs points out, Jonson had written a "comedy about millenarian Protestants [*The Alchemist*] and a tragedy about seditious cryptopapists [*Catiline*]."[16] Viewed from this perspective, the respective dedications of these plays to Wroth and Pembroke may indicate that Jonson was also using these texts as a means of engaging in religious debate with his patrons rather than merely seeking their literary approval and material support for his plays.

On another level, this "self-contained aristocratic community ... answerable only to its own ancestral traditions," as Jonson so earnestly sought to depict the Sidneys and Herberts, provided him with an ideal environment in which to maintain the legend of Sir Philip Sidney as writer and courtier who had valued literature as a means of mediating upon personal relationships and morality, alongside broader issues of national and international politics.[17] It is clear that the historical reputation of the Sidney family and, in particular, Sir Philip Sidney's memory – not only as an inspiration to writers but also as a kind of Protestant patron-saint – began to exert a powerful hold over Jonson's imagination from about 1610 onwards. "To Penshurst," usually denoted generically as a "country house" poem and probably based upon Jonson's residence there as a guest in 1611, is also very much a "family" or "genealogical" panegyric in that Robert Sidney's virtuous lifestyle is seen to be firmly rooted in the historical geography of his own lineage. Penshurst, of course, was also for Lady Mary Wroth that most potent of remembered personal landscapes – her happy childhood home; and it is perhaps permissible to speculate briefly on how she might have read the poem when it was first offered as a gift to the family by Jonson in manuscript form (as it surely must have been).

Jonson playfully implies in "To Penshurst" that it is the Sidneys, with the virtuous innocence of Adam and Eve before the fall, who have entirely shaped and defined the natural landscape around Penshurst. He notes with admiration how family individuals have even lent their names in perpetuity to specific locations ("Thy copp's, too, nam'd of GAMAGE" and "SYDNEY's copp's," lines 19 and 26). In Jonson's poem, nominally addressed to a building, it is not merely the stones and understated architectural style of the house which endow Lady Mary's childhood home with its sense of purpose, continuity, and morality but also Penshurst's encapsulation and preservation of the memory of those, such as her grandparents, Sir Henry and Lady Mary Sidney, who in previous generations had contributed so much through their estate management and personal integrity to achieving the decorous and harmonious quality of the whole property. Penshurst, in Jonson's eyes a kind of prelapsarian Eden in which marital fecundity and family bonds are sacrosanct, is cast as an ideal environment in which to raise successive generations of Sidney children ("Thence / Their gentler spirits have suck'd innocence," lines 93–94), including, of course, Lady Mary herself. Here it is perhaps also relevant to note that during, or shortly after, Jonson's residence at Penshurst his only surviving legitimate son, Ben (named after himself and, poignantly, his first son who had died in 1603), died aged four and a half in November 1611. Jonson's poetry of this period naturally becomes much preoccupied with ideas of legitimate succession and family bereavement. When viewed from this perspective, "To Penshurst" suggests that he readily appreciated how Lady Mary would have regarded Penshurst, the central landscape of her family inheritance, as a symbol of the enduring continuity of her Sidneian heritage – unlike Jonson's own abruptly terminated familial line of descent.[18]

The origins of Jonson's explicit concern in "To Penshurst" with the dynastic and literary succession of the Sidneys can be traced back to as early as 1599. Jonson seems, understandably, to have at first regarded Sir Philip Sidney's only child, Elizabeth (1585–1612), who in early 1599 married Roger Manners (1576–1612), Earl of Rutland, as his most promising literary heir. In all, Jonson addressed three warmly complimentary poems to her and in informal conversations with Drummond of Hawthornden he was reported to have considered her to be "nothing inferior to her Father in poetry."[19] Jonson's "*Epistle. To Elizabeth Countesse of Rutland*" (*The Forest* 12, sent to her on New Year's Day 1600) had optimistically sought to underline the latent literary potential of this fourteen-year-old girl:

> For what a sinne 'gainst your great fathers spirit,
>   Were it to thinke, that you should not inherit
> His love unto the *Muses*, when his skill
> Almost you have, or may have, when you will?
>   (lines 31–34)[20]

Writing perhaps a decade later, Jonson placed a more than merely diplomatic emphasis in addressing epigram 79 to the Countess of Rutland on how the literary genius of Sir Philip Sidney, in the absence of a son, was still able to descend undiluted through the female line:

> Hence was it, that the *destinies* decreed
>   (Save that most masculine issue of his braine)
> No male unto him: who could so exceed
>   *Nature*, they thought, in all that he would faine:
> At which, shee happily displeas'd, made you[.]
>   (lines 5–9)[21]

This thought about the Countess of Rutland, of course, also implicitly paved the way for some of the tributes later paid to Lady Mary Wroth as the true inheritor of Sir Philip's literary genius. Perhaps at about the time when he composed epigram 79, Jonson was also writing for Lady Mary's eldest brother an "*Ode. To Sir William Sydney, On His Birth-day*" (*The Forest* 14). Jonson pointedly reminded William (1590–1612) – by all accounts something of a disappointment to the family – of his need to compete not only with his contemporaries but also with the memory of his illustrious ancestors.[22] But, as has already been noted, by the end of 1612 both the Countess of Rutland and her cousin, Sir William Sidney, were dead. Abruptly and perhaps partly through default, Lady Mary Wroth then found herself publicly cast as a figure of central importance to an intimate group of writers, including Jonson, who regarded the preservation of the memory of Sir Philip Sidney as a means of bolstering their own literary careers.

It is usually assumed that Jonson had completed most of his *Epigrams* by the spring of 1612 when he went abroad until the end of June 1613 as the tutor–companion of Sir Walter Raleigh's son, Wat.²⁴ The two poems in this collection on Lady Mary Wroth (epigrams 103 and 105), although not published until 1616, seem to strike a chord (and perhaps even set the tone) for other tributes in circulation from about 1611 onwards. Jonson's first poem (epigram 103) underlined her illustrious heritage as "a SYDNEY, though un-nam'd"; while the second (epigram 105) placed particular emphasis upon her prominence as a role model for other women, encompassing Diana's virtue, Athena's wisdom, and Juno's majesty.²⁵ In this latter epigram, probably completed by 1612, Jonson also included the line: "There's none so dull, that for your stile would aske" (line 15), which appears to refer to her skill with the Greek "stylus" or writing implement, symbolic of Pallas Athena's role as the goddess of wisdom. (Strangely, this interpretation is passed over in silence in some editions of Jonson's poetry.)²⁶ In his elegy *Lachrimæ Lachrimarum* (1613) on Sir William Sidney, Josuah Sylvester made what is usually interpreted as the first definite reference in print to Lady Mary Wroth's own poetry:

> Although I knowe None, but a *Sidney's* Muse
> Worthy to sing a *Sidney's* Worthyness:
> None but Your Owne *AL-WORTH* Sidnëides [i.e. La: Wroth]
> In whom, her *Uncle's* noble Veine renewes.

It seems possible that Sylvester was referring here to some of the sonnets which are now preserved in the Folger Manuscript of Lady Mary's sequence, *Pamphilia to Amphilanthus* (first published, with the *Urania*, in 1621).²⁷

From about 1611 onward it is clear that a handful of authors with either privileged access to her manuscript work, or a peripheral knowledge of her social circle, or merely an opportunistic desire to cultivate her favor, sought to give some passing prominence to her burgeoning literary interests. In 1611 George Chapman prefaced his translation of Homer with a poem describing her as "the comfort of learning, sphere of all vertues," confirming her as a newly venerated "Happy Starre discovered in our Sydneian Asterisme."²⁸ Also in 1611 the writing master John Davies of Hereford, who had transcribed for the family one of the major surviving manuscripts of the *Psalms of David* versified by Sir Philip

Sidney and the Countess of Pembroke, addressed to her a dedicatory sonnet "In the deserved praise of heavenly Musick: resembling it to God Himselfe," and penned another epigram in her honor.[29] By 1613 other writers associated with the Sidneys were also beginning to offer printed tributes to Lady Mary Wroth. George Wither praised her as *"Arts sweet Lover"* in his *Abuses Stript and Whipt*; and William Gamage offered a tribute to her in his collection of epigrams, *Linsi-Woolsie*, which was noticeably similar to Davies of Hereford's tribute.[30] Some other undated anonymous manuscript tributes to her may also date from this period, most notably a striking acrostic sonnet, decorated in gold leaf as a presentation poem, commending her commitment to the arts and literature in its final stanza:

> **W** ith you ther is a happines of fate
> **r** eaching att that to which Your hope aspires
> **o** ver Your life guidinge your Honor'd state
> **t** o tyme, to fortune and Your high desires
> **h** ow Nobly then sitts Vertue in your brest
> Richer adorn'd then is by mee exprest.[31]

Jonson's admiration for Lady Mary seems to have been a likely stimulus for at least some of these dedications. William Drummond of Hawthornden, for example, dedicated both an ode and a sonnet to Lady Mary, even though he readily confessed that they had never met. Nevertheless, perhaps relying on Jonson's judgment of her literary skills, he felt able to commend warmly her poetry in his ode: "Your spacious thoughts with choice inventiones free, / Show passiones power, affectiones severall straines" (lines 5–6). And in his sonnet he paid especial tribute to her intellectual qualities, playfully complimenting her with the same pun on her name as used by Sylvester: "worth accomplisht" and by Jonson himself in his own sonnet to "the Lady Mary Worth" (*The Underwood* 28).[32] Jonson knew Sylvester well, and had provided a commendatory poem (epigram 132) for Sylvester's translation of Guillaume du Bartas's *Divine Weeks and Works* (1605).[33] Chapman, of course, was one of Jonson's closest literary associates (and later a bitter rival) from the time of their collaboration on *Eastward Ho* (1605) and resulting imprisonment.[34] Davies of Hereford was intimate enough with Jonson to compliment him jovially on his health and on being "sound in Body."[35] Other reasons, of course, may have prompted some of these writers to praise Lady Mary. William Gamage was a relative on her mother's side and Wither, in later years despised by Jonson for his populist satires, may have simply been paying an opportunist compliment to her in his *Abuses* volume, a collection packed with tributes to a miscellany of prominent figures.

But if Sylvester's 1613 tribute to Lady Mary does refer to some of the sonnets now preserved in the Folger Manuscript of *Pamphilia to Amphilanthus*, this manuscript may then offer the earliest surviving evidence of how she viewed her interdependent roles as the preserver of the literary reputation of the Sidneys and as a pioneering woman writer. The act of writing an entire sonnet sequence (certainly by 1613 very much a passé literary form) was in itself a nostalgic gesture of reverence towards both Sir Philip Sidney's *Astrophil and Stella* and her father, Robert's own unpublished collection of sonnets, probably written during his service in Flushing during the 1590s.[36] The incidental details of the Folger Manuscript also offer ample physical evidence of Lady Mary's self-conscious pride in her Sidney ancestry, in that she decorates certain poems (e.g. fol. 1^r and 29^r) with a "slashed s" device, a pen-and-ink symbol also adopted by her aunt, Mary Herbert, Countess of Pembroke. Indeed, throughout her marriage to Robert Wroth, Lady Mary preferred to retain her heraldic status as a Sidney, as illustrated by the arrowhead coat of arms attached to her name in Henry Peacham's *The Complete Gentleman* (1622).[37]

Written out in her own formal italic hand, the Folger Manuscript contained 117 poems, gathered in a number of discrete clusters, the most important being the first of 55 poems. By the time of the printed text of *Pamphilia to Amphilanthus* (published with the *Urania* in 1621) the poems had been reordered and revised down to 102, with one new one added. As with Jonson and his *Epigrams*, probably first collected together in manuscript in about 1610–12 and then prepared for printing in 1615/16, the process of publication for Lady Mary formed a kind of monumental culmination to the manuscript circulation and careful revision of her poetry.[38] As a woman, Lady Mary also had to address the traditional Petrarchan model of the male lover wooing his lady. It was not feasible simply to reverse the formula with Pamphilia wooing Amphilanthus (= "lover of two") and so instead her sonnets tend to address mythological figures such as Cupid, or the abstractions of fortune, grief, and time. Such a tactic recalls Jonson's own technique in some of the verses published in *The Forest* and *The Underwood*, most notably the untitled "And must I sing? What subject shall I chuse?" (*The Forest* 10), which actually debates the poetic tactic of addressing such figures as Phoebus, Pallas, Venus, and Cupid (whom Jonson himself addresses in "*His discourse with* Cupid" ("A Celebration of CHARIS in Ten Lyrick Peeces," *The Underwood*, 2.v). Furthermore, Jonson was one of the few dominant male poets of the period to attempt a convincing poetic representation of the woman's perspective on such topics as love (as in his "*A Nymphs Passion*," *The Underwood* 7), the ideal man ("A Celebration of CHARIS in Ten Lyrick Peeces," *The Underwood*, 2.ix, "*Her man described by her owne Dictamen*" and 2.x "*Another Ladyes exception, present at the hearing*"), the falsity of the world ("To The World. *A farewell for a Gentle-woman, vertuous and noble*," *The Forest* 4), inconstancy ("*Another. In defence of their Inconstancie. A Song*," *The Underwood* 6), and female song (see the pre-1618 version, originally for two female voices, of "*The Musicall strife; In a Pastorall Dialogue*," which was recast in the printed version (*The Underwood*, 3), for a female and male voice.

The death of her husband Sir Robert Wroth on 14 March 1614, left Lady Mary with the responsibilities of rearing his son, James (born only one month before the death of his father), and an estate encumbered with huge debts amounting to some £23,000. To make matters worse, her widowhood was compounded by the death of her two-year-old son, James, on 5 July 1616. As well as being an intense personal tragedy, this loss had the catastrophic effect (under the terms of her husband's will) of diverting much of what remained of her family assets to Sir Robert's brother, John Wroth.[39] And yet, despite (or perhaps as a means of coping with) these personal adversities, the period 1616 to 1620 turned out to be the most productive literary period of Lady Mary's life.

Lady Mary's state of mind when she first browsed, as she surely must have done, through the 1616 folio of Jonson's *Works* can only be a matter for speculation. But the elegiac tone of both the *Epigrams* and *The Forest*, especially for a member of the Sidney family who was a personal friend of Jonson, is unmistakable. Jonson's powerful poems "On My First Daughter" (epigram 22) and "On My First Sonne" (epigram 45) would have proved especially painful reading for a woman whose only child had just died. Lady Mary would also have been reminded of the deaths in 1612 of her cousin, Elizabeth, Countess of Rutland (epigram 79 and *The Forest* 12) and her brother, William Sidney (*The Forest* 14). Similarly, Jonson's warm praise of the Wroth family seat at Durrance in "To Sir Robert Wroth" was strategically placed by the author in the 1616 folio to follow immediately on from "To Penshurst" (*The Forest* 2 and 3) – both locations from Lady Mary's better and happier past as she now struggled after 1616 with widowhood, bereavement, and mounting debts.

In a more general sense, Jonson's folio, although a triumphant public statement of his authority as a writer, could also have been viewed by those close to him as a memorial testament of his firm intention to withdraw as a poet from the public stage (apart from *The Devil is an Ass*, performed in 1616) and from the world of print (apart from those few masques privately published after 1616). At the time of its publication, Jonson would have still regarded himself, in some respects, as a dependent upon the aristocratic hospitality of Esmé Stuart, Lord D'Aubigny. For Lady Mary Wroth, probably then herself almost entirely dependent upon the domestic support of her cousin the Earl of Pembroke at his London home, Baynard's Castle, the masques included in the folio – opening with *The Masque of Blackness* in which she had played the part of Baryte – along with the two epigrams to her and the dedication of *The Alchemist*, would have offered a poignant reminder of her own lost prominence and enforced departure from court life. As a woman exiled from the public world of courtly display, the messages of withdrawal and remembrance encoded in Jonson's folio volume (perhaps explicit only to those early readers privileged by their intimacy with him) would have struck an especially sympathetic chord with Lady Mary.

Of no less significance to her would have been Jonson's grandiose dedication of his *Epigrams* to her cousin, William Herbert, third Earl of Pembroke. Lady Mary had known William since she was a child through her family's frequent visits to the Herberts' London home, Baynard's Castle. It also seems likely that she had often stayed there after her marriage in 1604, especially whenever she was involved in court masques. Following her husband's demise – and perhaps even earlier – she had formed an intimate liaison with William Herbert, resulting in two children, William and Katherine.[40] Although the exact date of the birth of their first child, William, is not known, the period 1617 to 1618 is the most likely since their second child was born in about 1619 and her semi-permanent residence at Baynard's Castle had probably been occasioned by the entail of the Wroth estate away from her to John Wroth, following the death of her son James in July 1616. It seems likely, then, that her illicit sexual relationship with the "*Epigramme*, on all man-kind" (epigram 102) (i.e. the Earl of Pembroke) may have begun just about at the time of the publication of Jonson's folio.[41] Their personal intimacy, which was informally recognized within family circles, also seems to have been very much on Jonson's mind when he determined the final ordering of the plays included in the folio.[42] Of the nine plays printed in the *Works* (1616), the collection culminated, in dedicatory terms, with Pembroke (*Catiline*), immediately preceded by Lady Mary (*The Alchemist*). David Riggs has observed that the "ascendancy of Pembroke and his circle is an important motif in the folio as a whole," celebrating the Earl's appointment in December 1615 as the new Lord Chamberlain; and the specific wording of Jonson's dedications to Pembroke preceding both *Catiline* and the *Epigrams* ("TO THE GREAT EXAMPLE OF HONOR AND VERTUE, THE MOST NOBLE WILLIAM EARLE OF PEMBROKE, L. CHAMBERLAYNE, &c.") must have been added while the folio was still at press.[43] As Jonson carefully made these last minute adjustments to the dedicatory apparatus of the folio to make the most of Pembroke's growing prominence, he must have also borne in mind that his friend and former literary collaborator, Lady Mary Wroth, was now in an exceptionally powerful position of personal influence with the Earl, whose own epigram (102) immediately preceded and "protected" Lady Mary's first epigram (103). Similarly, her second epigram (105) was preceded and "protected" by that to Susan, Countess of Montgomery (104), Pembroke's sister-in-law, who had married his brother, Philip, Earl of Montgomery, in 1604. Through Jonson's deliberate ordering of this small cluster of epigrams, Lady Mary was securely cocooned in the permanence of print, as it were, within the power and protection of the Pembroke and Montgomery earldoms. At the same time, this strategic placement could also be taken to suggest that in about late-1615 she was perhaps Jonson's most important route of personal access to the increasingly influential Pembroke and Montgomery powerbase – since she was the first cousin of both Earls, the sexual partner of one, and the close friend of the other's wife, with whom she had danced in *The Masque of Blackness* in 1605 and to whom she dedicated her *Urania* volume in 1621.

To describe Lady Mary as a "former literary collaborator" with Jonson is not to disguise the fact that she would have been very much dependent upon his literary guidance rather than the other way around. It is clear, for example, that Lady Mary pointedly drew upon several of Jonson's published writings in the compilation of her own works. In the *Urania* she imitated the marginal commentary included in both the quarto and folio texts of the *Masques of Blackness* and *Beauty* and also seems to have borrowed details of settings from several other masques, including *Hymenaei, Lord Hay's Masque, The Masque of Queens, Tethys' Festival,* and *Oberon*.[44] Her poem in *Pamphilia to Amphilanthus*, "Like to the Indians, scorched with the sunne" (22, P25), may recall her participation in the *Masque of Blackness*; and Dolorindus's melancholic poetic lament in the 1621 *Urania* (U9), "Sweete solitarines, joy to those hearts" (titled "Penshurst Mount" in an earlier manuscript copy) may deliberately echo Jonson's "To Penshurst" which mentions exactly the same spot on the Sidneys' estate ("Thou hast thy walkes for health, as well as sport: / Thy *Mount*, to which the *Dryads* doe resort," lines 9–10).[45] R. E. Pritchard has also recently pointed out some striking similarities between her *Urania* poem, "If a cleere foun-taine" (U49) and 1.ii.65–9 of Jonson's *Cynthia's Revels* (1601), and her *Pamphilia to Amphilanthus* sonnet, "An end fond jealousie alas I know" (7, P69) and Jonson's "To the World. *A farewell for a Gentle-woman, vertuous and noble*" (*The Forest* 4).[46] More predictably, her pastoral drama, *Love's Victory* may also reveal the influence of Jonson's masques in its depiction of Cupid (e.g. V.555) and the vicissitudes of love's triumphs (e.g. II.101, 312).[47] In the broader context of the 1621 *Urania* volume Elaine Beilin has persuasively argued that "some key Jonsonian themes, steadfastness, and the 'centered self' may have influenced Wroth's conception of heroic virtue."[48]

Jonson is famously supposed to have written his "*Song. That Women Are But Mens Shaddowes*" (*The Forest* 7) as a punishment for support-ing the Earl of Pembroke's claim encapsulated in the title of the poem. But the exact wording of the source of this story is worth examin-ing here. In his record of his conversations with Jonson, Drummond of Hawthornden noted: "Pembrok and his lady discoursing the Earl said that Woemen were mens shadowes, and she maintained *them*, both appealing to Johnson, he affirmed it true, for which my Lady gave a pen-nance to prove it in Verse: hence his Epigrame."[49] The phrase "his lady" is usually assumed to indicate the Countess of Pembroke, Mary Talbot, whom William Herbert had married in 1604, even though there is no other evidence to show that this somewhat distanced and ill-matched couple ever participated in shared literary interests. In contrast, Lady Mary Wroth (certainly after 1616 worthy of being denoted as Pembroke's "lady," in view of her frequent residence at Baynard's Castle and her illegitimate children by the Earl) seems a much more likely candidate to place in such a light-hearted scenario, enjoying poetic banter with Pembroke and Jonson. Furthermore, it could be argued that the issues of gender inequality inherent in Jonson's jocular "throw-away" verse also lie, cast in much more somber tones, at the very heart of Lady Mary's preoccupations in the *Urania* with the tensions between men and women occasioned by their social inequality.[50]

It is tempting to assume that the publication of Wroth's own folio *Urania* was deliberately timed to coincide with the 1621 folio edition of Sidney's *Arcadia*. The fact that the latter was published in Dublin, however, makes this hypothesis rather unlikely. Of more significance is the possibility that Lady Mary was inspired to collect her poetry and prose together in printed folio form by Sir William Alexander's folio supplement to the *Arcadia* which was on sale in London probably from early in 1617. But perhaps the single most influential publication in this respect was Jonson's 1616 folio, with its insistent commemoration of the Sidneys' literary prominence, moral worth, and cultural significance. Above all, in the folio's epigrams and its pointed conjunction of *The Alchemist* with *Catiline*, Lady Mary Wroth would have seen herself figured not only as the literary heiress of Sir Philip Sidney, as well as of his daughter the Countess of Rutland and her father Sir Robert Sidney, but also as the unofficial consort or "lady" of the ultimate patron and protector of important sections of Jonson's folio, William Herbert, Earl of Pembroke.

Furthermore, as Martin Butler has explained, Jonson's folio was "the first important English book systematically to exploit the symbolic potential of typography and the technicalities of print." It may also prefigure some of the visual qualities of Lady Mary's own 1621 folio "collected works," with its minutely thought-out title-page engraved by the Dutch artist, Simon van de Passe (who was well known to the Sidney and Herbert circle), and its remarkably thorough and meticulous correction during the entire printing process.[51] Although Lady Mary later claimed that the *Urania* had been published without her knowledge, someone clearly ensured that great care was taken in the technical production of the entire volume.[52] Josephine A. Roberts has identified over 1,060 stop-press variants in the 1621 edition, more than double the number located by Charlton Hinman in his analysis of the Shakespeare first folio. This Jonsonian level of meticulous care over the stop-press correction of Lady Mary's writings cannot be examined in detail here. But it is suggestive of a determination to produce a printed volume which, in effect, would be a fitting, authoritative, and lasting monument to her Sidneian creativity. Even if Lady Mary's involvement in the production and proof-reading of this 1621 edition cannot be definitely established, then thanks to the recent discovery by Josephine A. Roberts of Lady Mary's own annotated printed copy of the *Urania* volume, it is at least clear, despite the scandalous outcry which greeted the publication of the *Urania* and her offer to the Duke of Buckingham to have the entire edition withdrawn, that Lady Mary continued after 1621 meticulously to work over and improve the printed texts of her published works.[53]

Within the context of the publication of the 1621 *Urania*, Jonson's "*A Sonnet, To the Noble Lady, the Lady MARY WORTH*," first printed in the posthumous 1640 edition of *The Underwood* (28), becomes of special significance. Katherine Duncan-Jones has plausibly suggested that this poem may have once been intended as one of the prefatory verses to the printed edition of the *Urania*.[54] For reasons that are not entirely clear, the 1621 edition of the *Urania* ultimately did not contain any preliminaries, even though the signatures (the text abruptly begins on signature B) indicate that such material was almost certainly anticipated by the printers.[55] The fact that Jonson – never a sonneteer by preference – chose to pen a sonnet in praise of England's first female compiler of a sonnet sequence is certainly intriguing. Furthermore, he specifically states that he has been copying out (presumably either from a manuscript source or printed page-proofs if this sonnet predates the 1621 publication of the *Urania*) some of Lady Mary's own poems:

> I, That have beene a lover, and could shew it,
> Though not in these, in rithmes not wholly dumbe,
> Since I exscribe your Sonnets, am become
> A better lover, and much better Poët.

In this carefully worded sonnet Jonson goes on to define the two central qualities of Lady Mary's love poetry as its expansive exploration of the constant interplays between the power of Cupid and Venus; and (perhaps as a self-conscious reminder of the central personifications of Cupid and Venus in her pastoral drama *Love's Victory*) her poetry's ultimate assertion of Love's eternal victory over all transitory vicissitudes:

> For in your verse all *Cupids* Armorie,
> His flames, his shafts, his Quiver, and his Bow,
> His very eyes are yours to overthrow.
> But then his Mother's sweets you so apply,
> Her joyes, her smiles, her loves, as readers take
> For *Venus Ceston* every line you make.

The image of "*Venus Ceston*" (i.e. girdle) may even be a specific reference to the group of Lady Mary's sonnets entitled "A Crowne of Sonnets Dedicated to Love" included in the *Urania* volume. If Jonson's sonnet was written to be printed with the 1621 folio of the *Urania* and *Pamphilia to Amphilanthus* (as opposed to being Jonson's generous response to reading through the printed text), then it seems all the more likely that Lady Mary, the Earl of Pembroke, and Jonson were in friendly communication about literary matters in the half-decade following the publication of Jonson's own folio. Following the death of Queen Anne in 1619, Lady Mary (like the "Gentlewoman" in Jonson's "To The World. *A farewell*," *The Forest* 4) seems to have dropped out of court prominence and there is no conclusive evidence to link her to Jonson during the mid- to late-1620s.[56] Nor has any evidence survived (other than perhaps *The Underwood* 28) to indicate how Jonson may have regarded the publication of her *Urania* and *Pamphilia to Amphilanthus*. But by 1621 Lady Mary had at least fulfilled the claims made in Jonson's two epigrams addressed to her a decade earlier. She had not only lived up to her literary reputation as "a SYDNEY, though un-nam'd" (epigram 103) but had also established an independent literary reputation of her own as "*Natures Index*," transcending the traditional boundaries that restricted women to translations and works of religious devotion, thereby restoring "I' your selfe, all treasure lost of th'age before" (epigram 105), when in a semi-mythologized classical age women such as Lady Mary's literary *alter ego* Pamphilia, a Roman author under Nero, could be openly admired and respected by men and women alike for writing poetry and history.[57]

NOTES

I am grateful to Margaret P. Hannay, Noel J. Kinnamon, and colleagues in the Renaissance Seminar group of the School of English, University of Leeds, especially Martin Butler, for illuminating comments and references to secondary sources during the compilation of this chapter.

1 Jonson, *Works*, eds. C. H. Herford and P. and E. Simpson, 11 vols. (Oxford: Oxford University Press, 1925–52), 8:66, "To Mary Lady Wroth," epigram 103, line 4. All quotations from Jonson's works are taken from this edition, although its use of 'v'/'u' and 'i'/'j' has been modernized.

2 Jonson, *Works*, 5:289, *The Alchemist*, dedication "To the Lady, Most Deserving Her Name, and Bloud: Mary, La. Wroth."

3 Lady Mary's married life is considered by Josephine A. Roberts in her pioneering edition of *The Poems of Lady Mary Wroth* (Baton Rouge: Louisiana State University Press, 1983), 9–12; in her article "Lady Mary Wroth," in the *Dictionary of Literary Biography. Volume One Hundred and Twenty-One. Seventeenth-Century British Nondramatic Poets. First Series*, ed. M. Thomas Hester (Detroit and London: Gale Research Inc., 1992), 296–309; and in her edition of *The First Part of The Countess of Montgomery's Urania by Lady Mary Wroth* (Binghamton: MRTS/RETS, 1995), lxxii–lxxiii, lxxxix–xci.

4 For Lady Mary Wroth's literary debts to her relatives, see (for Robert Sidney) Wroth, *Poems*, 47–48, Wroth, *Urania*, xcii–xciii, and Naomi J. Miller, *Changing the Subject: Mary Wroth and Figurations of Gender in Early Modern England* (Lexington: University Press of Kentucky, 1996), 42–44, 82–87, 156–60; (for Mary Herbert, Countess of Pembroke) Wroth, *Urania*, lxxxiv–lxxxv, Margaret P. Hannay, "'Your vertuous and learned Aunt': the Countess of Pembroke as a Mentor to Mary Wroth," *Reading Mary Wroth: Representing Alternatives in Early Modern England*, eds. Naomi J. Miller and Gary

Waller (Knoxville: University of Tennessee Press, 1991), 15–35; (for William Herbert, Earl of Pembroke) Wroth, *Poems*, 23–25, Gary Waller, *The Sidney Family Romance: Mary Wroth, William Herbert, and the Early Modern Construction of Gender* (Detroit: Wayne State University Press, 1993), 140–41, 159–88, and Wroth, *Urania*, xlv, lxxiv–lxxv, lxxxvi.

5 Millicent V. Hay, *The Life of Robert Sidney, Earl of Leicester (1563–1620)* (Washington, DC: Folger Shakespeare Library, 1984), 207, 210. Sir Robert Sidney clearly maintained a keen personal interest in Jonson's writings for court entertainments. In 1608, for example, he apologized to the Earl of Shrewsbury for the delay in sending him a copy of the verses from *The Masque of Beauty* because Jonson was too preoccupied with his part in *Lord Haddington's Masque (The Hue and Cry After Cupid)* to supply them. See Wroth, *Poems*, 14.

6 Roberts, "Lady Mary Wroth," 298. Roberts also notes (307) that Lady Mary, according to William Drummond's "Conversations," performed in Jonson's lost pastoral drama, *The May Lord*. See also Stephen Orgel and Roy Strong, *Inigo Jones: the Theatre of the Stuart Court* (London: Sotheby Parke Bernet, 1973), 1:89–93 (for *Blackness*) and 1:93–96 (for *Beauty*); and John Orrell, "Antimo Galli's Description of *The Masque of Beauty*," *The Huntington Library Quarterly* 43 (1979–80), 13–23.

7 Hay, *Life of Robert Sidney*, 184.

8 This point is made by Katherine Duncan-Jones (in her review of) *The Poems of Lady Mary Wroth*, ed. Josephine A. Roberts, *RES* n.s. 36 (1985), 565–66.

9 Robert C. Evans, *Ben Jonson and the Poetics of Patronage* (Lewisburg: Bucknell University Press, 1989), 107–18. Dick Taylor, Jr., has also made a case for William Herbert acting as a conciliatory influence in Jonson's frequently fraught dealings over masques with both Inigo Jones and Samuel Daniel, "The Masque and the Lance: the Third Earl of Pembroke in Jacobean Court Entertainments," *Tulane Studies in English* 8 (1958), 21–53. See also Michael G. Brennan, *Literary Patronage in the English Renaissance: the Pembroke Family* (London: Routledge, 1988), 103–11.

10 Jonson, *Works*, 5:431.

11 See Lisle Cecil John, "Ben Jonson's 'To Sir William Sidney on His Birthday,'" *Modern Language Review* 52 (1957), 168–76.

12 Jonson's *Epigrams*, dedicated to William Herbert, Earl of Pembroke, and entered in the *Stationers' Register* to John Stepneth in May 1612 (see *Works*, 9:14–15), included tributes to Sir Philip Sidney's only child, Elizabeth, Countess of Rutland (79); William Herbert, third Earl of Pembroke (102); Pembroke's sister-in-law, Susan, Countess of Montgomery (104); and Sir Robert Sidney's daughters, Lady Mary Wroth (103, 105) and Lady Philip Sidney (114). See David Riggs, *Ben Jonson: a Life* (Cambridge: Harvard University Press, 1989), 230, and Don E. Wayne, "Jonson's Sidney: Legacy and Legitimation in *The Forrest*," *Sir Philip Sidney and the Interpretation of Renaissance Culture*, eds. G. F. Waller and M. D. Moore (London: Croom Helm, 1984), 227–50, for further analysis of this family cluster of poems.

Jonson also addressed Benjamin Rudyerd (121), later a poet, politician and friend of the Earl of Pembroke. Around this period, however, Jonson is more likely to have known Rudyerd as the traveling companion of Sir William Sidney for his tour abroad in 1610. See Hay, *Robert Sidney*, 184.

13 *The Alchemist* was first performed at the Globe Theatre in 1610, almost certainly before the plague hit London in July. It was then entered in the *Stationers' Register* on 3 October 1610, presumably to prevent any illegal printing while it was still commercially viable as a play for performance. The King's Men, for example, on their autumn tour, staged the play at Oxford in September 1610. Jonson is known to have been personally involved in the printing and correcting of the 1612 quarto edition of the play.

14 Riggs, *Life*, 179–80, notes that Jonson had not made any significant gains from his cultivation of Cecil since 1609 and that he also remained distanced from the two influential groups gathered around Prince Henry and Henry Howard, Earl of Northampton, whom Jonson regarded as "his mortall enemie."

15 I use the word "outwardly" here because, as I have argued elsewhere, the Sidneys were privately very much aware of their Catholic origins. See my "'First rais'de by thy blest hand, and what is mine / inspird by thee': the 'Sidney Psalter' and the Countess of Pembroke's completion of the Sidneian Psalms," *Sidney Newsletter & Journal*, 14.1 (1996), 37–44.

16 Riggs, *Life*, 176–78.

17 Ibid., 180.

18 For an important assessment of the connections between literary and family genealogies in addresses to Lady Mary Wroth, see Gavin Robert Alexander, "Five Responses to Sir Philip Sidney 1586–1628," Ph.D. thesis, University of Cambridge (1996), chapter 5, "Mary Wroth's Constant Work," 141–87.

19 Jonson, *Works*, 1:138.

20 Evans, *Ben Jonson*, 39, points out that this epistle was penned when Jonson himself was "attempting to make the transition from writer of popular plays to genuine 'poet' with an appeal to more sophisticated tastes." Whether intentionally or not, Jonson's epistle also echoes several points about the value of poetry made in Sidney's *Defence*. See Evans, *Ben Jonson*, 45.

21 Jonson also addressed *The Underwood* 50 to the Countess of Rutland, in which he praised her scholarly pursuits: "And when you want those friends, or neere in blood, / Or your Allies, you make your bookes your friends, / And studie them unto the noblest ends, / Searching for knowledge, and to keepe your mind / The same it was inspir'd, rich, and refin'd" (lines 26–30). He also seemed to imply that she was able to apply this learning to her own writings: "These Graces, when the rest of Ladyes view / Not boasted in your life, but practis'd true" (lines 31–32). See also Wroth, *Poems*, 16–17, for the possibility that the Countess of Rutland may also have figured in Jonson's various poems to Celia.

22 Evans, *Ben Jonson*, 124–27. J. C. A. Rathmell, "Jonson, Lord L'Isle and Penshurst," *English Literary Renaissance* 1 (1971): 251, suggests that Jonson may have had a "quasi-tutorial relationship" with William Sidney.

23 Jonson, *Works*, 8:68, epigram 105, "To Mary Lady Wroth," lines 19–20.

24 Riggs, *Life*, 188–91. John Stepneth died soon after the *Epigrams* were entered to him in May 1612 in the *Stationers' Register* and there is no conclusive evidence to show that they were ever in print before the 1616 folio, despite Drummond of Hawthornden's reference to "Ben Jhonsons epigrams" among a list of "bookes red be me anno 1612" and some verses by "R. C." which refer to them as a pamphlet. See Jonson, *Works*, 8:16, and 11:356.

25 See Wroth, *Poems*, 16–17, and Evans, *Ben Jonson*, 127–28.

26 This reading of "stile," for example, is offered in Ben Jonson, *The Complete Poems*, ed. George Parfitt (Harmondsworth: Penguin Books, 1975; rpt. 1980), 499, but not mentioned in *Ben Jonson: Poems*, ed. Ian Donaldson (London: Oxford University Press, 1975), 59, where the word is simply modernized to "style."

27 Josuah Sylvester, *Lachrimæ Lachrimarum* (1613), STC 23578, sig. H; quoted from Wroth, *Poems*, 18–19. Alexander, "Five Responses to Sir Philip Sidney 1586–1628," 142, sensibly warns against reading this passage as absolutely conclusive proof that Lady Mary's writings were then in circulation.

28 George Chapman, *The Iliads of Homer* (1611), STC 13634, sig. Gg4v. See Wroth, *Poems*, 18. This poem had been first included, in two extra singleton leaves, in some copies of Chapman's *Homer Prince of Poets*, probably published in 1609. These additions are now found only in the Folger and Cambridge University Library copies and Gavin Alexander has suggested that the latter may have been Lady Mary's own presentation copy. See his "Constant Works: a Framework for Reading Mary Wroth," *Sidney Newsletter & Journal* 14.2 (1996), 5–32, 26: note 26.

29 *Complete Works of John Davies*, ed. Grosart, 2:56, 63; quoted in Wroth, *Poems*, 18.

30 George Wither, *Abuses Stript and Whipt* (1613), STC 25891, sig. V2. William Gamage, *Linsi-Woolsie* (1613), STC 11544, sig. D1^v. See Wroth, *Poems*, 18.

31 The text of this poem is quoted from Wroth, *Poems*, 18. This manuscript, now preserved in the Muniment Room of Belvoir Castle, the seat of the Duke of Rutland, perhaps provides another implicit indication of the literary links between Lady Mary Wroth and Elizabeth, Countess of Rutland. *HMC Rutland*, I.418.

32 *The Poetical Works of William Drummond of Hawthornden*, ed. L. E. Kastner, 2 vols. (Manchester: Manchester University Press, 1913), 2:271, 277. See Wroth, *Poems*, 17.

33 Riggs, *Ben Jonson*, 164. Riggs later states that Sylvester "had joined Pembroke's circle by 1614" (232).

34 Ibid., 122–26, 288. See also Jonson's "To My Worthy and Honoured Friend, Mr. George Chapman, On His Translation of Hesiod's *Works and Days*," prefacing Chapman's *The Georgics of Hesiod* (1618) (*Ungathered Verse* 23).

35 Riggs, *Ben Jonson*, 206.

36 See *The Poems of Robert Sidney*, ed. P. J. Croft (Oxford: Clarendon Press, 1984), Appendix C, "Echoes of Robert's Sequence in his Daughter Mary Wroth's Verse," 342–45.

37 Henry Peacham, *The Complete Gentleman* (1622), STC 19502, 161. For Lady Mary's personal allegiance to this Sidney family device, see Wroth, *Poems*, 11; Margaret P. Hannay, "Your vertuous and learned Aunt," 18.

38 For a detailed analysis of the groupings of sonnets in the Folger Manuscript, see Alexander, "Constant Works," 5–15.

39 See Wroth, *Poems*, 22–23.

40 Ibid., 24–26, and Wroth, *Urania*, lxxiv–lxxv.

41 The possibility that her son James, born after ten previously pregancy-free years of marriage and only a month before her husband's death, was also fathered by Pembroke cannot be discounted here.

42 These illegitimate children are recorded by Sir Thomas Herbert of Tintern in his manuscript history of the Herbert family, "Herbertorum Prosapia" and in Edward Lord Herbert of Cherbury's lighthearted poem, "A Merry Rime Sent to Lady Mary Wroth upon the birth of my Lord of Pembroke's Child. born in the spring." See Wroth, *Poems*, 24–26, and Wroth, *Urania*, xlv, lxxiv–lxxv, lxxxvi.

43 Riggs, *Ben Jonson*, 226. Martin Butler, "Jonson's Folio and the Politics of Patronage," *Criticism* 35 (1993), 381.

44 See Wroth, *Urania*, xxxi, 399, lines 2–3. The two masques were first printed in *The Characters of Two Royall Masques. The one of Blacknesse, The other of Beautie* (1608).

45 It should be noted, however, that Wroth's poem specifically refers to "Indians" rather than the "Ethiopians" of the fable of Blackness and that this link may not be as definite as some readers previously have assumed. See Wroth, *Poems*, 99, 153. "Penshurst Mount" is in BL Additional MS 23229, fols. 91–92.

46 *Lady Mary Wroth Poems: a Modernized Edition*, ed. R. E. Pritchard (Keele: Keele University Press, 1996), 181; and "'I Exscribe Your Sonnets': Jonson and Lady Mary Wroth," *Notes & Queries*, n.s. 242 (1997), 526–28.

47 See *Lady Mary Wroth's "Love's Victory." The Penshurst Manuscript*, ed. Michael G. Brennan (London: The Roxburghe Club, 1988), 232–36.

48 *Redeeming Eve: Women Writers of the English Renaissance* (Princeton: Princeton University Press, 1987), 210.

49 Jonson, *Works*, 1:142, *Conversations*, lines 364–67.

50 It is, of course, equally possible that this poem was occasioned by Pembroke's literary society with another female friend, such as Lucy Russell, Countess of Bedford (c. 1581–1627), a prominent performer in Jacobean masques and the patroness, among others, of Jonson, Donne, Drayton, and Daniel. Furthermore, I do not intend in this essay to enter the longstanding debate, first instigated by Frederick G. Fleay in his *Biographical Chronicle of the English Drama 1559–1642*, 2 vols. (London: Reeves and Turner, 1891), 1:327–28,

over the identification of Lady Mary Wroth with Jonson's Celia. For recent comment on this identification, see Pritchard, "I Exscribe Your Sonnets," 526–28.

51 Butler, "Jonson's Folio and the Politics of Patronage," 378. The symbolism of the *Urania* title page is analyzed by Wroth, *Urania*, cxi, and Alexander, "Five Responses to Sir Philip Sidney 1586–1628," 145–46.

52 See Alexander, "Five Responses to Sir Philip Sidney 1586–1628," 142–43, for a succinct summary of the debate over Lady Mary's possible involvement in the publication of the *Urania*.

53 Wroth, *Urania*, cxii–cxviii.

54 Duncan-Jones, review of *The Poems of Lady Mary Wroth*, ed. Roberts, *RES* ns 36 (1985), 565.

55 No convincing reason for this puzzling omission of preliminary and/or commendatory materials to the 1621 edition has as yet been offered. It is possible, however, to speculate that possible rumors of a breakdown in Lady Mary's relationship with Pembroke, just at the time when the work was being printed, could have prompted those authors (perhaps even including Jonson) who were intending to contribute commendatory verses, tactfully to withdraw their offerings. Even though there is no evidence to prove one way or the other the state of their relationship in 1621 it is noticeable that Pembroke seems to have played no part, as he easily could have done, in defending her against Edward Denny's violent attacks on her reputation following the publication of the *Urania*.

56 See Pritchard, "I Exscribe Your Sonnets," 526–28, which argues that Lady Mary's own position may have been figured in Jonson's "To The World."

57 See Wroth, *Works*, 42–43.

CHAPTER 5

Medium and meaning in the manuscripts of Anne, Lady Southwell

Victoria E. Burke

for mee, I write but to my self & mee
what gods good grace doth in my soule imprint
British Library, Lansdowne MS 740, fol. 161r, lines 289–90

In her lengthy poem on the fourth commandment, Anne, Lady Southwell[1] scorns those who write for reward, claiming that she writes to express what comes to her from God and for no one but for herself. Even if Southwell was sincere in writing those words, doubtful when they appear in what is ostensibly a presentation copy to the king, her second husband seems to have been very interested in ensuring the preservation of his wife's reputation. Evidence for this argument can be found in the physical characteristics of two extant manuscripts which are associated with Southwell's authorship. In considering how these manuscripts were compiled, bound, and possibly read, one can investigate the political dimensions of how Southwell's work came to be scribally published. A large part of such analysis must include Southwell's political contacts and relationships.

When we consider questions of how, when, and by whom a manuscript was compiled and bound we can gain further insight into its function and the status it held. Folger Shakespeare Library MS V.b.198, entitled "The workes of the Lady Ann Sothwell Decemb: 2° 1626" on the first folio, is a bound volume of seventy-four folios whose cover measures 355 mm by 233 mm. The sheets derive from different paper stocks which vary in size and their watermarks date from before 1600, with the exception of the final two folios. It was offered for sale by Thomas Thorpe as lot 938 in his 1834 catalogue of the Southwell papers. From Thorpe it passed to other booksellers, and was purchased by Henry Folger in 1927.[2]

The dates associated with Southwell's miscellany are from 1587 to 1636. Southwell probably acquired the book upon her marriage to her second husband Captain Henry Sibthorpe in 1626 (since that date appears in the title on the first folio and since memoranda in the late sixteenth-century hand of a John Sibthorpe appear in its pages), but some of her poetry was written earlier than 1626 and copied later into its pages. Though Southwell died on 2 October 1636, the memorial verses and epitaph by Sibthorpe and Roger Cox, the local curate, must obviously postdate that date, if only by a few days. I do want to argue, however, that it was after Southwell's death that the collecting and binding of this manuscript took place, by Sibthorpe as he sought to commemorate his wife's literary activities. Southwell's lengthy Decalogue poetry dominates the volume, but the rest of the poetry is a mixture of shorter religious and love lyrics, elegies, and verse depictions of historical or philosophical matters, some of it almost certainly authored by Southwell, though a few poems have been found among printed and manuscript sources. The first, second, and fourth poems on folio 1r appear in song books printed in 1605 and 1609 by Robert Jones and Alfonso Ferrabosco. One poem by Sir Arthur Gorges, two by Henry King, and one commonly attributed to Sir Walter Raleigh also appear in her pages, unattributed in the first three cases and misattributed to Southwell in the fourth.[3] Poems attributed to Southwell but not written by her may be her husband's attempt to make her more prolific than she was. She has also written an acrostic to the poet Francis Quarles.[4] The prose pieces in the miscellany can be divided into letters, philosophical terms (the five predicables and the ten predicaments of Aristotle), sermons, an exposition of Augustine's *City of God*, a mini-bestiary (extracted from Edward Topsell's *The Historie of Foure-Footed Beastes* [1607] and its companion volume *The Historie of Serpents* [1608]), and apothegms. The memoranda are military receipts, inventories of Southwell's goods, a list of books owned by Southwell and her second husband,[5] and receipts for property rental and domestic wages.

The main hand in the Folger manuscript is not Southwell's. Hers is the angular italic script found scattered through the manuscript, adding and deleting the words of other scribes, and writing editorial instructions (e.g. "thes four uersic [i.e. verses] cum in hear," fol. 34v). She has also written her name (fol. 2r), nearly illegible drafts of her poetry (fols. 44v–46r and 57r–58v), and a stanza, neatly and legibly, in the midst of her poem on the fourth commandment (fol. 40r).[6] But several other hands are prominent. A John Sibthorpe wrote military receipts in 1587 and 1588 (fols. 5r, 6r–6v) and a second sixteenth-century secretary hand recorded the payment of servants (fols. 62r–64r).[7] Several members of Southwell's household, such as Samuel Rowson and John Bowker, have signed receipts for rents paid in later pages of the manuscript (fols. 71r–71v, 72v) and their hands seem to match portions of the manuscript. At least two other unidentified hands appear among the Folger manuscript's pages, including one rounded, very polished hand which has transcribed Southwell's letter to Cicely, Lady Ridgeway (fols. 3r–3v) and all of the Lansdowne manuscript (except for corrections, possibly by Henry Sibthorpe, and for one extra stanza, written possibly by Joseph Hopton, another witness to the rental receipts). The letter to Ridgeway is subscribed in Latin as a true copy by "Io." (the rest of the inscription has been crossed out); perhaps this "John" was a secretary of Southwell's and her husband, and since he was the most skilled of all the scribes he was chosen to prepare the Lansdowne manuscript with its possible royal audience. A final important hand in the manuscript is Henry Sibthorpe, who has written out Southwell's epitaph and two commemorative verses by himself and Roger Cox (fols. 73r and 74r), as well as earlier pages and notes.[8]

British Library Lansdowne MS 740 contains expanded versions of Southwell's verses on the third and fourth commandments. These poems of 101 and 109 stanzas, respectively, are prefaced by a dedicatory poem, "To the kinges most excellent Ma^{tye}," attributed to Southwell. The poems are followed by praise of Southwell's skill as a poet in verse, and signed by "H." The sections of this manuscript relating to Southwell are found on fols. 142r–167v; this composite quarto manuscript of 173 leaves contains at least seven discrete sections, one of which is an important collection of poetry by John Donne.[9] Like the other Lansdowne manuscripts, this was acquired by the British Library in 1807, from William Petty, first Marquess of Lansdowne, Lord Shelburne (1737–1805). It is unclear who collected the disparate booklets together, but it may have been a late seventeenth-century person, since the last items in the manuscript date from that period. It was rebound by the British Library in the nineteenth century, when most of the leaves in the Southwell section were mounted separately. The cover measures 224 mm by 175 mm, and the page sizes vary for each section, though the pages in the Southwell section evidently came from the same stock and are approximately 200 mm by 150 mm (the height of the pages varies from 205 mm to 199 mm, depending on the wear to the page, and since the bifolia have been cut out and tipped in, these measurements cannot be completely accurate). The pot watermark in this section of the manuscript resembles Heawood's number 3561 (though the letters on the pot are different), which is dated 1600.[10] The watermarks and bibliographical formats are different for these two volumes of Southwell's, and other writers', work.

The presence of lot 959 in the Thorpe catalogue entitled, "Lectures on the Commandments and Moral Ethics, the Collections of Lady Anne Southwell, Wife of Sir Thomas Southwell, Uncle of Sir Robert Southwell,"[11] must refer to a lost manuscript of her works. One might assume that this refers to what is now the Lansdowne manuscript, but that manuscript was obtained by the British Library in 1807 and it is a quarto volume bound with disparate manuscripts, and not a folio bound in Russia leather, as the description in the Thorpe catalogue indicates. A third substantial manuscript of Southwell's work may remain to be found. Could this manuscript be another attempt by Southwell's second husband to publicize her literary activities after her death?

At least four letters written by Southwell are extant: two have been copied into the Folger miscellany and two exist at Chatsworth in Derbyshire among the Lismore papers (vol. XIV, nos. 160 and 174). In addition, at least two letters have been written about her: by a Captain Skinner, charged with escorting her home from Berwick where she went to greet the new queen in 1603, and by her first husband Sir Thomas Southwell, who wrote to clear his wife's name after that incident.[12] The letters tipped onto a guard in the Folger manuscript are addressed to Cicely, Lady Ridgeway on the subject of poetry (and must predate her death in 1627), and to Henry Cary, Viscount Falkland, Lord Deputy of Ireland, on the subject of his downfall in 1629. The Lismore letters are of 1623; in one written on 11 October Southwell asks Sir Richard Boyle, Earl of Cork to restore the lands of Sir Richard Edgecombe, and in the second, written on 23 October, Southwell addresses the same subject with Sir Thomas Browne, Sir Richard Boyle's cousin (not the English writer).

From the evidence of these manuscripts and letters, Southwell did not want to keep her verses or political dealings private. A woman of reasonable gentry standing herself, she sought favor from higher placed individuals throughout her life. She was the daughter of Sir Thomas Harris of Cornworthy in Devon and of Elizabeth Pomeroy. Anne, their oldest child of four, was baptized on 22 August 1574. Her father, a prominent lawyer and Member of Parliament, was knighted by King James at his coronation at Whitehall, as was her first husband, Sir Thomas Southwell, whom she married in 1594.[13] Thorpe claims that she was maid of honor to Queen Elizabeth, but no evidence has been found to support this.[14]

Sir Thomas was the eldest son of Alice, a daughter of Sir Thomas Cornwallis of Brome in Suffolk, and Richard Southwell, eldest son of Richard Southwell of Horsham St. Faith's in Norfolk.[15] Thomas Southwell was related to prominent Catholics (his uncle was Robert

Southwell the poet and martyr), but his wife had nothing but scorn for papists in her religious verse. Moving to Ireland with his brother soon after James I's accession, Sir Thomas was a member of the council of the president of Munster[16] and lived at Poulnalong Castle, near Kinsale, in the county of Cork. Thomas and Anne Southwell had two daughters, Elizabeth and Frances.[17]

Her second marriage to Captain Henry Sibthorpe took place soon after Thomas Southwell's death on 12 June 1626 (Sibthorpe refers to him and Southwell having been married for ten years at her death on 2 October 1636). Sibthorpe inscribes himself sergeant major and privy councilor on the pages which contain Southwell's epitaph (Folger manuscript, fols. 73r and 74r). The Sibthorpes of Essex were a well-established family in Ireland at this time to whom Southwell's husband may have been related; alternately he may have been a younger son of John Sibthorpe of Laneham, Nottinghamshire.[18] Sibthorpe's military career flourished after 1618 when Sir Dudley Carleton, Lord Ambassador at The Hague, granted John Chamberlain's request on behalf of Henry's uncle, John West, to "see him well placed in some companie."[19] He was an officer under Sir Edward Villiers in Youghal as of at least 1 August 1626 and his company was billeted at Cork from 1 September 1626 to 10 August 1627. They may have left Ireland soon after the last recorded payment to Sibthorpe from the Corporation of Cork on 12 December 1627.[20] They moved to Clerkenwell, an area of London they left in 1631 (as an inventory on fols. 59r and 60v–61r of the Folger manuscript indicates). Given the evidence of the list of books of Lady Southwell, Captain Sibthorpe lived until at least 1650; he is probably the Henry Sibthorpe of St. Dunstan-in-the-West, London whose will was proved on 16 December 1672.[21]

Anne Southwell's acquaintance was a wide one, judging from the personal references in her miscellany. A verse epistle is addressed to "Doctor Adam B[pp] of Limerick" (fols. 18r–19r); this was Dr. Bernard Adams, who was the Bishop of Limerick from April 1604 until his death on 22 March 1626.[22] The first Earl of Castlehaven, George Touchet, once governor of Utrecht, was a planter in Ulster, and on 6 September 1616 was created a peer of Ireland as Baron Audley of Orier, in the county of Armaugh, and Earl of Castlehaven, in the county of Cork.[23] Perhaps that connection with Cork led to Southwell's acquaintance with the Earl. A translation of Psalm 25, evidently written before 1617 when he died, is entitled "<Dauids> Confiden<ce i>n <prayer> he prayeth for <remissi>on of sinns and <for helpe i>n afliction"[24] (fol. 7r). Although it is difficult to read the author's name in the top right-hand corner of the page, the words "writen by the ladie Anne <..........>" make it possible that South-well is its author, but Klene suggests that the missing letters might refer to Touchet's daughter Lady Anne Blount.[25] If Southwell knew of one daughter of Touchet's perhaps she knew a second, Lady Eleanor Davies, the prophet. She spent time in Ireland before her marriage to Sir John Davies, Attorney General of Ireland, in 1609. The couple spent extensive periods in England, finally returning to London in 1619 when Davies was relieved of his duties in Ireland.[26] Southwell may have known Eleanor Davies's husband (who was a poet as well as a lawyer) through the political contacts of her husband Thomas; she may also have known her father.

In a letter to the "deputye ffalkland of Ireland," dated 1628, she writes that although Falkland says he is "depriued of all," she and Captain Sibthorpe are among his servants. Fortune gave him his position and fortune took it away; Southwell honors him for his goodness and not his fortunes. Henry Cary, first Viscount Falkland, was sworn in as Lord Deputy of Ireland on 18 September 1622. He was forced to relinquish his authority in 1629 due to several controversial acts in his final years in office, one of which was his attempt to deprive the Byrnes of Wicklow of their lands.[27] The letter has been wrongly dated 1628 by another hand (possibly Sibthorpe's). It must date from after 1 April 1629. In a letter of 4 October 1627 to the king, Henry Cary, Viscount Falkland supported Sibthorpe's petition to be given a command, reminding Charles that Sibthorpe led a company in the Cadiz expedition and that he kept that company for two years in Ireland until it was delivered to Sir Ralph Bingley for the expedition to France.[28] It is not known whether Southwell knew Falkland's wife, Elizabeth Cary, the playwright, translator, and poet. She accompanied her husband to Dublin at his appointment but left in 1625; if Southwell did know her she could only have disapproved of her conversion to Roman Catholicism.[29]

Three separate items in the Folger manuscript refer to Cicely, Lady Ridgeway, and seem to indicate a personal relationship. Southwell's letter to Ridgeway in defense of poetry, apparently a response to a letter from Ridgeway which denounced poetry, may have been carefully chosen to appear at the front of the volume, a fitting place to announce Southwell's stance on the worth of poetry. Southwell's two elegies on the countess (one playfully chiding her for her silence and one mourning her death) try to establish the closeness of their relationship. Like Thomas Southwell, Sir Thomas Ridgeway was employed by James I in Ireland; he became Earl of Londonderry on 23 August 1623.[30] Southwell's letter to Ridgeway indicates some type of relationship, but it may not have been a close one, since the title of her epitaph refers to Cassandra MacWilliams (the name of her daughter and sister) instead of Cicely.[31]

Roger Cox was the assistant curate at St. Mary's church for most of Dr. Daniel Featley's term as rector, 1628–42. He is undoubtedly the "m^r Coxe (the Lecturer of Acton)" whom Lady Southwell praises in her poem on folio 21r for his book on the birth of Christ. Roger Cox's literary output was significant. His *Hebdomada Sacra* of 1630 comprises meditations for each day of the week based on chapter two of St. Matthew's gospel. He also wrote a pamphlet in response to Sir Edward Peyton's *A Discourse Concerning the Fitnesse of the Posture* of 1642 (number 52 on the list of books owned by Southwell and Sibthorpe).[32] Cox and George Herbert, contemporaries at Trinity College, Cambridge, both contributed a Latin poem to a printed volume commemorating the death of Henry, Prince of Wales in 1612.[33] Cox wrote at least one poem in the Folger miscellany: his punning elegy on Anne, Lady Southwell, beginning, "The South winde blew vpon a springing Well" (fol. 73r), and at least two of his sermons appear in its pages, including a funeral sermon about Robert Johnson, the court musician discussed below.[34]

Southwell had some kind of literary relationship with an unnamed neighbor and Daniel Featley, given the evidence of two verse epistles in the miscellany. The letter to Bishop Adams of Limerick (fols. 18r–19r) and the poem on folios 26r–26v share significant passages. Like the epistle to Bishop Adams, this poem is aimed at a specific audience, a person she calls "My noble Neighbour" (as opposed to "Good reuerend Father," her term of address to the Bishop). Whereas two lines on folio 18r tell the reader to correct the poem, twelve lines on folio 26r tell her neighbor to correct it and/or to pass it on to Dr. Featley.[35] This neighbor would probably have been Roger Cox, the only conceivable person who would have had Featley's ear given Featley's limited contact with the parish. Daniel Featley was the rector of St. Mary's from 1627 until his arrest in 1642 for his views. As well as being a Puritan preacher who was loyal to the Church of England, he was a scholar, writer, and prominent disputer, both in Europe and England.[36] One of his works, published posthumously, appears in the Sibthorpes' library list: *Dippers Dipt. Or the Anabaptists Duck'd and Plung'd Over Head and Eares* (1645–60). Copies of many of his letters and theological pieces exist in a Bodleian manuscript but none are addressed to Anne Southwell.[37] Evidently Cox, if he is the "noble Neighbour," had enough contact with Featley to enable Southwell to ask him to act as a type of literary mediator between herself and Featley.

The Robert Johnson referred to on later pages in the manuscript was lutenist to James I, musician to Prince Henry, and lutenist and court composer to Charles I. He composed music for songs for the plays of Shakespeare (*Cymbeline, A Winter's Tale*, and *The Tempest*), Ben Jonson, Beaumont and Fletcher, and Middleton, as well as for masques. He came from an old Acton family and probably set up house in the village before 1620 when his first child by his wife Ann was baptized. He was churchwarden in 1622 and an active member until his last mention in the churchwardens' books in 1631. The Johnsons and their five children moved to the Rectory in the churchyard in 1627 from Bank House, which they later let to Anne, Lady Southwell and her husband (see their memoranda on fols. 71r–71v and 72v). His widow, Ann Johnson, has written receipts (dated 1634–36) in the later pages of the manuscript indicating that both Lady Southwell and Captain Sibthorpe have paid their rent for the tenements "Scituated vpon the Stean in Acton" (fol. 71v). The Steyne was a croft or close which existed in 1522 and which later gave its name to the area north of the church and nearby houses. He died on 18 November 1633. His funeral sermon, given by Roger Cox, appears on folio 72r of the miscellany. After Southwell died in 1636, Johnson's widow Ann sold both houses and all her property.[38]

Evidence in the manuscript tells us that Southwell had contact with Roger Cox, Daniel Featley, and Robert and Ann Johnson, but it is also likely that she knew another notable Acton figure, Catherine, Lady Conway, widow of Edward Conway, Chief Secretary of State to both James I and Charles I and President of the Council. Like the Sibthorpes, the Conways had an Irish connection; Sir Edward was created Viscount Killultagh of Killultagh in county Antrim in 1626 and Viscount Conway of Conway Castle in Carnarvonshire in 1627. There is some dispute over the identity of Conway's second wife, but she was most likely the Catherine whose first husband was John Fust, a member of the Grocers' Company. She married Conway in 1619 and died in 1639.[39] Smith has suggested that a likely place where these people would have met was at church. Bank House was provided with a special pew at St. Mary's.[40]

The poetry copied into the miscellany is often valued for its connections with certain people, not necessarily for those who wrote it. Henry King's elegy on the death of his wife is not entitled "An Exequy To his Matchlesse never to be forgotten Freind" and attributed to King; instead the poem has been called "An Elegie writen by m^r Barnard brother to m.^{rs} Jern<ingham> y^t dy<ed at> Ac<ton>" (fol. 21v). This indicates that the poem was appropriated by a brother to mourn a sister who was probably known to Southwell.[41] The most significant alteration in Southwell's versions of both this poem and "An Elegy Upon the most victorious King of Sweden Gustavus Adolphus" follows a strain in other manuscript versions.[42] The point was not to record the author of the poem, but instead to note how it was used to mourn a local person.

A potentially more explosive poem, "The Lie," usually attributed to Sir Walter Raleigh, appears on the second folio of the Folger miscellany. As Klene has noted, Raleigh owned lands in Devon near Cornworthy, and sat in Parliament with Southwell's father, joining forces for their Devon constituents in 1593 and 1597, and so he was known to the Harris family.[43] The poem was circulating in manuscript by 1595, and was a popular presence in miscellanies of the early seventeenth century.[44] Southwell has signed the poem, probably transcribed by Joseph Hopton, most likely after 1626, the date announced on the previous page, demonstrating how earlier poetry could be appropriated by later readers for similar ends.[45] Later poetry in the miscellany by Southwell shares Raleigh's bitter tone about courtly privilege. Answering poems were written to "The Lie," and it was often significantly altered as it was transcribed. Lady Southwell's version of the poem (transcribed by an amanuensis, but corrected twice in her own hand) is a significant departure from known manuscript and printed copies in several ways. Using the 1611 printed version (which appeared anonymously in the third edition of Francis Davison's *A Poetical Rhapsodie*) as a benchmark, the scribe has copied stanzas one through five, then eleven, then a combination of stanzas nine and ten, then one apparently of Southwell's invention, and then ended with stanza thirteen, the final stanza of the printed version. She has eliminated the other stanzas. This in itself is not uncommon in manuscript versions of the poem (Bodleian MS Ashmole 51, for example, the miscellany of Ann Bowyer, omits stanza three, one-third of stanza five, and stanzas six through twelve), but some of her phrases seem particular to her (e.g. she uses "deny," in lieu of the more common "reply" and "lie," three times in the poem), and her eighth stanza appears to be unique.

The largest amount of Southwell's poetry is religious in nature, and based specifically on the Decalogue, not a common topic for poetry. Slightly later in the century An Collins addressed this topic in her poem "The Discourse." She describes the process the Christian must undergo for faith to be planted in his or her heart. God must first take the hammer of his law (i.e. the ten commandments) and break the heart; the seduced soul will then feel awe and submit; it will see its sin and sorrow over it; and in this state of humility it will be prepared for God. Each of the ten commandments is described in a 7-line stanza, rhyming ababbcc. This form is not too far from Southwell's for her Decalogue poetry, but otherwise the poetry is strikingly different. Southwell is less interested in the individual soul's embracing of God and more in the myriad ways that humanity breaks from God's laws.[46] In the miscellany Southwell has written poems of multiple six-line stanzas, rhyming ababcc, for the first, second, third, fourth, fifth, seventh, and eighth commandments, ranging from ten to seventy stanzas. The Lansdowne manuscript gives us expanded versions of meditations on the third and fourth commandments found in her miscellany. Written in a polished hand and with a dedicatory poem to the king, as well as a commendatory poem on Southwell's poetic achievement (probably by Henry Sibthorpe, the "H" of its attribution) the section of the manuscript associated with Southwell resembles a presentation copy. But there are rough elements as well: Sibthorpe's hand has made corrections throughout the volume (including those at the bottom of fol. 165r, "These verses & those that follow though crossed out are fitt to stand"); stanzas are crossed out; one stanza in another hand, reversed, appears on fol. 142v; and on fol. 158v, lines 155–56 are incomplete. This may have been an intermediate copy – surely it wouldn't have been given to the king in less than perfect form. Perhaps it never reached the king, in any of its incarnations. Several references in the Lansdowne manuscript, both early and late in its pages, suggest that this poetry was composed while Southwell lived in Ireland: "yf in Hibernia god will haue mee dye" (fol. 148r), and "at home a surplesse [of radical sects] makes them sitt & mourne / but heere fiue churchmens s^{t}ates serues not one turne" (fol. 165v). In the first passage, she expresses her contempt and pity for the Irish, calling them wretched souls who experience mad fits, saying "the Pope doth cozen them of wealth & wittes." In the following stanza she prays to God to "giue them more light / & cutt of theyr seducer from his throane" (fol. 148r). Perhaps portions were composed in Ireland and then copied by a scribe at a later date, with Sibthorpe's input, either correcting from another copy written by Southwell or adding his own words.

Southwell trod a precarious line between private devotional poet and politic flatterer. The Duchess of Lennox may not have been a personal acquaintance; Southwell's poem addressed to her may have been an attempt to curry favor (fol. 22r). Klene has pointed out that Ludovick Stuart, second Duke of Lennox was appointed to attend Princess Elizabeth in 1613 to Germany after her marriage to the Elector Palatine.[47] But since he did not seem to stay with the Princess long, and since his second wife had died by 1610 and he did not marry his third wife until 1621, the identity of the Duchess, if the poem dates from this period, is a mystery. It may be more likely that the poem dates from the 1630s, making it contemporary with the two poems which follow, in which case the Duchess may be Catherine Clifton, who married Esmé, the third Duke in 1607. She remarried in 1632, but the fourth Duke did not marry until 1637 (a year after Southwell's death), making it likely that Clifton is the addressee of the poem.[48] Southwell asks that her regards be given to the princess and ends by drawing attention to her own position: "Nor shall I faile; to let the world ^{to} knowe / How much vnto; her gracefull grace; I owe." Southwell's elaborate compliment reinforces her own high standing in the courtly community – or at least indicates that she seeks to be rewarded by those in positions of power.

Below this poem are two which must date from 1632, since they commemorate two heroes of the Protestant cause. The kings of Bohemia and Sweden both died in the autumn of 1632 at separate battles during what has been called the Swedish phase of the Thirty Years War.[49] In the elegy on the King of Bohemia, Southwell focuses on the grief of his wife, Elizabeth, also referred to in the preceding poem, whom she calls goodness distressed. Gustavus Adolphus, the son of Charles IX of Sweden, succeeded him as king in 1611, and campaigned on the Continent from 1621. After the great victory at Breitenfield in 1631 he became the embodiment of the Protestant cause, and a huge industry built up around him, involving the mass production of ivory reliefs, silver statues, gold rings, pendants, and medallions.[50] Literary tributes abounded as well. In England Aurelian Townshend and Thomas Carew conducted a verse correspondence on the subject, and ten elegies were appended to the beginning of the third part of *The Swedish Intelligencer* (one being Henry King's, which has been copied into Southwell's miscellany).[51] It is not inappropriate that Southwell's elegies on Frederick and Gustavus should appear near each other in her miscellany because of the way the two figures became linked in the popular imagination; Frederick was later remembered as "the prince for whom *Gustavus* fell."[52] Southwell evidently saw herself as equal to the task of eulogizing these great men.

There are sections in both manuscripts which praise the king. Addressed "To the kinges most excellent Ma^{tye}," the prefatory poem in the Lansdowne manuscript praises him in rhymed couplets, and is signed "your ma^{tyes} most humble & faythfull subiect Anne Southwell," though not in her hand (fol. 142r). This praise of the king recalls her eulogistic stanzas in the poem on the fourth commandment in the Folger manuscript (fol. 42v, see fig. 2), in which Southwell compares "that blest

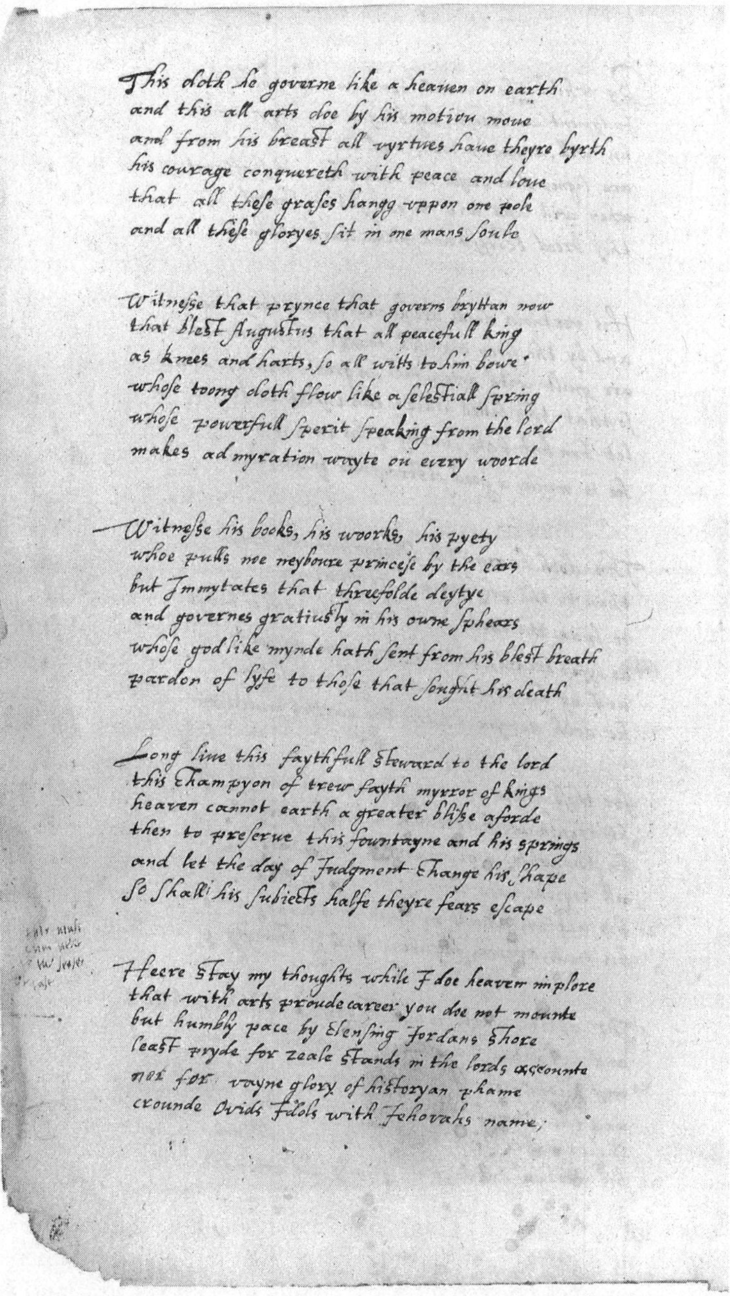

This doth so governe like a heaven on earth
and this all arts doe by his motion moue
and from his breast all vyrtues haue theyre byrth
his courage conquereth with peace and loue
that all these grases hangg vppon one pole
and all these gloryes sit in one mans soule

Witnesse that prynce that governs bryttan now
that blest Augustus that all peacefull king
as knees and harts, so all witts to him bowe
whose toong doth flow like a selestiall spring
whose powerfull sperit speaking from the lord
makes admyration wayte on every woorde

Witnesse his books, his woorks, his pyety
whoe pulls noe neyboure princese by the eare
but Immytates that threefolde deytye
and governes gratiusly in his owne sphears
whose godlike mynde hath sent from his blest breath
pardon of lyfe to those that soufht his death

Long liue this faythfull steward to the lord
this Champyon of trew fayth myrror of kings
heaven cannot earth a greater blisse aforde
then to preserue this fountayne and his springs
and let the day of Judgment Change his shape
So shall his subiects halfe theyre fears escape

Heere stay my thoughts while I doe heaven implore
that with arts proude career you doe not mounte
but humbly pace by blessing Jordans shore
least pryde for zeale stands in the lords accounte
not for vayne glory of historyan phame
crounde Ovids Idols with Jehovahs name,

Figure 1. British Library MS Lansdowne 740, fol. 151v: stanzas 69–72 of Southwell's
poem on the third commandment, which praise the king.

Augustus that all peacefull king" who rules Britain with God. He is celebrated for his books, works, and piety, and for his great forgiveness in pardoning those who sought his death. In the Lansdowne manuscript, the king is similarly praised for his accomplishments not just in ruling peacefully but in the arts as well ("in whome all artes reside"). He is also compared with God ("I know in God there doth noe ill abide / nor in his true Epitome, noe pride" [Lansdowne manuscript]; "Immytates that threefolde deytye" [Folger manuscript]), though interestingly that tendency is checked in the Folger manuscript. Directly after she asks God to preserve "this fowntayne and his springs" she asks forgiveness for crowning Ovid's idols with Jehovah's name; she must not "try Seneca and Paule with one tutchstone / waygh Aristotell with wise Salomon" (fol. 43r; these lines and others surrounding it also appear on fols. 28r–28v in her poem on the first commandment). The intention of Southwell, or Sibthorpe, to gain royal attention necessitated that no similar reservations about praising mere earthlings appeared in the dedicatory epistle of the Lansdowne manuscript. Later in the Lansdowne manuscript, she prays that England's Augustus might flourish, and she asks God to be the king's "tower, his fortresse, & defence," to bless him and his posterity (fol. 151v, see fig. 1). Though Southwell could be addressing either James I or Charles I, James is more likely her intended subject in the Folger manuscript, given his works on the art of government, theology, and his poetry in Latin, Scots, and English. In the Lansdowne manuscript his works are not specifically mentioned, and neither is the attempt on his life, possibly a reference to the gunpowder plot, and so Charles may be the intended recipient of the verse, a likely proposition if the Lansdowne manuscript was prepared after Southwell's death.

Although the main hand in the Lansdowne manuscript cannot be securely matched with a person in Southwell's circle, the hand of what might be Joseph Hopton appears once in the Lansdowne manuscript. It has written one stanza on the reverse of the dedicatory poem to the king (fol. 142v). This stanza is nearly identical to the ninth stanza in the Folger manuscript's versification of the first commandment (fol. 28v), and refers to Christ, but given that it has been copied on a sheet addressed to the king, it may refer as well to her desire to be one of his court. The word "court" is mentioned in both, suggesting a possible political dimension. The first four lines correspond very closely in both versions and warn against the presumption of entering the most holy place, or looking at the sun, but the last two lines vary slightly. The Folger manuscript has,

69. for mee, I haue of all but litle reason
to flatter gaynst my harte that happy land
where I was borne, who like fruit out of seaso~
hath layd on mee an envious stepdames hand,
yett doe I pray all Catelines may perish
& our Augustus happily may florish.

70. Thou most almightye powerfull & imense
thou that makest kinges, & rulst on sea & land
bee thou his tower his fortresse & defence
& euer keepe him wth thy gratious hand.
& blesse that christall orbe wherein did lye
th'invallued gemes of his posterityè.

71. who for his owne sake seekes his cuntryes good
doth beare a face but like a painted dreub
such doe I wish were choked in her mudd,
whose smoothed faces haue a harte all skabb
but for christes spouse sake wish her happy grace
who not where els dares shew her frighted face.

72. for I by booke haue travell'd all the world
to find out the religions of all landes,
eich where I see how ignorance hath hurt
her foggye mantle vppon all theyr strandes
I will not dare to iudge theyr misteryes
yett I will euer fly theyr villanyes.

Figure 2. Folger Shakespeare Library MS V.b.198, fol. 42v: stanzas 53–57
of Southwell's poem on the fourth commandment, which praise the king.

"let mee be of ^{thy} Court, there will I rest / leauing thy secrets, to thy
sacred brest" while the Lansdowne version differs slightly: "if off thy
court I am, there will I rest / leaueing sacred^{secret} councell to thy sacred
brest." She asks permission to join his court in the Folger manuscript,

whereas in the Lansdowne manuscript she asks if she is a member. *Secret* and *sacred* are used in both versions, but *counsel* is used in the more political extract, reminding us of the potential political meaning of that word.

Since the Lansdowne manuscript is presented for a royal audience, one might assume that criticism of the court and its leader might be minimal, and that the Folger manuscript might show more license. In her main defense of women in the Folger manuscript, Southwell asks if women lack the ability to deceive political enemies, to buy crowns and thrones, or to ordain laws, concluding that these are all meaningless in heaven (fol. 26v, lines 35–40). In her meditations on the third commandment Southwell lists among the various ways in which we take God's name in vain, "kings breake theyre lawes subiects neglect theyre duty" (fol. 36r, line 50), balancing the duties of rulers and subjects. A further stanza, however, ventures a critique of excessive veneration of earthly leaders. Southwell writes that if one is slandered to the king or queen, one should make use of this affliction, for "what doest thou know but that thy princes grace / may in thy harte gods Image quite deface" (fol. 36r, lines 65–66). These lines do not appear in the Lansdowne manuscript, not surprisingly given their alleged royal audience.[53] This couplet is repeated on folio 57r, just above Southwell's drafts of stanzas in her own hand. She has altered the first line of the stanza from "Admyte a sycophant that stands in place" to "Admyte a sycophant much grast in cort," making her scorn of courtly flattery even stronger than the scribal hand has written.

Again, harsh criticism of evil monarchs is expressed in the first twenty-four lines of Southwell's poem on the eighth commandment, thou shalt not steal (Folger manuscript, fol. 52r). She calls "potentates and mighty kinggs" the greatest thieves of all – and she addresses them explicitly throughout this introductory portion of the poem: your "ambytious covetous desyre" leads men to war, and your "wicked pouder policyes" try to trick good, religious people. Your policies cause death, starvation, and want, but God will destroy corrupt rulers, and so advance his praise.

Southwell is contemptuous of courtly women, as well as men. On keeping the sabbath day holy, Southwell warns her readers not to let their sons be deluded by "a wanto[n] parrit…that ietts in coorte" (fol. 39r). She describes how this soulless creature entraps men, with her perfumes, seductive words, curled hair, and kisses. Southwell's greatest scorn is for the wife who leaves her husband and family to live at court and gets venereal disease:

> Marke hir that leaues hir lord and laufull mate
> to daunce to paynt to bee the stamp of fashions
> forsakes hir famyly to liue in state
> and getts infection by hir wanton passions.
>   (Folger manuscript, fol. 39v, lines 141–44)

Southwell would have had a careful line to tread since some of her own poetic efforts sometimes request courtly advancement. Perhaps lines of this nature do not appear in the Lansdowne manuscript because of its potential courtly audience. Instead, amidst the lengthy defense of women which she offers in her second poem in the Lansdowne manuscript (on the fourth commandment) Southwell offers the example of Queen Elizabeth, who "stellifyed" the female sex, scorned Rome and fortified the true church (fol. 164r, lines 463–68).

Criticism of the court finds its way into the Lansdowne manuscript as well, but less venomously. Southwell writes that she refuses to flatter or stoop by seeking the grace of a bad person; she would rather go without what she seeks (fol. 147r, lines 205–16). She writes that it is better to be thought a liar by your king than to swear a false oath (fol. 149v, lines 319–24). If kings and princes blaspheme, it is better to sit with dogs at Lazarus's meats, "then beare a scepter wth such reseruation" (fol. 150r, lines 336–41). When kings are cruel they cause chaos; when subjects are false, they are accursed (fol. 150v, lines 373–84). She criticizes those who ignore "the kind aspect of maiestye," calling them Judases who cannot recognize when a good king is gone (fol. 151r, lines 385–96). She critiques the ruler who seeks his country's good for his own sake, calling such a person "a painted drabb," but ends by saying that she wishes this person grace for the sake of Christ's spouse, that is, the church (fol. 151v, lines 421–26).

Southwell's work seems to have appeared not only in manuscripts but also in printed material. Jean Klene suggests that she may have been the "A. S." who contributed to the second impression of *A Wife Novv the Widdow of Sir Thomas Overbvrye. Being a Most Exquisite and Singular Poem of the Choice of a Wife. Wherevnto are Added Many Witty Characters, and Conceited Newes, Written by Himselfe and other Learned Gentlemen his Friends* (1614).[54] "A. S." provided "Answers" to Sir Thomas Overbury's "Newes from Court" and to John Donne's "Newes from the very Countery." In later impressions, her initials for the "Answer to the Court newes" were omitted, but "A. S." continued to be attributed as the author of the "Answer to the very Country Newes" until its last impression in 1664. She may also have been the author of "Certaine Edicts from a Parliament in *Eutopia*; Written by the Lady *Southwell*" which first appeared in the sixth impression of 1615, in a section entitled, "An Addition of Other Characters, or Lively Descriptions of Persons."

Louise Schleiner describes the parlor games, "Newes" and "Edicts," which this volume of witty sayings records. "Newes" required the player to produce clever sayings on a theme, like the court, as if they were "newes from" that place, incorporating gossip and political intrigue. An opponent would then compose an answer. "Edicts" were a series of criticisms of male and female behavior laid out as laws.[55] No evidence has been found as yet which firmly links Southwell with the group of poets and courtiers who played these games at Queen Anne's court, and which included Overbury, Donne, Lucy Russell Countess of Bedford, and Cecily Bulstrode. Southwell may have had some contact with Donne and Overbury; poetry by both men appeared in Lansdowne MS 740, bound together with Southwell's, though a later hand may have grouped those booklets together. There is a link, albeit indirect, between Overbury and Southwell in the Folger miscellany: Southwell has written an elegy on the death of Frances Howard, the woman who was charged (with her lover and future husband Robert Carr, Earl of Somerset) with Overbury's murder (fol. 23r). The elegy hints at none of this scandal, a political statement in itself.

Various candidates have been proposed for these attributions: Schleiner agrees with Klene that A.S. may be Anne Southwell but discounts James E. Savage's suggestion that A. S. is Lady Anne Clifford (her first husband was Richard Sackville, Earl of Dorset). She agrees with Savage that the highly placed Lady Elizabeth Southwell (who is wrongly called Frances by Savage) is a candidate for authorship of the Edicts. She was lady in waiting to Queen Elizabeth and later to Queen Anne.[56] Cecily Bulstrode's contribution to the volume, "Newes of my morning worke," is attributed to "Mris B." That might suggest that "A. S." is assumed to be male.[57] The answer of "A. S." to the court "Newes" contains statements critical of women, something which does not preclude Southwell's authorship, because in her Decalogue poetry women are a common target for censure. Savage posits 1609, when Cecily Bulstrode died, as the likely date when the "Newes" games stopped. These items had some circulation in manuscript. One hundred and forty-five passages in the "Newes" style were written in the commonplace book of Sir Henry

Wotton. They date from 1610 or earlier, and the first thirty-four of them were taken from the items of "Newes" written by Overbury, Donne, and Sir Benjamin Rudyerd, years before the date of publication of the earliest extant version in 1614.[58]

The response to Donne's "Newes" is headed "Answere to the very Country Newes." In the answer "A. S." has written, "That life, death, and time, do with short cudgels dance the Matachine," which sounds very like Southwell's letter to Viscount Falkland on folio 4r of the Folger miscellany: "Yo^r perspicuous eye see's dayly, how Nature, chance, and death doe dance the Matechyne about all Mortalls till they haue stript vs of those borrowed plumes y^t begett admiration onely in Ignorance." As Klene has noted, *matechyne* is an unusual word[59] (the matachin is a type of sword dance), though it is used by Sidney, Harington, Sylvester, Webster, and Heywood (OED). A verbal echo also appears in the "Edicts" of the 1615 edition; "corriuall" (meaning a rival in a position of equality) appears at least twice in the Folger miscellany (fols. 29v and 33r). Her "Answere to the very Country Newes" ends with a reference to the writer's place of residence: "That I liuing neere the Church-yard, where many are buried of the Pest, yet my infection commeth from Spaine, and it is feared it will disperse further into the Kingdome." Southwell had a house in London at Clerkenwell, an area indeed near St. Paul's, from which she moved in 1631. She probably obtained this house after her second marriage when she moved back to England, but she may have had earlier connections with a neighborhood like Clerkenwell as early as 1609, through the family of her first husband, when she was apparently writing this (Thomas Southwell's aunt and uncle on his mother's side, Elizabeth, Lady Kytson, and Sir William Cornwallis, lived in Clerkenwell, as did his grandfather on his father's side, Richard).[60]

Her "Answere to the Court Newes" includes sentiments similar to those found in her Decalogue poetry: "That Titles of Honor, are rattles to still ambition. That to be a King, is *Fames Butte*, and feares *Quiuer*." Savage has pointed out that writers of the "Newes" intend to critique the corruption of courtiers and the worthlessness of titles. In the "Edicts," Southwell scorns the bankrupt knight who becomes a parasite or buffoon to a great Lord, saying that he can no longer swear by his honor, only by his knighthood.[61] A few verbal echoes in Southwell's writing, as well as a similar attitude about the court, strengthen the case for her authorship of these passages, but her contact with this group can only remain speculative at this point.

Interestingly, the eighth impression of *Sir Thomas Ouerburie His Wife* in the Bodleian Library (Malone 483) contains some poetry written in a seventeenth-century hand, directly after the "Edicts." This may have more to do with the blank space available on that page, but it may be significant that the few lines of verse are attributed to someone with the first name Ann. A few lines of prose ("and in time he shall ope<n>ly professe to raile on her: but with Such a modesty") are followed by a drawing of a woman, in profile, which in turn surmounts a few lines of verse ("when this you / See remember mee / and keep mee Still in / mind for unto you iwill / proufe <t...> trow and / neuer be ^on^kinde / Ann S........"). It is not Southwell's hand nor any of her scribes', but it is noteworthy that a woman felt moved to fill this page, one of the few associated with a woman's authorship, with a few lines.

Anne, Lady Southwell's miscellany originated in the family of her second husband. To it Sibthorpe added loose sheets of Southwell's works, some in his own hand. Though the binding of the Folger manuscript is now nineteenth-century, he most likely had the volume bound together in its current order. He is also probably the force behind the Lansdowne manuscript, since emendations appear in his hand, and since he is probably the author of the flattering poem on Southwell's poetry which concludes the booklet. Wishing to highlight his wife's ties with highly placed people (or at least her attempts to garner links with them by addressing poetry to them), Sibthorpe includes pieces addressed to (or concerning) the Countess of Londonderry, Viscount Falkland, the first Earl of Castlehaven, the Bishop of Limerick, the Duchess of Lennox, the Countess of Somerset, and the kings of Bohemia and Sweden. While stressing his wife's links with these people, he nevertheless does not soften her often biting criticism of the court. At various points her manuscript seems intended for some kind of audience: much of the poetry is beautifully presented in a neat italic script, and Southwell's own corrections are minimal. But at other points her own hand takes over for entire pages, resulting in nearly illegible additions to her Decalogue poetry, which were no doubt intended to be her own private annotations and not to be seen by other eyes. The fact that Sibthorpe would include those rougher pages, and that the "presentation" copy contains so many rough elements, suggests that we may be seeing an intermediate stage in Sibthorpe's attempts to scribally publish his wife's works.

Many questions remain to be answered about both Southwell's and Sibthorpe's scribal practice. The Thorpe catalogue throws up several

interesting questions about provenance: if Henry Sibthorpe is responsible for the gathering and binding of the Folger manuscript, as I am
arguing, then how did it revert to the possession of the family of her first
husband? Did Southwell know that her expanded poetry on the third and
fourth commandments would be destined for a royal audience, or was
that decision made after her death by Sibthorpe? To what extent were the
couple successful in garnering royal and aristocratic attention? Sibthorpe
claims in her epitaph that Southwell was "Publiquely honoured by her
soveraigne / Passionately affected by her equalles / Observantly reuer-
enced by her inferiours / Worthyly Admired by all" (fol. 74r; these lines
also appear on fol. 73r). Whether she was or not, Sibthorpe's desires that
she should be are reflected in both extant manuscripts associated with
her name.

NOTES

All transcriptions have been taken from British Library Lansdowne MS
740 and Folger Shakespeare Library MS v.b.198, but checked against Jean
Klene (ed.), *The Southwell-Sibthorpe Commonplace Book: Folger MS v.b.198* (Tempe:
Renaissance English Text Society, 1997).

1 Though Southwell is referred to as Lady Anne Southwell in the manuscript,
I have elected to call her Anne, Lady Southwell because her father and
first husband were knighted by James I. The order of knight is not elevated
enough to provide a title for one's children. The title "Lady" must come
from her husband, and so should be joined to her husband's last name (Lady
Southwell), and not her first name (Lady Anne), as would be the case if her
father had been of an aristocratic rank.

2 Jean Klene (ed.), *The Southwell-Sibthorpe Commonplace Book: Folger MS
V.b.198* (Tempe: Renaissance English Text Society, 1997), xxxiii–xxxvi;
Thomas Thorpe, *Catalogus Librorum Manuscriptorum Bibliothecae Southwellianae*
([London], 1834), 520–23. Klene's source, Seymour De Ricci and W. J.
Wilson, *Census of Medieval and Renaissance Manuscripts in the United States and
Canada*, 2 vols. (New York: The H. W. Wilson Company, 1935), 1:419, no.
1669.1, claims that Thorpe sold the manuscript as number 1032 in 1836.

3 The first song, beginning "ffly from the world, o fly, thow poore distrest,"
has been set to music in Ferrabosco's *Ayres* of 1609 and in Jones's 1605
edition of airs (*Ultimum Vale*). The second poem, beginning "When I sitt
reading all alone that secret booke" appears in Jones's *A Musicall Dreame. Or
the Fourth Booke of Ayres* of 1609, as does the fourth poem, "If in the flesh where
thow indrench'd do'st ly." "Like to a lampe wherein the light is dead" was
composed by Arthur Gorges in the 1580s. The two Henry King poems are
his elegies on his wife and on Gustavus Adolphus. The poem associated with
Raleigh's authorship is "The Lie."

4 Linda L. Dove has described Southwell's poetic indebtedness to Quarles in "Composing (to) a Man of Letters: Lady Anne Southwell's Acrostic to Francis Quarles," *ANQ* 11 (1998), 12–17.

5 For a discussion of this list see Jean C. Cavanaugh, "The Library of Lady Southwell and Captain Sibthorpe," *Studies in Bibliography* 20 (1967), 243–54.

6 Klene has noted that Southwell's hand occurs forty-three times in the manuscript, *Southwell-Sibthorpe Commonplace Book*, 123.

7 Thomas Thorpe, in his catalog of the Southwell manuscripts, asserts that this volume belonged to Colonel John Sibthorpe when he served in Flanders with Robert Dudley, Earl of Leicester in January and February of 1587/8. The volume contains reckonings with Leicester for the maintenance of prisoners, etc., at various locales. There are also notes of servants receiving their pay for January 1588/9, *Catalogus*, 522–23.

8 See Klene's invaluable chart of suggested scribes in the Folger manuscript, *Southwell-Sibthorpe Commonplace Book*, 117–23. Sibthorpe's hand varies greatly throughout the Folger manuscript, but I am not convinced that this hand is responsible for the entire list of books in their library; I can only confidently link his hand with entries 35–76 (fols. 65v–66r).

9 Peter Beal has described it in his *Index of English Literary Manuscripts*, 4 vols., (London: Bowker and Mansell, 1980), 1:part 1, 250–51. Ernest W. Sullivan, II, explains its links with the Dalhousie manuscripts, demonstrating that it derives like the first Dalhousie manuscript from papers preserved by the Essex family; *The First and Second Dalhousie Manuscripts: Poems and Prose by John Donne and Others, A Facsimile Edition* (Columbia: University of Missouri Press, 1988), 1–12. Both sources cited in Klene, *Southwell-Sibthorpe Commonplace Book*, xxxii and 188.

10 Edward Heawood, *Watermarks, Mainly of the seventeenth and eighteenth Centuries* (Hilversum, Holland: The Paper Publications Society, 1950).

11 Thorpe, *Catalogus*, 532.

12 All of these letters are described in Jean Klene, "Recreating the Letters of Lady Anne Southwell," *New Ways of Looking at Old Texts: Papers of the Renaissance English Text Society, 1985–1991*, ed. W. Speed Hill (Binghamton: Renaissance English Text Society, 1993), 239–52. Transcriptions of the two letters written about Southwell have been preserved in *Historical Manuscripts Commission Calendar of the Manuscripts of the Most Hon. the Marquess of Salisbury Preserved at Hatfield House, Hertfordshire*, part 15 (London: HMSO, 1930), 90–91, 124, and 388. In the first, of 15 May 1603, Captain John Skinner writes to William Cecil, Lord Burghley, that Mrs. Southwell refused to travel from Berwick to London without escorts for her protection. A list of traveling charges submitted by Southwell's "keeper" Thomas Meade indicates that the trip was made later that month. In the second letter her newly knighted husband petitions to have the Southwell name cleared since the Queen's letters urged his wife's journey.

13 J. L. Vivian (ed.), *The Visitations of the County of Devon, Comprising the Herald's Visitations of 1531, 1564 and 1620* (Exeter, 1889–95), 452; William A. Shaw, *The

Knights of England, 2 vols. (London: Sherrat and Hughes, 1906), 2:124; Richard Polwhele, *The History of Devonshire in Three Volumes*, 3 vols. (1797 and 1806; London: Kohler & Coombes, 1977), 1:266; John Prince, *Danmonii Orientales Illustres: Or, the Worthies of Devon* (Exeter, 1701), 378; Klene, *Southwell-Sibthorpe Commonplace Book*, xiii–xxiii.

14 Thorpe, *Catalogus*, 520–21. She is not listed among women at court in Joan Goldsmith, "All the Queen's Women: the Changing Place and Perception of Aristocratic Women in Elizabethan England, 1558–1620," Ph.D. thesis, Northwestern University (1987), Appendix B; nor in Charlotte Merton, "The Women Who Served Queen Mary and Queen Elizabeth: Ladies, Gentlewomen, and Maids of the Privy Chamber, 1553–1603," Ph.D. thesis, University of Cambridge (1992), Appendix 1. Thorpe may have confused Anne Southwell with three other Southwells who served at court: Nazareth Newton Southwell Lady Paget, Lady Elizabeth Howard Southwell, and her daughter Elizabeth Southwell Dudley.

15 Charles Parkin, *An Essay towards a Topographical History of the County of Norfolk* (London, 1809), 10:275; Mervyn Archdall (ed.), *The Peerage of Ireland*, by John Lodge, rev. edn. (Dublin, 1789), 6:6–7.

16 Sir Thomas Southwell's name appears on two documents in "The Counsell booke for the prouince of Mounster contayninge all the Actes. Recordes and entries. of that Provinciall state from the xx[th] daie of August 1601...", BL Harl. MS 697. The first, of 24 April 1620, authorizes the Sheriff of the county of Cork to collect £60 from the families of the traitors Murrieghs and Owens, which are to be distributed as rewards to those who bring the heads of the traitors to the Lord President and Council of Munster (fol. 104r). The second, of 12 April 1620, orders the burgesses of Kinsale to seize all priests, friars, and Jesuits, to put them in safe custody, to seize the houses they used and all the relics therein, and to learn who harbors them (fol. 106v). Both Thomas Southwell and Edward Harris (Southwell's brother-in-law) are signatories to these documents.

17 Elizabeth's first husband may have been a member of the Gray family in Shropshire, a descendant of Lord Powis. Her second was Sir John Dowdall and her third was Donogh O'Brien, son and heir of Sir Daniel O'Brien of Carrigichoulta in county Clare. Frances married William Lenthal of Lachford in Oxfordshire. She had two sons and died in 1643, Archdall, *Peerage of Ireland*, 6:7. John Lindsay Darling lists only one daughter, Elizabeth, *St. Multose Church, Kinsale* (Cork, 1895), 30, as does the death certificate of Thomas Southwell, BL Add. MS 4820, fol. 98v; Alexander B. Grosart (ed.), *The Lismore Papers (First Series), viz., Autobiographical Notes, Remembrances and Diaries of Sir Richard Boyle, First and "Great" Earl of Cork*, 5 vols. (Private Circulation Only, 1886), 2:346; referred to in Klene, *Southwell-Sibthorpe Commonplace Book*, xix. A passage in the Lansdowne manuscript may refer to her children and how they have kept her from her writing (it begins, "You litle brattes that hange about my knees," fol. 145r); if this reference reflects reality, she likely had more than one child.

18 Arthur R. Maddison, *An Account of the Sibthorp Family* (Lincoln, 1896), 8–9.
The Sibthorpe arms which Daniel Lysons gives for Anne Southwell match
those of the Sibthorpes of Laneham, Nottinghamshire. Tom Harper Smith
(a local historian of Acton), personal communication, 16 January 1996;
Daniel Lysons, *The Environs of London* (London, 1795), 2:8. Those arms are
"argent two bars gules a border sable" (i.e. two red bars on a silver or
white background enclosed in a black border). The arms for Sir Christopher
Sibthorpe, Justice of the King's Bench in Ireland are the same, except with
a mullet (the rowel of a spur) added to them, Bernard Burke, *The General
Armory of England, Scotland, Ireland and Wales* (London, 1884), 926. If Lysons is
correct in his description of Sibthorpe's arms, Henry was probably related
to the Sibthorpes of Laneham rather than the Essex branch. John Sibthorpe
of Laneham was born in 1546 and married Rosamund Bellamy in 1578.
A Henry does not figure among their children, however; their offspring are
listed as Robert, Gervase, Agnes, William, and George. Arthur R. Maddison
(ed.), *Lincolnshire Pedigrees* (London: Harleian Society, 1904), 3:877.

19 Norman Egbert McClure (ed.), *The Letters of John Chamberlain*, 2 vols.
(Philadelphia: American Philosophical Society, 1939), 2:166. In a letter of
25 June 1625, Chamberlain expresses to Carleton both John West's and
Henry Sibthorpe's gratefulness for Carleton's favours (624).

20 *Calendar of the State Papers Relating to Ireland, of the Reign of Charles I, 1625–32*,
ed. Robert Pentland Mahaffy (London: HMSO, 1900) 145, 261, and 293.
See 158, 165, 172, 173, 194, 206, and 220 for receipts and records of salary
payment.

21 Cavanaugh, "Library," 244. Thorpe, *Catalogus*, 521 asserts that he died in
London in or about 1664. Tom Harper Smith (personal communication, 16
January 1996) suggests that Henry Sibthorpe died in 1672. In his will (PRO,
PROB 11/340), written 30 December 1670, he describes an obligation dated
13 January 1638/9 entered into by William Viscount Grandison, Edward
Hyde Earl of Clarendon, and others in the penal sum of £1,200 for the
payment of £624 owed to him. He divided this sum into bequests for his
West cousins, his Crosby cousins, his friend Colonel Edward Gray of Grays
Inn, his friend Mrs. Anne Francklyn and her daughter Alice, his landlord
Mr. Bryan Sharpe and his wife Frances, John Cooke his attorney (so that
he could assist Sibthorpe's executor, Charles Francklyn, in procuring the
money owed to him), his servant Joan Muleyes, and the poor of the parish.
To his executor Francklyn, Sibthorpe left the residue of his estate, as well
as his "Little Truncke with the Bookes conteyned therein." Perhaps one of
the books was Anne Southwell's miscellany. Support is given to the theory
that the Henry Sibthorpe who wrote this will is our Henry Sibthorpe by the
fact that he had cousins named West; our Sibthorpe had an uncle John West
who helped him secure a post early in his career.

22 Brendan Bradshaw, J. C. Simms, and C. J. Woods, "Bishops of the Church of
Ireland from 1534," *A New History of Ireland*, eds. T. W. Moody, F. X. Martin,
and F. J. Byrne (Oxford: Clarendon Press, 1984), 9:420. Adams wrote three

tracts on the union of the crowns of England and Scotland (printed in 1604, 1605, and 1641), a treatise on alchemy (printed in 1621), and a discourse on the Sacrament (printed in 1630). A further work, *Pax Vobis, A Treastise on the Unity and Peace of the Church*, has never been printed. Henry Cotton, *Fasti Ecclesiae Hibernicae. The Succession of the Prelates and Members of the Cathedral Bodies of Ireland*, 2nd edn. (Dublin, 1851), 1:383.

23 Leslie Stephen and Sidney Lee (eds.), *Dictionary of National Biography*, 22 vols. (Oxford: Oxford University Press, 1917), 19:1004; George Edward Cokayne (ed.), *The Complete Peerage*, rev. edn., 14 vols. (London: St. Catherine Press, 1910–59), 3:86.

24 Letters enclosed in < > are damaged, cropped, or lost in the gutter.

25 Klene, *Southwell-Sibthorpe Commonplace Book*, 190.

26 Esther S. Cope (ed.), *Prophetic Writings of Lady Eleanor Davies* (Oxford: Oxford University Press, 1995), xi–xii, 20–23; Esther S. Cope, *Handmaid of the Holy Spirit: Dame Eleanor Davies, Never Soe Mad A Ladie* (Ann Arbor: University of Michigan Press, 1992), 15–16. Cope writes, "With her marriage to Sir John Davies in the spring of 1609, Lady Eleanor entered a social circle in Ireland that included key figures among the English officials there," *Handmaid*, 19. She does not, however, give any specifics.

27 Stephen and Lee (eds.), *Dictionary of National Biography*, 3:1149–51; Cokayne, *Complete Peerage*, 5:239–40.

28 *CSPI, 1625–32*, 273. This refers to the disastrous Cadiz expedition of October–November 1625 under Sir Edward Cecil. Richard W. Stewart, "Arms and Expeditions: The Ordnance Office and the Assaults on Cadiz (1625) and the Isle of Rhé (1627)," *War and Government in Britain, 1598–1650*, ed. Mark Charles Fissel (Manchester: Manchester University Press, 1991), 115–21; and Charles Dalton, *Life and Times of General Sir Edward Cecil* (London, 1885), 2:152–97.

29 Stephen and Lee (eds.), *Dictionary of National Biography*, 3:1151. Diane Purkiss explains that the date of her conversion to Catholicism is unknown, but suggests that living in Catholic Ireland may have been an influence. Diane Purkiss (ed.), *Renaissance Women: The Plays of Elizabeth Cary. The Poems of Aemilia Lanyer* (London: Pickering, 1994), xiv.

30 Prince, *Danmonii Orientales Illustres*, 549; Stephen and Lee (eds.), *Dictionary of National Biography*, 16:1165–67; Cokayne (ed.), *Complete Peerage*, 8:105–06.

31 Cicely was the fifth daughter of Henry MacWilliam and Mary, Lady Cheke of Stambourne Hall, Essex. William Tighe, personal communication, 21 December 1995; his source is Lady Cheke's inquisition post mortem. In Vivian's *Visitations of…Devon* Cicely is called a maid of honor to Queen Elizabeth (647) but she does not appear among Goldsmith's or Merton's lists. Three women of her maiden name did serve at court: Margaret MacWilliam, Lady Mary Cheke MacWilliam, and Elizabeth MacWilliam. The first two women are Cicely's sister and mother.

32 *The Victoria History of the Counties of England: a History of the County of Middlesex*, ed. T. F. T. Baker, 9 vols. (London: Oxford University Press, 1982), 7:36; T. and A.

Harper Smith, *Acton People 1200–1700* (Acton: Local History Society, 1989), 6; Roger Cocks, *Hebdomada Sacra: a Weekes Devotion: or, Seven Poeticall Meditations, Vpon the Second Chapter of St. Matthewes Gospell* (London, 1630); Roger Cocks, *An Answer to a Book Set Forth By Sir Edward Peyton, Knight and Baronet, Carrying this Title, a Discourse Concerning the Fitnesse of the Posture, Necessary to be Used, in Taking the Bread and Wine at the Sacrament* (London, 1642).

33 John Venn and J. A. Venn, *Alumni Cantabrigienses* (Cambridge: Cambridge University Press, 1922), part 1, 1:408; Amy M. Charles, *A Life of George Herbert* (Ithaca: Cornell University Press, 1977), 15–16. Herbert's and Cox's poems appear in *Epicedivm Cantabrigiense, In Obitum Immaturum, Semperque; Deflendum, Henrici, Illustrissimi Principis Walliae, &c.* (Cambridge, 1612), sig. I3–4 and O3.

34 The title of fol. 66v is cropped, but one can make out what is probably "Preacher of acton" and a letter C preceding it; this most likely refers to Mr. Cox, and is dated "the 3th of ffebruary 1632." An exposition of Matthew 11:16–17 follows. Roger Cox's funeral sermon on Robert Johnson, who died on 18 November 1633 and was buried on the 21st, appears on fol. 72r.

35   fol. 18r: Good reuerend Father I will doe my best
        and where I fayle doe yow supply the rest.

                                           (lines 15–16)

        fol. 26r: My noble Neighbour I will doe my best
        and wheare I faile, please you supplye the rest,
        Whoe hath a minde and hoards it vp in store
        is poorer then a beggar at the doore
        Let your cleare Iudgment, and well tempered soule
        Condemne, amend, or rattifye this scrole
        Twi'll prooue your fairest Monument and when
        your Marble ffailes, liue with the best of men
        If you haue lost your fflowinge sweete humiddities
        and in a dust disdaine theise quantities
        Pass it to oure beloued Docter Featlye
        his tongue dropps honnye, and can doe it neatlye.

                                           (lines 11–22)

36 T. and A. Harper Smith, *A Brief History of Acton* (Acton: Local History Society, 1993), 7.

37 Bodlein MS Rawl. D. 47. Copies of five love-letters from Featley to a "Mrs Anne" appear on fols. 48v–52r, but this is not the twice-married Anne Southwell. The recipient of Featley's affection was a Frenchwoman named Anne Mouline to whose virginity Featley alludes.

38 *The New Grove Dictionary of Music and Musicians*, ed. Stanley Sadie, 20 vols. (London: Macmillan, 1980), 9:681; *Victoria County History of Middlesex*, 7:8; Smith, *Acton People*, 2–3.

39 T. and A. Harper Smith, *St. Mary's Acton: a Guide* (Acton: Local History Society, 1985), 4; John Bowack, *The Second Part of the Antiquities of Middlesex*

(London, 1706), 49–50; and *Victoria County History of Middlesex*, 7:36–37. Lady Conway bequeathed a rent charge for the teaching of six poor children, *Victoria County History of Middlesex*, 7:42. See, *Dictionary of National Biography*, eds. Stephen and Lee, 4:975–6, although that source has his wife's name as Dorothy. A piece of evidence can be gleaned from a letter of 1 March 1638, in which Lady Brilliana Harley writes to her son Edward that he should write a letter to "my lady Conway": "I thinke the carryer goo by Acton, wheare my lady Conway dwells, when they goo to Loundon." Brilliana Harley, *Letters of the Lady Brilliana Harley*, ed. Thomas Taylor Lewis (London: Camden Society, 1854), 33. This Lady Conway must have been Harley's stepmother; Harley was the second daughter of Sir Edward Conway and Dorothy Tracy. Brilliana Harley compiled her own commonplace book, now in the Nottingham University Library Portland Collection.

40 Smith, *Acton People*, 5.

41 Klene notes that Sir Henry Jernegan occupied a house at Acton in 1636, *Victoria County History of Middlesex*, 7:21, and that a Mrs. Mary Jernegan of Acton died in 1633. *Abstracts of Probate Acts in the Prerogative Court of Canterbury*, eds. John Matthews and George F. Matthews (London: Chancery Lane, [1902]), 1:218; Klene, *Southwell-Sibthorpe Commonplace Book*, 195.

42 Margaret Crum (ed.), *The Poems of Henry King* (Oxford: Clarendon Press, 1965), 68–72 and 197–98.

43 J. E. Neale, *Elizabeth I and her Parliaments* (New York: St. Martin's Press, 1958), 300 and 344; J. H. Adamson and H. F. Folland, *The Shepherd of the Ocean: an Account of Sir Walter Ralegh and His Times* (London: The Bodley Head, 1969), 286; Klene, *Southwell-Sibthorpe Commonplace Book*, xii–xiii.

44 Steven W. May, *Sir Walter Ralegh*, Twayne English Authors Series (Boston: Twayne, 1989), 61; *Index of English Literary Manuscripts*, ed. Peter Beal, 2 vols., 2 parts (London: Mansell; New York: R. R. Bowker Company, 1980), 1: part 2, 390–92. Michael Rudick discusses "The Lie" and prints three different manuscript versions of the poem with responses in *The Poems of Sir Walter Ralegh: A Historical Edition* (Tempe: Renaissance English Text Society, 1999), xlii–xlvii and 30–44.

45 Anna R. Beer, in *Sir Walter Ralegh and his Readers in the Seventeenth Century: Speaking to the People* (Basingstoke: Macmillan, 1997), discusses the political effects of Raleigh's writing, and those produced in response to his works, during the seventeenth century.

46 An Collins, *Divine Songs and Meditacions* (London, 1653), sig. B1v–sig. C6r.

47 Klene, *Southwell-Sibthorpe Commonplace Book*, 195; Cokayne, *Complete Peerage*, 7:604–05.

48 *The Scots Peerage Founded on Wood's Edition of Sir Robert Douglas's Peerage of Scotland*, ed. James Balfour Paul, 8 vols. (Edinburgh: Douglas, 1908), 5:358.

49 Stephen J. Lee, *The Thirty Years War* (London: Routledge, 1991), 6.

50 Geoffrey Parker, *The Thirty Years' War* (London: Routledge, 1984), 322, plates 11 and 14.

51 Ethel Seaton, *Literary Relations of England and Scandinavia in the Seventeenth Century* (Oxford: Clarendon Press, 1935), 84–86; *The Swedish Intelligencer. The Third Part* (London, 1633).

52 This is the final line of the single elegy which commemorates the King of Bohemia in *The Swedish Intelligencer*; quoted in Seaton, *Literary Relations*, 83 and Parker, *The Thirty Years' War*, 131.

53 Both of the stanzas in which these lines appear in the Folger manuscript (and others around them) have been lightly crossed out, suggesting that Southwell thought them perhaps too contentious to be included in future drafts.

54 Klene, *Southwell-Sibthorpe Commonplace Book*, xxviii–xxxi.

55 Louise Schleiner, *Tudor and Stuart Women Writers* (Bloomington: Indiana University Press, 1994), 113–16.

56 Ibid., 265–66 n. 1; James E. Savage (ed.), *The "Conceited Newes" of Sir Thomas Overbury and His Friends. A Facsimile Reproduction of the Ninth Impression of 1616 of Sir Thomas Ouerbury His Wife* (Gainesville: Scholars' Facsimiles, 1968), xxxviii–xli. Lady Elizabeth Southwell's daughter, Elizabeth, followed Sir Robert Dudley to Italy in 1605, where they converted to Roman Catholicism; her description of the death of Queen Elizabeth from a manuscript of 1607 has been edited by Catherine Loomis, "Elizabeth Southwell's Manuscript Account of the Death of Queen Elizabeth [with text]," *English Literary Renaissance* 26 (1996), 482–509.

57 Schleiner's suggestion that after 1615 (the first appearance of the "Edicts") Southwell could be called Lady Southwell but before that just "A. S." would be appropriate is based on misinformation about her first husband, Schleiner, *Tudor and Stuart Women Writers*, 265–66. As Klene has shown, Southwell was married to the Thomas Southwell who was knighted in 1603, not the one knighted in 1615, *Southwell-Sibthorpe Commonplace Book*, xiv.

58 Savage, *Conceited Newes*, xxvi and xliv–xlv; Logan Pearsall Smith, *The Life and Letters of Sir Henry Wotton*, 2 vols., Oxford: Clarendon Press, 1907, 2:489–500; Evelyn M. Simpson, "John Donne and Sir Thomas Overbury's 'Characters,'" *Modern Language Review* 18 (1923), 410–15. Wotton's commonplace book was among the papers of G. H. Finch, esq., at Burley-on-the-Hill in Rutland in 1879 (*Seventh Report of the Royal Commission on Historical Manuscripts*, 2 parts [London: HMSO, 1879], 1:516; [Smith, *Life and Letters*, 489–90]).

59 Klene, *Southwell-Sibthorpe Commonplace Book*, xxix.

60 Nancy Pollard Brown, "Paperchase: the Dissemination of Catholic Texts in Elizabethan England," *English Manuscript Studies 1100–1700* 1 (1989), 132; *the Private Correspondence of Jane Lady Cornwallis; 1613–1644. From the Originals in the Possession of the Family* (London, 1842), xxxiv–xxxv. The latter is cited in Klene, *Southwell-Sibthorpe Commonplace Book*, xiv.

61 Savage, *Conceited Newes*, 226, lix, and 219.

CHAPTER 6

The posthumous publication of women's manuscripts and the history of authorship

Margaret J. M. Ezell

Amber has been viewed as a talismanic substance since ancient times, and those pieces containing the captured remains of insects supposedly "provided more protection and more magical powers than others."[1] "If thou couldst but speak, little fly," Immanuel Kant observed, "how much more would we know about the past!"[2] Today, scientists are pushing the edge of science fiction with the successful extraction of DNA from the trapped citizens of an amber world. Such investigators share Kant's curiosity: in these unintentional insect monuments, a brief life accidentally caught and hermetically sealed in time, scientists interested in life forms today see a new opportunity to discover more about our relationship with a past world, through one of its serendipitously preserved artifacts.

As one of the many who have worked on recovering early modern women writers over the last two decades, I do sometimes feel that I, too, am searching for the literary equivalent of amber. How excellent it would be if one discovered some new source to provide access to the literary culture of early modern Britain, one which has been preserved intact, but without the intervening layers of commentary from generations of editors and scholars explaining its lack of significance or denying its presence. With the help of those pioneers in the field of manuscript recovery such as Peter Beal who spearheaded the massive series cataloging English literary manuscripts and current electronic projects such as the Perdita Project whose goal is to construct databases of women's manuscript texts, we are gradually coming to a point where we will have the tools to permit us to begin to make different generalizations about women's participation in literary culture from traditional ones based on only printed works. I would suggest, however, that in addition to such archival manuscript texts there are still some remaining sources of information already in our grasp. These sources may prove valuable as we attempt to reconceptualize and reconstruct the dynamics of literary culture (as opposed to the effort merely to chronicle major authors) during the period just preceding the development, institutionalization, and enforcement of the notion of proprietary authorship embodied in copyright law.

In 1685, Damaris Masham wrote to John Locke apologizing for not sending any of her verse to him in her letter; she speculates, however, that perhaps in the future Locke might be able to read her verse in print rather than waiting on her correspondence. On the other hand, she notes, while publishing one's verse has "growne much the fashion of late for our sex, . . . I confess it has not much of my Approbation because (Principally) the Mode is for one to Dye First."[3] Masham never did publish her verse although she did publish two prose treatises some fifteen years after this letter.

Masham's ironic comment serves to draw our attention to a phenomenon which for the modern reader seems a rather curious although unstudied facet of early modern authorship, posthumous publication. I once opened a talk before a group of American academics by urging them to consider the possibilities of posthumous publication, which was greeted with a wave of laughter. I, who had been thinking about something else entirely, had not expected such a response; but, really, I should have, given the massive importance in an American academic's career of being a published author. Indeed, we coined the phrase "publish or perish," and although the grave's a fine and private place, but none, I think, do there receive tenure or promotion, although as we shall see, perhaps even that is becoming a possibility. For an early modern writer, perhaps especially for a woman writer or any writer not living in London or one of the University cities, however, posthumous publication must be considered as one part of a complex system of authorship practices and manuscript coterie dynamics. In posthumous editions, collections of verse or prose by both men and women which were printed only after the author's death, the structure and apparatus – called by some the paratexts – as well as the volume's contents, can make suggestive revelations concerning the text's previous existence as part of a social literary practice.

Before turning directly to texts which exemplify women's involvement with coterie literary practices and the significance of posthumous print editions for those interested in women's manuscript texts, let us look first at the whole, to us odd, phenomenon of posthumous publication. If one uses the "key-word" function on a library computer index to perform the entertaining task of calling forth materials whose virtues are signified under the term "posthumous," an interesting range of dramas suddenly unfolds. Before looking at a set of examples from the period in question,

I think it is important to look at the anticipated "stories" we associate both with the artist and with the posthumous artifact, and to become aware of the discourse we are accustomed to use when analyzing the phenomenon.

For example, there is the poignant story of the mother's determination to see her wronged son's novel in print, which resulted in the posthumous publication of John Kennedy Toole's novel *A Confederacy of Dunces* (1980) and its subsequent winning of the Pulitzer Prize. Likewise, there are stories of artist Inez Helen Seibert, who was confined in a mental asylum for most of her life, but whose works responding to Picasso and Mondrian done in the 1930–49 period were carefully stored and after her death received their first public exhibition in 1996.[4] Still other articles point to the posthumous rise to "superstardom" of the painter Frida Kahlo, described as "the strikingly beautiful but tragically handicapped artist" known during her life mostly as the wife of the painter Diego Rivera, but whose own creations after her death now command extraordinary prices and have created for her a cult following far outstripping her husband's reputation.[5]

In modern stories such as these, the narrative of the artist is that of the damaged, alienated sensibility who can only be accepted and appreciated after death. Only in posthumous publication or exhibition can such individuals claim the public's rightful admiration. Certainly, those of us working on early modern women's texts are familiar with this narrative being associated with early modern women's texts and the practice of posthumous publication. In the 1970s and 80s, those working on women's texts frequently structured their discussions of women and print culture by attempting to describe the forces that would prevent a meritorious woman from publishing her texts, theorizing that a pervasive social code of "feminine modesty" would effectively silence most women with literary ambition. If a woman did write, such a code of "feminine modesty" ("the feeling that publication of one's work symbolically violated feminine modesty by exposing private thoughts to the world"[6]) would thwart most from attempting publication, and thus result in the practice of posthumous publication. Elaine Hobby's early analysis of seventeenth-century women's writing, of course, makes note of the posthumous publication of women's texts: but her interest in her study lay in answering the questions, "in the light of all these restrictions, how did seventeenth-century women manage to write and publish?" Hobby's groundbreaking constructive analysis of "how different women faced with different circumstances managed to write" and to publish within cultural systems of restraint provided the stable platform from which a reassessment of women's place in the literary world in the latter part of the seventeenth century could be launched.[7] The issue of posthumous publication mentioned in this study, however, has since been left unexamined.

This chapter is engaged in a different task, and it is part of a longer project concerned with recovering the nature of social literary culture. In turning our gaze from the professional and the commercial world of authorship and considering other alternatives for literary life, earlier equations of print and literary voice for women writers, or such a privileging of print over script, must be called into question. It is not unlikely, however, that when encountering posthumous editions of women's writings from the latter part of the seventeenth and early eighteenth centuries we may be still predisposed to view them as manifestations of the restrictive power of the hegemony of "feminine modesty" and to see their authors as cultural victims who lacked the nerve, will, or means, as Patricia Crawford expressed it in her checklist of women's publications 1600–1700, "to value themselves" and "to write for publication."[8]

Obviously, posthumous editions by women can be used to further this model; however, I believe that they contain another type of information which might be considered. While the early studies of women's participation in the world of print carved out the field of early modern women's studies, through reconstructing the relationship between manuscript and print texts, author and audience, we can possibly continue to broaden the field of women's literary history.

Finally, to return to our assessment of the implications contained within the act of posthumous publication, the figure of controversy also emerges in modern posthumous dramas over the impact and interpretation of the material, speaking as it were, from the grave to the living. The postmodern/modern reader asks: What are the rights of the departed artist? For example, does the late photographer Man Ray's assistant have the authority to issue and exhibit posthumous prints which he made as being by Man Ray? Lucient Treillard defended himself asserting that by reproducing the prints, he was following Man Ray's "artistic philosophy, which gave no particular weight to 'vintage' over 'nonvintage' prints," but collectors, on the other hand, wonder whether prints made by Treillard could actually be considered to be by the original artist.[9]

Some modern artists clearly recognized the dangers of the mechanical reproduction of their art after their death. The sculptor Henry Moore was so concerned over this possibility that before his death he instituted a foundation to insure that none of his sculptures would be recast after his death. Literary reviewers and Ernest Hemingway admirers united in wishing that Hemingway's final novel, *The Garden of Eden*, had not been published in the format of a novel, because it was felt that the rough, undeveloped text was not a true reflection of his talents, and also perhaps because the misogynistic representation of the female characters severely disrupted any attempt to represent Hemingway in a kinder, gentler light. In a similar scenario, critics and fans alike express their outrage over a new type of posthumous publication, literally "ghost written" novels "based on" outlines or "ideas" left in the working papers of popular writers such as Ian Fleming and Dashiel Hammett. The underlying story about this type of posthumous publication concerns whether it was the intent of the author to publish and be public and whether subsequent generations have the right to appropriate and exploit artistic materials for reproduction without the express consent of the artist.

Not completely dissimilar questions arise when one performs the same computer conjuring trick, restricting the sweep to a period between 1650 and 1720. However, while anxieties over posthumous acts do overlap in many areas with modern ones, it is clear that the act of posthumous publication of manuscript texts in the early modern period also had quite different connotations from the ones I have just presented featuring modern artists.

It is interesting to note first that the term "posthumous" is relatively scarce in titles associated with the publication of texts in the seventeenth and early eighteenth centuries. Instead, what one finds in quantity are peoples' "remains" and "reliques." Starting with the choice of titles of posthumous texts, then, we can see a different and suggestive discourse being used to represent the practice, the author, and the compiler or printer of the resulting volume.

The question for us, therefore, is to determine the implications behind an early modern text's posthumous appearance in print as part of a study of manuscript culture and, in particular, to look closely at women's texts which were posthumously printed. While in the twentieth century, we find the act of posthumous recognition to be ambivalent – either it seems a belated attempt to adjust claims for merit or it seems an invasion of the writer's or artist's privacy by bringing to the public and exploiting works not intended by the author for that type of presentation – we find three parallel types of posthumous practices in the latter part of the seventeenth and early part of the eighteenth centuries, which nevertheless reveal very different assumptions about authorial voice and the recognition of merit.

First and closest to the modern anxiety over posthumous publication is the printing of a deceased writer's papers by a commercial agent primarily for the benefit of the publisher or bookseller. Such an exploitative relationship with the deceased author underpins the construction of the experience of female authorship in the "Introduction" to Germaine Greer *et al.*'s anthology *Kissing the Rod*, which opens with the assertion that "the book-selling trade has always made use of women."[10] Specific examples are easily found in the life and adventures of John Dunton and Edmund Curll, the latter who provoked one author to observe, "For Booksellers vile Vipers are, / On Brains of Wits they prey; / The very Worms they will not spare, / When Wits to Worms decay."[11] Such posthumous editions, as Greer notes, typically depended on the deceased having sufficient name recognition that it would make sense to publish them for a profit. We find the same practice of a deceased author's work being purchased for printing by a commercial agent in a rather more savory fashion in the publication pattern of Humphrey Moseley, who, as he announced in his prefaces to posthumously printed works of John Donne and Beaumont and Fletcher in the 1650s, produced such editions as a mark of his love for the English language.

Second, we have the practice of posthumous publication of an author's papers which involved the author's participation in preparing the texts before his or her death with the anticipation they would be printed. This can be seen, for example, in Lady Sarah Freeman's preface to her husband Sir George Freeman's essays, which she opens by informing the reader that "the great charity the Author had for souls . . . and the desire he had of making what restitution he could, was the reason he desired me to set out his Treatise against Drinking after his Death."[12]

More soberly, we can also find the hand of the author in the preparation of manuscript materials for posthumous publication in the writings of Ann, Lady Halkett. Halkett left behind on her death a large number of folio and quarto manuscript volumes containing her prayers, meditations, and an autobiographical sketch; following her death, a short biography of her by "S. C." was printed by Andrew Sympson in Edinburgh in 1701 along with three other texts by Halkett, *Instructions for Youth*, *Meditations on the Twentieth and Fifth Psalm*, and *Mediations and Prayers Upon the First Week*. As I have written elsewhere, there is some evidence that Halkett herself took steps to facilitate the printing of her texts, in spite of her repeated declarations to herself in her manuscript texts that she was not writing with the intent that they be for public consumption but instead for her own private edification.

This stated, we do find in her manuscript volume she records that "if the Lord think fitt to manifest them when I am Dead, I hope (whose ever hands they fall in) that ye blessed spirit of God will so influence what himselfe hath wrought in mee, that it shall make them studious to perform... what make[s] harmony & Concord with the Glorified spirits."[13] It subsequently appears that she did not rely entirely on the Lord to prepare her texts for print, however, since her biographer records that "a few Years before her Death,... she made known to some, in whom she reposed great confidence, that she had Written such Books; being moved to make the discovery by hearing of several Persons, who died suddenly."[14] The publisher of these posthumous texts alerts the reader in the preface that "the words and expressions are very little varied" from Halkett's original manuscripts, which also suggests that Halkett left texts in a format which permitted them to be easily transformed from manuscript to print.

Third, we have the papers of a suddenly deceased author being published by the family or friends as a "monument" to the departed merits, without any direct indication that the author wished the texts to be presented in this format. These volumes are an attempt to set forth a coherent collection of ordered papers and/or poetry and frequently have conventional paratexts such as commendatory verses and testimonials about the departed. Such would be the case with the Freeman volume cited before, which Lady Sarah Freeman entitled *Golden Remains* (1682), and where, in addition to presenting her husband's essays on diverse topics, she prefaces the volume with a laudatory account of his rather dissolute life. Another obvious example of the posthumous edition as a memorial marker would be the posthumous publications of Richard Lovelace's *Lucasta. Posthumous Poems* (1659), which has as its epigram on the title page Martial's observation that "Those Honours come too late, / That on our Ashes Waite." Likewise, *Fragmenta Aurea*, published by Moseley in 1646, contains according to its title page "A collection of all the Incomparable Peeces, Written by Sir John Suckling. And published by a Friend to Perpetuate his memory." In the preface "To the Reader," Suckling's unidentified friend asserts that "it had been a prejudice to Posterity they should have slept longer, and an injury to his own ashes"; furthermore, the compiler asserts, those individuals who knew Suckling in life will "honour these posthume Idea's of their friend."[15]

One finds the same type of rhetoric in the presentation of women's volumes of prose and verse. The title page of Lady Gethin's *Misery's Virtue's Whet-stone*, subtitled *Reliquiae Gethinianae or Some Remains of the Most*

Ingenious and Excellent Lady Grace Gethin (1699), states that it was "published by her nearest relationships to preserve her memory."[16] In the dedication of the volume to her father, Sir George Norton, the compiler "J. M." declares that the contents will "be look'd upon as an in estimable Treasure by all her Friends; and as even the Filings of Gold are precious, and carefully preserved, so will these *Golden Remains* of the most Excellent Lady, be carefully laid up and valued as they deserve by all that knew her." The compiler concludes that Gethin "can never die so long as this monument of her Vertue, Wit, and Ingenuity shall continue, which I prophecy, shall out-live the Marble Monument" erected in Westminster Abbey by her grieving parents.

On a less elaborate level, the posthumous edition of the Quaker Mary Mollineaux's verse entitled *Fruits of Retirement* (1702), opens with testimonials from her cousin Frances Owen, her friend Tryall Ryder, and her husband concerning the author's pious virtues and secular accomplishments in classical languages and medicine. Ryder notes in his preface that Mollineaux sought "to communicate the Exercise of peculiar Gifts amongst her near Friends and Acquaintances"; he concludes, however, that since her death, "I think it would be ungrateful to her Memory, and also a wronging of others, to keep such Worthy Things unpublished."[17]

In short, volumes such as Freeman's, Lovelace's, Suckling's, Gethin's, and Mollineaux's are contained within a discursive framework where the printed text stands as a physical memorial monument to the author, erected by his or her friends and justly representing his or her literary merits. It is interesting that the prefaces and dedication frequently stress the fidelity of the printed text to the departed author's living voice, that those who knew the author in life will "recognize" the printed text as authentic through its characteristic "voice." It is also significant to note that the prefaces typically address the volumes specifically towards an audience of family and friends, who are best able to appreciate this fidelity of the printed text to the manuscript and the living author, and for whom it will serve as a lasting monument to a departed friend, regardless of the sex of the author. One could say that the posthumous editions which frame their dedications of the printed texts so specifically to those with whom the living author had had relationships, whether familial, friendly, or intellectual, continue a type of selected, social readership found in coterie or social literary practices. The posthumous text, therefore, could be seen as an attempt to continue the "living" voice of the author's manuscript writings rather than as an indication of any lack of

"self-worth" by the writer, who apparently did not need print publication
to define him- or herself as author.

Obviously, it is also of particular interest to note for this audience
that the sex of the author does not appear to have barred or dimin-
ished the value of the posthumous volume as a memorial marker nor
distinguished its contents as being more or less "literary" or any less the
product of an "author" as such. Indeed, it is explicitly stated that the
posthumously printed text, through mimicking the manuscript voice of
the living woman, enables the reader to appreciate the quality of the
woman writer's virtues, intellectual as well as spiritual. The very designation of such volumes as "reliques" and "remains" suggests to us that
they were conceptually contained in discourse not as a "posthumous"
act – defined as an event occurring after the death of the figurative
"father" – but instead a continuation of that presence which survives
destruction, that matter which the living are permitted still to embrace.
Although I am here adopting a different perspective than that used by
Wendy Wall in her study of authorship and publication in earlier periods,
it is clear that as she premises for earlier Renaissance texts "when writers,
publishers, and printers adapted material for the press, they simultaneously activated an intertwined social, textual, and sexual politics and
promoted a particular concept of literary authority."[18] What the posthumous editions of texts by women in the latter part of the seventeenth and
first part of the eighteenth centuries call into question is what, more precisely, is the nature of the literary authority so summoned and whether
Wall's observation that "it is commonplace to observe that the author
and the subject are male" was still true for the later part of that century.
These posthumous transformations of women's texts by their relatives
also invite us to rethink whether what Wall sees as being a characteris-
tically Renaissance gender coding of literary authority expressed in the
act of printing manuscript materials did indeed result in the "developing
concept of authorship [as] masculine" (4).

Finally for our consideration, we have the posthumous publication
of a varied assortment of papers connected with a single author, but
not necessarily solely by that author. In short, in such volumes we are
presented not with a single voice, but instead with a network of literary
conversations, whose dynamics are suspended eternally in print, like our
flies in amber. This type of composite volume has long proved the bane
of bibliographers given the difficulties in attribution it typically brings,
but if one lets go of the issue of proprietary authorship, such volumes
may reveal further examples of women's participation in literary culture.

Again, to start with a familiar example of this type of posthumous work in the male canon of seventeenth-century literature, we can examine the presentation of John Cleveland's writings in the 1659 posthumous edition. The title page suggests some of the issues: *J. Cleaveland* [sic] *Revived: Poems, Orations, and Epistles, and other of his Genuine Incomparable Pieces, never before publisht. With some other Exquisite Remains of the most eminent Wits of both the Universities that were his Contemporaries.*[19] The preface addressed "to the Discerning Reader" is signed by "E. Williamson"; it opens "Worthy Friend" and reveals that because of the "intimacie I had with Mr. Cleaveland, before and since these civill wars," Williamson was able to gather together the contents of the volume. This proved a difficult task because "out of the love he had to pleasure his friends, [Cleveland was often] unfurnisht with his own manuscripts, as I have heard him say often, he was not so happy, as to have any considerable collection of his own papers, they being despersed amongst his friends." Although individual pieces had been printed during Cleveland's lifetime without his supervision, Williamson declares that "out of a true affection to my deceased friend," he decided to publish this posthumous volume, "to prevent surreptitious Editions [and] . . . that by erecting this Pyramide of Honour, I might oblige posterity to perpetuate their memories."

Of interest here is that in the process of collecting the dispersed manuscripts from Cleveland's friends, Williamson managed also to collect poems by them, too, and thus Cleveland's friends' pieces came to be "intermixed" in the collection. Once again, it is significant for us that the compiler is sure that "the world cannot be so far mistaken in his Genuine Muse, as not to discern his pieces from any of the other Poems." Again, the voice of authorial authenticity is assumed to shine from the posthumous printed text, regardless of the presence of verse by those with whom Cleveland had so generously shared his verse; it is not felt inappropriate or a diminution that the verse of Cleveland's friends accompany his into print.

Perhaps the most interesting two examples of this type of posthumous editions by women are those of Anne Killigrew and Mary Monck. Anne Killigrew served as a Maid of Honour to Mary of Modena at the same time as Anne Finch and Sarah Jennings; the writer of the entry for her in Todd's *Dictionary of British and American Women Writers* speculates that Killigrew's work "takes its cue from her life at court."[20] After her death at age 25 from small pox, her father had published in 1686 a small volume entitled *Poems by Mrs. Anne Killigrew.* This collection is undoubtedly much more famous for its inclusion of a poem not by her, but about her;

as Richard Morton, who wrote the introduction to the 1967 facsimile edition of Killigrew's poems to which all subsequent accounts of this text appear heavily indebted, observes, "her book of verses is known essentially because of John Dryden's Commendatory Ode."[21] The most extended account of the contents of the volume by Ann Killigrew rather than by Dryden is found in a chapter by Ann Messenger: "it is easy to dismiss Anne Killigrew's poetry as insignificant," Messenger opens ominously, but Messenger feels that Killigrew's poetic talents, especially the quality of "wit" in her work, demand respect separate from the nature of the praise by Dryden.[22]

In her analysis of the poetic qualities or lack thereof in Killigrew's verse, Messenger makes the interesting observation that the volume itself was a "slim one hundred pages long, fifteen pages of which are said to have been written by someone else" (14). Messenger observes that the final three poems in the volume are prefaced by a note, placed there Messenger imagines by either Killigrew's father or her publisher, declaring that "these Three following ODES being found among Mrs. Killigrews Papers, I was willing to Print though none of hers." In Messenger's view, however, the "tone, and a number of close verbal echoes all suggest that these poems came from the same hand as the rest of the volume" (29). These three poems contain two directly praising "Eudora," a woman whose charms rescued the speaker from tormented love of "Chloris" and whose "soft and gentle Motions" are music itself; she also figures in an ode "Upon a Little Lady Under the Discipline of an Excellent Person," who is able to transform a child's tears to music.

I am afraid I find Messenger's stylistic analysis of these three poems unconvincing. I do so in part for her summary of their contents as "a tragic love for a woman and the poet's rescue from despair by another woman, who in turn practiced flagellation on yet another woman," and her conclusion that "if these poems are indeed autobiographical, one can easily see why a discreet father or cautious publisher would choose to disavow them" (29). But I do so also because of Messenger's dismissal of Killigrew's participation in manuscript verse exchange which is clearly evident in the remaining contents of the volume.

What is the evidence that Killigrew's texts, like Cleveland's, may have been mingled with those of her literary associates in this posthumous volume? Messenger herself points to the "autobiographical nature" of poems such as "Upon the Saying that my Verses were made by another." In this poem, Killigrew laments that "Embolden thus, to Fame I did commit, / (By some few hands) my most Unlucky Wit /... / My Laurels thus an Others Brow adorn'd, / My Numbers they Admir'd, but Me they scorn'd" (45–46). Interestingly, Killigrew states that it was other women reading her verse who denied Killigrew her place as author: in comparing her fate to Katherine Philips, Killigrew observes that "Nor did her Sex at all obstruct her Fame, / But higher 'mong the Stars it fixt her Name." It would be interesting to speculate which other Maids of Honour might be her readers and which might have claimed credit for Killigrew's verses.

Further evidence for Killigrew's participation in a literary network of versifiers comes in the poem "To my Lord Colrane, in Answer to his Complemental Verses sent me under the Name of Cleanor." The title certainly gives a clear occasion for this social poem, where Killigrew credits reading Colrane's verses with awakening her own "slumbering" muse. Morton identifies "Cleanor" as Henry Hare, second Baron Coleraine (1636–1708) whom he describes as "a distinguished antiquary," a view shared by the editors of *Kissing the Rod*, which adds that he resided in Tottenham, Middlesex (*Rod*, 308). Morton notes that an edition of the *Poems* with his bookplate in it dated 1702 is held by the University of Michigan library; this is particularly interesting because the Folger Shakespeare Library also holds a copy of the volume with the bookplate of "The Right Honble Henry Lord Colerane of Colerane in ye Kingdom of Ireland 1702."[23] This volume contains handwritten corrections and emendations of two of the poems which are not those included on the printed errata sheet for the volume: in "Upon the Saying that my Verses were made by another," someone has helpfully inserted a missing "c" in the word "struk," but in "Extempory Counsel given to a Young Gallant in a Frolick," the unknown hand has crossed through the word "Quarrels" in line two and substituted the phrase "but broils." The poems which immediately follow this one in the volume are the "Eudora" odes which were "found among Mrs. Killigrew's papers." Obviously, it is tempting to speculate that Coleraine was correcting the posthumous copy based on his own manuscript texts which he and Killigrew exchanged; whether Coleraine is the author of the "Eudora" odes I leave to someone else to ponder.

We find the same intertwining of texts in my final example, the posthumous edition of Mary Monck's verse entitled after her poetic name, *Marinda. Poems and Translations upon several Occasions* (1716). As with Killigrew's volume, the edition was caused to be printed by her father. Richard Molesworth, the first Viscount Molesworth, and in 1714 Privy Councillor for Ireland, prefaced the volume with an extremely long dedication to Princess Carolina, Princess of Wales, of the evils of flattery in dedications. Eventually, he arrives at "those Poems which give me the Opportunity of Addressing myself to your Royal Highness," which he characterizes as "the Product of the leisure Hours of a Young Gentlewoman lately Dead, who in a Remote Country Retirement, without any Assistance but that of a good Library, and without omitting the daily Care due to a large Family, . . . perfectly acquired the several Languages here made use of."[24] Molesworth concludes in the fashion we have already seen associated with posthumous editions which were intended as a memorial: "I cannot do a greater Honour to her Memory, than by Consecrating her labours or rather her Diversion to your Royal Highness."

Interestingly for us, Molesworth says that he is transmitting the materials to print "as we found most of them in her Scrittore after her Death, written with her own Hand, little expecting, and as little desiring the Publick shou'd have any Opportunity either of Applauding or Condemning them." As I have noted elsewhere, the contents of this volume, as with that of the Cleveland and Killigrew volumes, intermingle poems by Monck with poems to her: her entry in Todd's *Dictionary* calculates that of the sixty-three poems in the volume, eleven of them are directly addressed to "Marinda" (220). Of particular interest in delineating Monck's participation in a literary network are pieces such "Upon an Impromptu of Marinda's, in answer to a Copy of Verses" (94) and a series of epistles to Marinda.

In one of these epistles, the author self-consciously reflects on the nature and goals of being a poet and in the process gives a glimpse of literary culture of which Mary Monck was a part. "A Just Applause, and an Immortal Name/Is the true Object of the Poet's Aim" (85); in search of Fame, however, the poet must subject his or her verse to the readings of others. If one is a conceited young poet, the writer warns, one is liable to be crushed when one's verses do not meet the anticipated, imagined reception. The author of the epistle offers advice on how one can tell "false Applause" from true: "Be sure you press the Circle to declare/Their Sentiments, ev'n where they doubt you Err." Interestingly, the "circle" of evaluators are depicted not as reading the poet's work, but instead listening to him or her perform it.

> Trust less to their Tongue, than to their Eyes.
> Here wide glaz'd Opticks openly betray
> The forc'd Attention which your Hearer pay,
> Who strive at last by all ill-tim'd Applause
> To make up for a long suspicious Pause.

The poem concludes that the ideal reader of a poet's work or hearer of his verse is Marinda:

> *Marinda*, let your steady Judgment guide
> Your Poet thro' those Dangers, steer him wide
> Of all these Shelves, let your unerring Taste
> Secure him from the Malice of the Rest.

Although Mary Monck is routinely depicted as being an "Irish" author, it is of no small significance that she died from a "languishing sickness" in Bath. One of the poems by her not printed by her father was a set of verses which the eighteenth-century chronicler of learned ladies, George Ballard, records as having been written on her deathbed in Bath and sent to her husband in London.[25] How long she was in Bath during this time may prove of interest to those working on women's participation in manuscript literary culture; as Elizabeth Child discusses in her article, "'To Sing the Town': Women, Place, and Print Culture in Eighteenth-Century Bath," Bath was the locus of provincial literary activity. While Child's focus is on women publishing commercially in Bath over the course of the eighteenth century, the article is nevertheless illuminating in reminding us that in terms of literary history, "Bath was a particularly important site by sheer dint of the number of women authors who lived, wrote, and published there."[26]

The posthumous volume of Mary Monck's verse, as with Killigrew's, highlights several issues for those interested in the manuscript practices of early modern women. For example, in the same fashion that we have traditionally privileged the printed text over the manuscript one, we have too little sense at present about literary life outside London. Volumes such as Monck's not only confirm the possibility of conducting a literary life worth a monument while in a remote provincial retirement, but also remind us to consider the site of the compositions, whether in Ireland or in Bath, and to start perhaps to look further for women's participation in manuscript culture outside the expected venues.

Volumes such as these, too, remind us to consider the ways in which manuscript texts were circulated and perhaps also performed, whether among Maids of Honor or family members. They also remind us to consider the circumstances surrounding their preservation as well as their mode of presentation. In short, the contents of posthumous volumes, like the little flies in amber, offer more than a literary curiosity to those interested in early modern women writers; they offer a new way in which an artifact from the past can speak to the present and a possible means for reconstructing and reanimating a long-since deceased literary landscape.

NOTES

1 George O. Poinar, Jr., *Life in Amber* (Stanford: Stanford University Press, 1992), 3.
2 Quoted in David A. Grimaldi, *Amber: Window to the Past* (New York: American Museum of Natural History, 1996), 126.
3 *The Correspondence of John Locke*, ed. E. S. de Beer, 8 vols. (Oxford: Clarendon Press), 2:762.
4 Penelope Rowlands, "A Posthumous Recovery," *Art News* 95 (1996), 40.
5 Judd Tully, "The Kahlo Cult," *Art News* 93 (1994), 126–33.
6 Angeline Goreau, *The Whole Duty of a Woman: Female Writers in Seventeenth-Century England* (Garden City: Dial Press, 1985), 15.
7 Elaine Hobby, *Virtue of Necessity: English Women's Writing 1649–1688* (Ann Arbor: University of Michigan Press, 1989), 6. Such a position privileging print as a literary medium still conventionally shaped 1990s scholarship, for example in Charlotte F. Otten's assertion that "a woman going into print was a challenge to the theological and medical grounds that supported the inferiority of women – an inferiority that demanded silence," *English Women's Voices, 1540–1700* (Miami: Florida International University Press, 1992), 1.
8 Patricia Crawford, "Women's Published Writings 1600–1700," *Women in English Society 1500–1800*, ed. Mary Prior (London: Methuen, 1985), 231.
9 Peter Hay-Halpert, "Who says it's a Man Ray?" *American Photographer* 6 (1995), 22–24.
10 *Kissing the Rod: an Anthology of Seventeenth Century Women's Verse*, eds. Germaine Greer *et al.* (London: Virago Press, 1988), 1.
11 "Moore Worms for the Learned Mr. Curll, Bookseller," quoted in Ralph Straus, *The Unspeakeable Curll* (London: Chapman and Hall, 1927), 59.
12 Lady Sarah Freeman, "Preface" to *The Golden Remains of Sir George Freeman* (London: 1682).
13 Halkett MSS, The National Library of Scotland, MS 6495, fol. ii.
14 S. C., *The Life of the Lady Halket* [sic] (Edinburgh, 1701), 59.
15 "To the Reader" in Sir John Suckling, *Fragmenta Aurea. A Collection of all the Incomparable Peeces Written by Sir John Suckling* (London: 1646).
16 Title page, Lady Gethin, *Misery's Virtue's Whet-stone* (London: 1699).
17 Mary Mollineaux, *Fruits of Retirement* (London, 1702), sig. A7v.
18 Wendy Wall, *The Imprint of Gender: Authorship and Publication in the English Renaissance* (Ithaca: Cornell University Press, 1993), 4.
19 *J. Cleaveland* [sic] *Revived* (London: 1659).
20 "Anne Killigrew," in *A Dictionary of British and American Women Writers 1660–1800*, ed. Janet Todd (London: Methuen, 1987), 184–85; see also Killigrew's entry in *The Feminist Companion to Literature in English*, eds. Virginia Blain,

Isobel Grundy, and Patricia Clements (New Haven: Yale University Press, 1990), 610.

21 Richard Morton, "Introduction," *Poems by Mrs. Anne Killigrew*, 1686 (Gainesville: Scholar's Facsimiles & Reprints, 1967), v.

22 Ann Messenger, *His and Hers: Essays in Restoration and Eighteenth-Century Literature* (Lexington: University Press of Kentucky, 1986), 14.

23 Folger Library Shelfmark K442.

24 Mary Monck, *Marinda* (London: 1716), "Dedication."

25 George Ballard, *Memoirs of Several Ladies* (London: 1752), rpt. edn. (Detroit: Wayne State University Press, 1985), 363.

26 Elizabeth Child, "'To Sing the Town': Women, Place and Print Culture in Eighteenth-Century Bath," *Studies in Eighteenth-Century Culture* 28 (1999), 157.

CHAPTER 7

Jane Barker's Jacobite writings[1]

Leigh A. Eicke

In Jane Barker's *A Patch-Work Screen for the Ladies* (1723), one character conveys a secret letter to another by placing the letter inside the lining of a "curious fine Purse" (av).[2] Both the purse and the manuscript, "writ on fine Paper and in a small Character," seem an apt figure for Barker's own *Patch-Work Screen* and its 1726 sequel, *The Lining of the Patch-Work Screen*. Like the embroidered purse, these books evoke a culture in which secret manuscripts are passed covertly from writer to knowing reader; like the purse, the books also signify the earning power of print. Indeed, *The Patch-Work Screen* and *The Lining* embody Barker's astute manipulation of both manuscript and print conventions at a time when print carried certain liabilities: for Barker the Jacobite, print publication was politically dangerous; for Barker the woman, print publication still carried a social stigma.[3] I will argue that Barker ameliorates the stigma of print and encodes Jacobite messages by infusing into her printed works practices associated with the production and circulation of manuscripts. By composing her books as compendia of manuscripts, by presenting herself as a manuscript author and representing the processes of manuscript exchange, and by including in her printed works poems from her own manuscripts, Barker brings her experience as a manuscript author to all her subsequent work. As printed texts that embody manuscript culture, by which I mean those practices of authorship, composition, circulation, and collection used when manuscripts served as the primary means of literary and political communication, *A Patch-Work Screen* and *The Lining* are particularly vivid in marking the moment of transition from manuscript to print.

Recent critical attention both to Barker's work and to manuscript circulation makes it possible to recognize the intimate connection between her political beliefs and her literary career, and to elucidate the connections among the diverse materials that compose her "patch-work screen." Although manuscript culture has been studied extensively by scholars such as Harold Love, Arthur Marotti, and Margaret Ezell, there has not been sufficient attention to the interaction of manuscript culture with print culture in the transitional years from the late seventeenth century to the middle of the eighteenth century.[4] Barker's contemporaries Aphra Behn, Elizabeth Singer Rowe, and Anne Finch also published in both manuscript and print, but Barker is unusual in blending the two forms. This manuscript link permits Barker to present herself as a scribal author, hence a gentlewoman writer, rather than as a print author, a common hack. Moreover, Barker's use of manuscripts in her novels intensifies the novels' political import, since Barker associates scribal publication with Royalist and, after 1688, Jacobite beliefs. Strongly linking these novels to scribal culture thus allows Barker at once to use and to critique print publication as she advocates the Jacobite cause.

Barker's manuscripts already reveal her understanding of the systems and strategies of scribal publication that she later employs in her novels. An astute publisher as a manuscript author, she controls reception, limits circulation, and revises poems for different audiences. Barker developed this expertise in the late seventeenth century, when she was the center of a minor poetic coterie involving students at Cambridge, one of whom was her relative.[5] Participation in this group became the foundation for the fictional relationships she creates, and this group arranged (possibly without her permission) the first printing of her work, which composed the first half of a collaborative miscellany, *Poetical Recreations* (1687).[6]

Working from this early scribal background, Barker produced two highly political and formally accomplished poetic manuscripts. The first, "A Collection of Poems Refering to the times; since the Kings Accession to the Crown" (1700/01), contains Jacobite poetry dedicated to the Prince of Wales, James Francis Edward Stuart.[7] This manuscript includes prefatory epistles to the prince and to "the Reader," a table of contents, and marginal notes, and its lettering is large, legible, and detached rather than cursive, signifying formality. Barker states that a copy of the manuscript was presented to the Prince of Wales, and its appearance and apparatus make it suitable for presentation to the prince and for circulation among the Jacobite exiles residing at St. Germain.[8]

Barker's second poetic manuscript invites a more general audience than does "Poems Refering to the times." This manuscript, "Poems on several occasions in three parts" (c. 1704), contains revised versions of all the poems from both "Poems Refering to the times" and *Poetical Recreations*.[9] In the prefatory matter to "Poems on several occasions," Barker addresses neither individuals nor specific groups, but her notes and prefaces provide information suitable for an audience unacquainted with details of her life and career. For neither manuscript is a historical audience actually known, but she addresses or imagines one, whether a general contemporary audience or an audience of posterity. The volume presents and corrects all of Barker's poetic work to that time, and Barker's notes imply faithfulness to an original and reject compromises to suit specific audiences, suggesting a summative or historical purpose.[10]

In the case of Barker's most overtly Jacobite poems, manuscript publication allowed her not only to control circulation but to tailor copies for different audiences. One such poem reveals with particular clarity Barker's use of these manuscript capabilities. "Fidelia walking the Lady Abess comes to her" appears in both "Poems Refering to the times" and "Poems on several occasions" and was never printed. In the poem, Fidelia learns that the Jacobite military campaign has failed in Ireland and she therefore questions providence and the justness of religion. The Abbess explains that Heaven is always just and good, though sometimes hard to understand, and she suggests that the Stuarts and their supporters are being punished for other, earlier crimes. The poem seems to have existed in four distinct versions. First, what Barker terms the "original" poem, now lost, contained lines that she later suspected a Catholic Jacobite audience would dislike. In the first scribally published version, in "Poems Refering to the times," she removed these objectionable lines. Later, in "Poems on several occasions," Barker reinserted lines from "the original," but on the same manuscript page, she also revises these reinserted lines by sewing a revision over the first reinsertion, literally tailoring the manuscript.[11] In the third and fourth versions of the poem, transcribed in "Poems on several occasions," all but the reinserted lines are in what Kathryn King has identified as the hand of Barker's cousin William Connock; the additional lines are in Barker's hand.[12] A footnote, also in Barker's hand, explains the change she has stitched into the "Poems on several occasions": "note these athestical lines were not given to the Prince, but being in the original, they are here incerted" (fol. 57r). These restored and revised "athestical" lines, written on the stitched piece of paper, suggest that since God does not defend the Catholic faith, Catholics are lulled into a stupor:

> When Providence wants will or power to grant
> Our want of merit must supply that want
> Thus Providence cheats fooll, and fooll the wise
> Lulling us into stupid letergies,
> Till worthless fools the worthiest men dispise.
>
> (fol. 57r)

This revision suggests that Barker prepared the two manuscripts for different purposes, and she addressed the poems to the different expectations of her audiences. The exiled Jacobite audience of "Poems Refering to the times" expected loyal, orthodox poetry. Meant for the prince and court circle, and perhaps a request for patronage, "Poems Refering to the times" needed to meet this audience's sense of propriety. The sentiment in the lines quoted above certainly might have been inappropriate for the prince, then a child of twelve, and they also could have offended the devout. Less controversial was the second state of the poem in which Fidelia merely questions the inaction of Providence instead of accusing Providence of wrongdoing (fol. 52r). Barker's revisions of "Fidelia walking" for different audiences reveals her sophisticated understanding of scribal publication, and the stitches connecting the correction to the page remind us that the production of a manuscript was a material project, much like the production of a patch-work screen.

Most importantly, Barker's choice to publish "Poems Refering to the times" scribally rather than printing it intensifies the political character of this collection, since several aspects of manuscript publication made it an especially appropriate vehicle for these poems. Although manuscript circulation was used in early modern Britain for a wide range of political and not-so-political writings, when a political group was proscribed, scribal publication became the method of choice both because the personal connection a handwritten text suggests would have strengthened community ties, and though some inflammatory Jacobite materials were printed, it was highly dangerous to do so. The poems' uncompromising Jacobitism would suit a manuscript form because circulation could be better controlled. Moreover, a carefully prepared manuscript given at the New Year, as Barker states this collection was, evokes the tradition of the New Year's gift-exchange, which Jane Donawerth argues made it easier for women to publish their poetry.[13] Recalling an older political and social order, this monarchical ritual that flourished under the Tudors and Stuarts would have appealed to Jacobites, and by observing this ritual, Barker associates herself with this older aristocratic culture.

That both manuscripts were produced after *Poetical Recreations* also confirms that Barker preferred scribal publication for certain works: reversing the modern trajectory of publishing, Barker returned to manuscript publication after publishing in print form. Barker's manuscripts also skillfully employ features characteristic of print culture, such as a table of contents, prefaces, and large-size significant words analogous to italics in a printed text. This skilled use of print conventions not only further demonstrates a knowledge of manuscript and print publication strategies, but also confirms that for Barker, manuscript publication was a conscious choice. Many of Barker's female contemporaries felt similarly, according to Margaret Ezell: "women's participation in such practices is not so much a mark of 'modesty' as conservatism, the preference for the older form of literary transmission which left control of the text in the author's hands rather than signing it over to the bookseller."[14] Scribal publication also may have offered a stronger connection to Barker's model author, Katherine Philips, who was well-known for her manuscript publication and her resistance to appearing in print. For Barker, manuscript publishing, the gift-exchange tradition, Catholicism and adherence to the Stuart family all reflected a preference for older forms, an older culture. Scribal publication, in short, allowed Barker to exploit both the protective and the community-building aspects of manuscript and the visual conventions of print.

Conversely, in Barker's *Patch-Work* novels, the notable features of Barker's manuscript publications – their marked Jacobite nature, their awareness of audience, and their astute manipulation of textual appearance and apparatus – blend with characteristics of the novel to link the print world to the manuscript world. *A Patch-Work Screen for the Ladies* reveals its ties to scribal culture through its overt descriptions of manuscript exchange, its metaphor of manuscripts as patch-work, its intertextuality with Barker's own scribally published poems, and finally through the content and language of the individual patches, which mingle Galesia's story with short stories, recipes, poems, and moral observations. The patch-work metaphor enters the story when the Lady asks if Galesia would stay with her for a time and help her make a screen. Galesia offers fabric from her luggage to make the screen, but when her luggage arrives, it contains only: "Pieces of Romances, Poems, Love-Letters, and the like: At which the good Lady smil'd, saying, She would not have her Fancy balk'd, and therefore resolved to have these ranged and mixed in due Order, and thereof compose a SCREEN" (a5v). The materials that compose the screen, Galesia's literary manuscripts, range from "a Piece of a *Farce*" (1) to odes, letters, satires, ballads, and a prophecy, to the "*Receipt* for *Welsh* Flummery, Made at the Castle of *Montgomery*" (96). This wide range of manuscripts together with Galesia's oral stories combine to form a textually and politically significant book.

Galesia's manuscripts provide the occasion for the screen, but manuscripts written by others also crop up throughout the book, appearing in the preface, in the characters' tales from the inset stories, and in the frame narrative itself. This ubiquity of references to manuscripts within the text suggests Barker's desire to announce a connection to manuscripts and to the world of scribal publication. Barker evokes manuscript culture early in her preface when she fancifully describes her print persona's fall from an overwrought metaphor into a "joyful Throng" of patch-workers who upon "finding some Manuscript *Ballads* in my Pocket, rejected me as one of that Race of Mortals who live on a certain barren Mountain 'til they are turn'd into *Camelions*; so I was forc'd to get away, every one hunching and pushing me, with Scorn and Derision" (vi–vii). These ballad manuscripts are not identified – they may be Barker's own works-in-progress, or manuscript copies of works by others. It seems unlikely that the crowd would reject her simply for carrying or even for writing manuscripts; rather, it seems more likely that the content of the manuscripts offended the crowd.[15] The description of the crowd as working to compose a "*New Creation*, where all Sorts of People were to be *Happy*" suggests republicanism, and the term "Camelion," often applied to those who changed religion or party, makes the rejection politically charged. Of course, if this print persona Barker carried manuscript poems in the voice of Fidelia, the crowd could have rejected her as a Jacobite. In this fable of authorship, politics, and reception, Barker at once identifies her print persona with manuscripts and gives manuscripts a political weight.

Once the patch-work screen is completed, the book concludes with a climactic description of scribal publication. To comfort Galesia's sorrow on her mother's death, the Lady promises to "shew you a Poem that was presented me on New-Year's Day last, by an Excellent Hand, . . . Which, . . . I question not, but will give you as much Pleasure and Consolation, as it has frequently done me" (131). The Lady calls attention to the material manuscript when she praises the "Excellent Hand," which might refer either to the author of the poem or to its handwriting. In this case as in others, the manuscript is specifically noted and described, and it is part of daily life, but it reaches a wider audience when the creator or recipient shares it. The Lady owns a copy of a text she did not author, and she shares this copy with others, who in turn are able to make copies for themselves. This case and others in the book solidly fit the system of scribal practice Harold Love describes as "user publication."[16] The straightforward and detailed descriptions of characters circulating manuscripts suggest that Barker wants to underscore society's continued reliance on scribal publication in everyday use, as well as in literary endeavors.

The manuscripts that compose the screen provide a rich description of different kinds of scribally circulated materials and their social use. The screen as an artifact both conceals and reveals; it shields from a too-hot fire or displays the handiwork of its maker. Similarly, Galesia's screen metaphorically both hides and displays the political concepts in the text. It protects by surrounding politics with stories to interest other audiences, and it displays by using key words and phrases to signal a political stance to the partisan reader. The screen is also a shared project: although nearly all of the material for the screen is written by Galesia, the Lady draws out her confidences, selects and places the patches in the screen, acting the role of manuscript collector. The Lady takes this role seriously, rejecting Galesia's farce and critiquing Galesia's stories and poems: "a Landskip in a Screen, is very agreeable" (7) and "these melancholy *dark Patches*, set off the light Colours; making the Mixture the more agreeable" (21). Throughout the book, Galesia also constantly addresses the Lady directly, reminding the reader that a conversation and communal creation are occurring. This interaction between Galesia and the Lady evokes a history of women's scribal publication. Most manuscript books made by women include recipes for food and medicines and practical information for household management, and so does *A Patch-Work Screen*. Its three recipes and its medical descriptions suggest that the needlework of Galesia and the Lady reflects the creation of a similar commonplace or recipe book. This use of needlework as a metaphor for women's writing was not new in Barker, as Kathryn King has observed,[17] but in Barker's blend of manuscript, romance, and novel, the stitching of the screen resembles the composition of the commonplace book, making a clearer link between this printed text and its manuscript forbears.

The poems in *A Patch-Work Screen* further relate this printed text to its manuscript antecedents. Most of the poems originally appeared in *Poetical Recreations*. The revised and reprinted poems thus strongly link this printed text not only to the earlier printed text (itself an artifact of the historical coterie), but also to part three of "Poems on several occasions," which contains corrected versions of the same poems. In *A Patch-Work Screen*, all of the poems are identified as manuscripts, and Galesia recounts the history of these poetic manuscripts – how they came to be and what caused her to write the poems. In most cases modern critics must recreate the story of a collection's origin, but Barker has provided such a story in her fiction. Of course, as Kathryn King and Jeslyn Medoff remind us, Galesia's story *is* a story, not a simple autobiography of Jane Barker, and Galesia's story of her manuscript is that of a *manuscript* author; Galesia does not tell the story of how *Bosvil and Galesia* came to be printed, nor of how her manuscript poems became part of a printed miscellany. Rather, as Galesia and the Lady compose the screen, Galesia's poems and narration place the screen not in the grubby and common print marketplace but in the leisured and restricted world of scribal circulation.

Since Galesia's manuscripts are, with few exceptions, Jane Barker's own acknowledged manuscripts, Barker provides through Galesia's story a fictional account of a manuscript author's experience. Galesia describes the context of her poems, and in one case, presents an additional manuscript to explain a poem. She recounts receiving a letter from her Cambridge friends regarding her "*Ballad.* By Way of *Dialogue* between Two *Shepherd-Boys.*" The letter describes how one of them set her ballad to a tune, and they sang it, which disturbed the proctor, but "he finding no Female amongst us, drank the innocent Author's Health, and departed" (31). Including such an account from Galesia, along with the letter from her Cambridge friends, gives a history of the manuscripts while introducing the kind of realistic detail characteristic of the novel. This blend of manuscript poems with fiction hybridizes the form, allowing Barker to highlight a manuscript persona while enjoying the currency of print.

Barker also combines manuscript poetry with fiction to present her Jacobite politics indirectly, through detailed descriptions of the individual poetic "patches." One patch in particular draws together Galesia's personal history and her politics through the Lady's description of its manuscript form. The patch consists of a love poem and a religious poem on opposite sides of one sheet of paper; the love poem beginning "But what does most of all my Spirit grieve" (130), and on the reverse, "*On the* Difficulties *of* RELIGION"(127), which is a reduced version of "Fidelia arguing with her self on the difficulties of finding the true Religion," from "Poems Refering to the times" (fol. 21r). The Lady observes that the poems "seemed, by the Tenor of them, as well as by the Writing, to be the product of the same melancholy Frame of Mind with the former, as well as to be written at the same Time" (129). The Lady notes the similarity of writing, which could indicate the color of the ink and condition of the pen as well as the style of handwriting, further linking the two poems. Her interpretation of the manuscript's physical characteristics leads her to read for similarity of content. And the poems do share a sense of melancholy questioning: one speaker questions which religion is true, and the other speaker questions whether her love for Fidelius is just, and whether his love is confirming her in goodness or leading her astray. Both poems raise the issues of loyalty and legitimacy, and the difficulties of determining what is true. Though these topics were not limited to Jacobites, the revolution of 1688 led many Britons to ask these questions with increased intensity. Since manuscript so often had been the province of political contention, this strong evocation of manuscript publication in a printed work with clear Jacobite associations encourages a political reading.

Political contention clearly appears in the poems in *A Patch-Work Screen* that were drawn from "Poems Refering to the times" and "Poems on several occasions." Indeed, the poems from the profoundly political "Poems Refering to the times" bring a rare note of overt political commentary into the book. The most forceful of several instances occurs when Galesia recalls overhearing a neighbor praise the duke of Monmouth. Monmouth, the illegitimate Protestant son of Charles II, attempted to gain the throne from James II, and for many Jacobites, Monmouth's rebellion prefigured the successful revolution of 1688. This event was first related in the poem "Fidelia alone lamenting her parents lately dead, and her Relations gone into the west against Monmouth" (fol. 11 v) and a portion of the poem appears in *A Patch-Work Screen*, intensifying the description of the neighbor, the supporter of Monmouth's rebellion (120). The passage displays Fidelia's and Galesia's political ideas in contrast to those the moderate persona Jane Barker assumes in the preface, when she mentions various religious and political positions without adopting any herself. Fidelia and Galesia, the manuscript personae, freely express their politics, while the print persona Barker acts as a screen; this Barker both displays and protects these her own Jacobite ideas by presenting them through fictional characters. Though the poems and fictions did not exist as an intertext for most of Barker's contemporary readers, since the vast majority would not have known Barker's manuscript poems, for Barker herself, these differing personae enable her to express her political commitments and ambivalence about print.

Barker also highlights the political in her preface when she explains how to read the patch-work metaphor:

Ladies, in this latter Age, have pleas'd themselves with this sort of Entertainment; for, whenever one sees a Set of Ladies together, their Sentiments are as differently mix'd as the Patches in their Work: To wit, Whigs and Tories, High-Church and Low-Church, Jacobites and Williamites, and many more Distinctions, which they divide and subdivide, 'till at last they make this Dis-union meet in an harmonious Tea-Table Entertainment. This puts me in mind of what I have heard some Philosophers assert, about the Clashing of Atoms, which at last united to compose this glorious Fabrick of the Universe. (v–vi)

Making patch-work – group literary production – brings together people of various opinions. Whigs, Tories, High-Church, and Low-Church meet at the tea-table harmoniously, clash but unite, and they compose the nation both literally and figuratively. The distinction in political sympathies between the politically tolerant Jane Barker persona and the thoroughly Jacobite Galesia may also signal political content to a factional reader. Since Galesia has identified herself as from St. Germain, and therefore as a Jacobite, factional readers could recognize the temperate prefatory persona as a protective mechanism. And later in the preface, she provides this puzzling prophetic remark: "... *they* cou'd not see the *Danger themselves* and *their Posterity might be in, a Thousand Years hence, about I know not what* – But I will inquire against the next Edition; therefore, be sure to buy these *Patches* up quickly, if you intend to know the *Secret*" (viii). The market-savvy Barker's references to a secret, a distant future, danger and posterity all insinuate that should the current edition sell out, a political mystery will be revealed in a future edition. This playful hint both encourages purchasing the book and announces the upcoming political content.

Galesia often refers to Royalist, proto-Jacobite, and Jacobite topics in *A Patch-Work Screen*. Galesia's Catholic and proto-Jacobite sympathies are evident when she wishes that the supporters of the duke of Monmouth, like her neighbor, might have died "in their Infancy, before the Baptismal Water was dry'd off their Face!" (121). More commonly, though, Galesia conveys her political sentiments through praise. Every English writer she praises is a Royalist, and Galesia and others also refer positively to one's duty to the king, here meaning James II or his son, James Francis Edward Stuart, and to Roman Catholicism. For instance, one of the stagecoach passengers highly praises convent life: "that devout and heavenly Way of Living: Such Regularity and Exactitude in their Religious Performances: Such Patience; such Obedience: Such Purity of Manners" (65). Since convents were used regularly as locations for tales of passion and misery, this laudatory description significantly reverses the usual depiction. Praising the Catholic church and its institutions, and honoring individuals who served their exiled king, could strengthen and confirm ties within the hard-pressed Catholic Jacobite community, much as a circulated political manuscript would. Such specific political activism was rare in the early English novel, except in the scandalous roman à clef, which placed critique or slander of major figures in an imaginary setting. Indeed, at a time when few novels were set in a place or time recognizable to contemporaries, and fewer still explicitly critiqued national and international political issues, Barker's here-and-now descriptions and naming of names reflect the more open world of manuscript publication rather than the conventions of the emerging novel. In *A Patch-Work Screen*, at once a novel and a printed version of a manuscript collection, Barker employs some of scribal publication's political license in order to accomplish some of the political work more common in manuscript.

If *A Patch-Work Screen* deliberately bridges manuscript and print, *The Lining of the Patch-Work Screen* shares few of its predecessor's overt ties to manuscript culture, yet it ameliorates the stigma of print and encodes Jacobite messages through indirect references to manuscripts.[18] The opening metaphor, though its use is brief, does serve to link these books and to signal political content to those who found it in *A Patch-Work Screen*. In fact, the political content becomes even more visible, since most of the characters are identified as Jacobites, and the frequent use of a moral or proverb to end a story reinforces the didactic import. *The Lining* includes only one description of scribal publication, and printed books take precedence over manuscripts as a means of communication, though conceptions of manuscript authorship and publication remain. The shift to printed sources is clear: *The Lining* makes fewer intertextual references to Barker's manuscript work but more frequently evokes other print writers. The few poems in *The Lining* are original, appearing in neither of Barker's manuscript collections, and *The Lining* is composed of stories told or read, rather than manuscripts. While these stories reveal a consumption and enjoyment of print, their narrators' elisions and transformations suggest a discomfort with the world of print and its necessarily broadly public nature. Near the end of the book, Galesia's story again becomes central, and her story expresses great anxiety about print publication.

Though the books differ in several ways, they also share an intermingling of manuscript and print. Lacking *A Patch-Work Screen*'s direct association with manuscript, *The Lining* relies more on coded stories to present its message, but print does not usurp the place or status of manuscript publication. Though this book is printed, it criticizes print, and it retains the literary foundation of *A Patch-Work Screen*, structurally resembling a manuscript collection. The collection's inset stories become part of the book in a variety of ways: nine are related orally, four are read from printed sources, two are related orally from printed sources, and one is presented as a manuscript. The only represented manuscript exchange appears when Malhurissa shares with Galesia some verses she copied from another woman's manuscript (166). These manuscript verses, which follow a tale of an evil governess who is burnt as a witch, are highly appropriate to the inset story just told – they describe Saul and the Witch of Endor – and they are not present in Barker's manuscript collections. Since so many of the manuscripts in *A Patch-Work Screen* existed in Barker's manuscripts outside the novel, this use of a manuscript (perhaps from a lost Barker manuscript, from another author's works, or perhaps invented for this tale) in *The Lining* becomes an important and deliberate invocation of manuscript publication.

Manuscripts convey crucial information in the novel, such as when Mr. Goodman shows Galesia the letter he received from Malhurissa's uncle (155). The letter is necessary to save Malhurissa from a miserable fate, so within the context of the story, it testifies to the power of the handwritten word. In a similar case, manuscripts are strongly implied in "The Story of the Portugueze Nun," told by the Lady from St. Germain. The Lady calls attention to the manuscript or print status of the letters: she refuses to speculate on how the nun and her Huguenot lover "climb'd up to an extream Passion, such as her printed Letters demonstrate," but the Lady notes that they exchanged letters "not only those in Print, but divers others" through religious books, ostensibly intended to convert her lover to Catholicism (77–78). The distinction she makes between the printed letters and the divers others (presumably manuscript letters never printed) suggests that the printed letters are incomplete, that the manuscript letters are closer to the truth. The manuscript letters could explain how the nun and her lover reached their passion for each other, or how or whether the nun attempted to convert the lover to Catholicism. Manuscripts in *The Lining* thus retain their power and currency, though their number is smaller and their depiction is less overt.

The opening metaphor of *The Lining* announces this reduced presence of manuscripts, shapes the book's structure and suggests its sequential relationship to *A Patch-Work Screen*. Whereas Galesia and the Lady jointly composed the *Patch-Work Screen*, Jane Barker and Galesia compose *The Lining*: "[in London] it was I found her, and often had her Company, receiving from time to time an account of her Adventures; which I have kept together, in order to make a *Lining* for your *Patch-work Screen*. But these Pieces being much larger than the others, I think we must call it *Pane-work*" (A2v). While the patch-work metaphor calls attention to the material form of the "patches," the lining metaphor frames the "panes" as experiences, "an account of her Adventures," rather than manuscripts. The pane-work primarily consists of stories told or read by Galesia or her friends and acquaintances. Instead of serving as the author of the patches, as in *A Patch-Work Screen*, Galesia assumes the Lady's role and becomes the publisher or collector of the panes in *The Lining*. Whereas the patches represented individual literary manuscripts, the panes include oral tales, printed stories, and moral observations. Much as the compiler of a manuscript commonplace book would transcribe items, sometimes with, sometimes without attribution, combining and editing the items, so does Galesia with these inset stories in *The Lining*.[19] Galesia retells and adapts the items in her collection, selecting and arranging items to advance her Jacobite argument and to negotiate the unwelcome aspects of print.

The Lining contains little poetry, but in key places its prose echoes Barker's manuscript verse. Two thematically similar inset stories in *The Lining* employ language evocative of Barker's highly charged manuscript poetry when they echo a moral from the scribally published "Poems Refering to the times." The moral comes from the poem "A discourse between Englands ill Genius and his Companion," where the Genius and his Companion discuss British and European politics of the 1680's (fol. 21r). The Companion brings up the Covenant – the "She" below – to encourage the Genius in evil:

> As for the *Holy bretheren we know,
> She needs no more but her own face to show,
> For where the Devil leads or drives they go.
>   *the sectarys   (fol. 23r)[20]

This comparison between the Covenant and the Devil may seem like an overstatement, even for a Catholic Jacobite, but within the extraordinarily partisan context of "Poems Refering to the Times" it is scarcely an exaggeration, for in that manuscript volume, Lucifer actively attempts to influence world politics. Similarly, the first related story, "The STORY of **SUCCUBELLA**, Related by MALHURISSA," concludes with a nearly identical moral: "*Needs must, when the Devil drives*" (165). Succubella, as her name suggests, is the evil governess from Malhurissa's story, mentioned above. She tries to lure her pupil into witchcraft, but as they fly to a festive demonic rendezvous, the young woman absentmindedly crosses herself at the stroke of midnight and thus breaks the spell and falls to safety in a monastery. The young woman's internal and habitual Catholicism and the quick thinking of the religious brothers save her from witchcraft and apprehend Succubella before she can escape. This story shares the poem's demonizing of opponents to Catholicism and clearly presents the virtue and efficacy of Catholicism. This story's especially close relationship to manuscript is cemented by *The Lining*'s only overt example of manuscript publication, for it is this story that causes Malhurissa to copy the verses that she shares with Galesia.

The second related story from *The Lining* shares a nearly identical moral, includes a Jacobite story, and overtly discusses the practice of interpretation. *"The Cause of the* MOORS *Overrunning* SPAIN" describes how a Regent, using "many false invented stories," usurps the throne of Spain from his nephew (43).[21] The Queen, mother of the young prince, escapes to the Moors, who agree to help her regain the throne for her son. The usurper soon rapes the daughter of his noble and trusted general which causes the general, now his implacable enemy, to lead a revolt and join with the Moors. The usurper turns in desperation to the Devil's Tower, where he misinterprets a riddling warning written on a gate. Proceeding around the room, "on the Walls they found divers Inscriptions, all importing Warnings, Menaces and Miseries to those that came there. In reading which, they sometimes stopt to consider the Purport and dubious Meanings of these uncouth Writings" (50). The political situation recalls the Jacobite view of the Glorious Revolution, and rape is a common Jacobite metaphor for the unlawful taking of the throne – and Britain – from James II.[22] Just as the usurper's people had failed to interpret his "false invented stories," the usurper himself fails to interpret the warning correctly and so loses his throne. The writings inscribed in the tower resemble manuscript publication in their limited circulation, and the story's concluding proverb, *"Who drives the Devil's Stages, / Deserves the Devil's Wages"* recalls the line from the manuscript poem. Although this is a commonplace expression, Barker uses a version of it in three places to associate her religious and political opponents with the devil. The stories of Succubella and of the Moors overrunning Spain are the most sensational tales in the volume, echoing the quotidian political diabolism of the manuscript devils and transforming it into a print-friendly supernatural.

Though the sometimes sensational inset stories seem to be designed for entertainment rather than instruction, the reflective tone of *The Lining's* opening, the context of the stories, and the repetition of morals and proverbs all convey its didactic nature. *"The Cause of the* MOORS *Overrunning* SPAIN" is one of two principal episodes in *The Lining* that give the reader directions for interpretation. In Annabel Patterson's suggestive readings of early modern printed texts, one key to factional reading comes in the representation of secret cabinets and closets.[23] In *The Lining*, such a key comes in the secrets of the Devil's Tower, especially the simple riddle on the gate. A second short didactic story offers even more particular instructions for reading: the "old story of a Cobler" is partially told, then concludes, "What succeeded between them, matters not; We are to apply the Story to our *Galecia*" (180). Once we apply the story to Galesia, it seems possible to apply it to Barker as well, for Galesia's story discusses the dangers of print. That such instructions appear at all is a sign that these stories lie more completely within the world of print, where an author has much less control over circulation, audience, and reception.

Ironically, after venturing rather far into the world of print, collecting and adapting printed stories, *The Lining of the Patch-Work Screen* ends with a dream evocation of the glories of scribal publication and the stigma of print. Galesia's dream begins as a nightmare and then becomes more pleasant when her good genius takes her to the coronation of Orinda as Queen of Female Writers, where she sits and watches the singing and dancing with pleasure. The Fairy Queen, who presides over the ceremonies, spots Galesia and "whether she was angry to see a Mortal in that Assembly; or that she was excited by Charity, is unknown; but she took a Handful of Gold out of her Pocket, and gave it to one of her Gentlemen waiters, bidding him carry it to that Mortal, and command her away from thence" (177). Galesia wakes from her dream to find a gentleman presenting her with a bag of gold, which she happily accepts. Two interpretations of the Fairy Queen's action are provided, but if the Fairy Queen acted from charity, would she command Galesia away? It seems more likely that Galesia was dismissed because she is a mortal. Galesia is a mortal in the literal sense that she lives and will die, but also in the figurative sense that she is sullied by print and profit. Though Galesia may be a manuscript persona, she is certainly complicit in the print persona Jane Barker's profit from these books, since her writings and history compose the printed *Patch-Work Screen* and *Lining*. Orinda, Katherine Philips, who was Barker's model of a scribal author, did not print her works for money, yet the print persona Jane Barker did. Though the exact reason for the Fairy Queen's command is unclear, this difference in publishing form cannot be overlooked.

The rest of *The Lining* can be read as an extended meditation on the stigma of print, since unlike Orinda, Galesia has allowed the printing of some of her texts and received money for them. If we apply the story of the cobbler and usurer to Galesia, as we are told to do, we know that Galesia cannot be happy with this literary gold. Galesia decides to invest this gold in "the choicest, and nicest of the *Female Vertues*," repeating the question of whether it is acceptable to profit from writing, even the most virtuous kind. It seems difficult to do so: Galesia's factor, whom we can perhaps read as a bookseller, cannot find anyone who wants sincerity, chastity, or humility. Galesia finally succeeds in selling repentance and piety to prostitutes, but she has become discouraged with the city's lack of interest in virtue and hopes for better luck in the country. Galesia's attempt to promote virtue through commerce has been only somewhat successful, as if to underscore that even virtuous and didactic printed texts still carry a stigma. Her cares are removed when the kind Lady from *A Patch-Work Screen*, her companion in manuscript production, invites her to the country again. Galesia's dream is the only story not announced in the table of contents, and it seems appropriate that the aspect of *The Lining* that struggles with the dangers of print should not be advertised in the table, that hallmark of print.[24] Whether Barker felt a stigma of print or simply desired the status of a scribal author, invoking Orinda – widely known for virtue, Royalist politics, and a distaste for print – could only strengthen her position.

The return to the country at the end of *The Lining* offers a resolution to the transitions between manuscript and print in Jane Barker's works. Jacobites increasingly celebrated retreat from public life to the country as hopes for a restoration became fainter. The London location of *The Lining* and the difficulty of selling virtues there reinforces the undesirability of print publication. In the preface, the Jane Barker persona ironically describes the frivolous reasons that might have drawn Galesia there: "some Business of consequence call'd her to *London*, whether Masquerading, or Tossing of Coffee-Grounds, I know not; . . . whatever was the motive, our *Galecia* must needs ramble, like others, to take *London*-Air, when it is most to be distinguished, in the midst of Winter" (A2v). The ironic reference to popular amusements and the jab at London's poor winter air quality mark this Jane Barker as one who knows London but is not overly impressed by it. Once Galesia learned that female virtues were little desired in London, the country offered her hope, and perhaps a return to manuscript culture. Galesia's thought of the country, where her manuscript books were produced and where presumably her patch-work screen still stands in the Lady's country house, was "an inexpressible Joy" to her (201).

The Lining of the Patch-work Screen was Barker's final printed work, and her final known work of any kind.[25] It is possible that Barker was too infirm to write anything else in her final years, but it is tempting to read the conclusion of *The Lining* as a deliberate withdrawal from print publication. It is also tempting to read similarities in Barker's career in print and Galesia's career in merchantry: Galesia wishes to sell humility to the court and persuade prostitutes to repentance and piety; Barker's Jacobites wish to chasten the unlawful court and her Catholics advocate repentance, piety, and virtue to all.

In the end, *A Patch-Work Screen for the Ladies* and *The Lining of the Patch-Work Screen* both celebrate and resist the world of print. The novels retell stories from a range of printed texts, from chapbooks to Behn's works to *The Imitation of Christ*, and they laud the variety of works available in print. Yet the coronation of Orinda, the patch-work structure of both books, and the many references to scribal texts resist a wholesale conversion. While employing the necessarily broad and public nature of print, Barker also uses the oppositional and historical associations of manuscript to alleviate the remaining stigma of print and to present her political message. This case study of Barker's works suggests that examining the interaction of manuscript and print culture in the works of her contemporaries, such as Delarivier Manley or Anne Finch could yield equally productive results. Though the majority of Barker's contemporary writers did not share her politics, others did share her interest in representing manuscript culture. Conditions slowly changed, mitigating the stigma many women writers once felt, and the cause Barker served so faithfully withered and died with the son of her Prince of Wales. Even though Barker's specific concerns no longer occupy public discourse, questions of legitimate government and of women's place in politics remain compelling. And Barker's books still puzzle and fascinate: her poetry and fiction testify to the energy and innovation she brought to a time of great change in literary publishing.

NOTES

1 I would like to thank Susan Lanser, Kathryn King, Vincent Carretta, and William Sherman for commenting on drafts of this essay.
2 Jane Barker, *A Patch-Work Screen for the Ladies; Or Love and Virtue Recommended: In a Collection of Instructive Novels* (London: E. Curll, 1723). *The Lining of the Patch-Work Screen; Designed for the Farther Entertainment of the Ladies* (London: A. Bettesworth, 1726). Three of Barker's works, *A Patch-Work Screen for the Ladies*, *The Lining of the Patch-Work Screen*, and *Love Intrigues: Or, the History of the Amours of Bosvil and Galesia* are now available in a modern paperback edition, *The Galesia Trilogy and Selected Manuscript Poems of Jane Barker*, ed. Carol Shiner Wilson (Oxford: Oxford University Press, 1997). This edition makes Barker available to many new audiences.

3 J. W. Saunders, "The Stigma of Print: a Note on the Social Bases of Tudor Poetry," *Essays in Criticism* 1 (April 1951), 139–64. Saunders's essay concerns an earlier period in literary history than this study, but in many circles, the preference for scribal publication continued far beyond the Tudor era, as Harold Love notes in seventeenth-century women: "The stigma of print bore particularly hard on women writers, as they themselves pointed out," *Scribal Publication in Seventeenth-Century England* (Oxford: Clarendon Press, 1993), 54.

4 Harold Love provides an overview and analysis of seventeenth-century manuscript practices in his *Scribal Publication*. For women's manuscript circulation, see Chapter 3 in Margaret Ezell, *The Patriarch's Wife: Literary Evidence and the History of the Family* (Chapel Hill: University of North Carolina Press, 1987). Other important sources include Arthur Marotti, *Manuscript, Print, and the English Renaissance Lyric* (Ithaca: Cornell, 1995), and J. W. Saunders, "From Manuscript to Print: a Note on the Circulation of poetic MSS in the Sixteenth Century," *Proceedings of the Leeds Philosophical and Literary Society* 6:8 (May 1951), 507–28. Ezell and Love both convincingly demonstrate that manuscript literary activity thrived in late seventeenth-century Britain. Love argues that by the end of Queen Anne's reign, print had become the primary medium for literary and political expression (vi). Barker's texts support Ezell's argument that manuscript publication continued to be vitally important for women writers well into the eighteenth century.

5 Kathryn R. King's "Jane Barker, *Poetical Recreations*, and the Sociable Text," *ELH* 61 (1994), 551–70 provides an extremely valuable analysis of this coterie, its literary production, and the place of such a collection in literary history.

6 The second part contains a miscellany of poems by Barker's friends, her printer, and others. Barker may not have authorized their printing (King, "*Poetical Recreations*," discusses the possible interpretations of Barker's statement that the poems were printed without her permission), and Barker's name appears on the title page and in several poems to her. Pastoral pseudonyms reminiscent of Philips's coterie appear in the collection, primarily as the signatures of the male poets.

7 Jane Barker, "A Collection of Poems Refering to the times; since the Kings accession to the Crown. Occasionally writ according to the circumstance of time and place" (1700/01). British Library Add. MS 21,621.

   Kathryn R. King discusses this manuscript as well as the Magdalen manuscript in her highly rewarding "The Poems of Jane Barker: the Magdalen Manuscript," *Magdalen College Occasional Paper* 3, ed., C. Y. Ferdinand (Magdalen College, Oxford, 1998). King provides a thorough overview of the manuscripts, what is known of their composition and history, a first-line index, and she prints several poems from the Magdalen manuscript "Poems on several occasions."

8 While this collection apparently was not distributed widely enough to meet Harold Love's criteria for publication in what he calls the strong sense, it does meet the criteria for publication in what he calls the weak sense. Love, *Scribal Publication*, 37–39. King considers the possibilities of whether this copy

of the poems was a presentation copy given to the prince, or whether it was a retained copy or a draft version. *Magdalen College Paper*, 15.

9 Jane Barker, "Poems on several occasions in three parts: The first refering to the times. The second, are poems writ since the author was in France, or at least most of them. The third, are taken out of a miscellany heretofore printed, and writ by the same author," MS 343, Magdalen College, Oxford. The second part of this manuscript contains new work – poems from neither "Poems Refering to the times" nor *Poetical Recreations*. Kathryn King and Jeslyn Medoff date the manuscript approximately 1704. Kathryn R. King with Jeslyn Medoff, "Jane Barker (1652–1732) and Her Life: the Documentary Record," *Eighteenth-Century Life* 21 (November 1997), 30, n. 8. Their essay is extremely valuable for students of Barker and the literature of the time. King makes a crucial distinction between the historical Jane Barker, whom we can begin to know through King and Medoff's careful research, the "briskly ironic" Jane Barker of the prefaces to *A Patch-Work Screen* and *The Lining*, and the fictional Fidelia and Galesia. Perhaps one of the most valuable results of their careful scholarship will be a new emphasis on Fidelia and Galesia as characters, rather than simply as autobiographical representations. For a more detailed discussion of the date of composition and preparation of the poems in "Poems on several occasions," see King, *Magdalen College Paper*, 16–17.

10 Indeed, King sees the volume as a "personal poetic archive [that] became in time a working manuscript, subject to fresh revision," *Magdalen College Paper*, 5.

11 King provides a photograph of the page and discusses this revision to support her argument that the manuscript became a "working book" for Barker. *Magdalen College Paper*, 11, 15.

12 King and Medoff, "Jane Barker and Her Life," 30, n. 8; for a more extended discussion of the hand, see King, *Magdalen College Paper*, 8–9.

13 Jane Donawerth discusses how women participated in the system. "Many women writers offered their poetry as a gift to circulate in the gift exchange system. Seeing poetry as part of this system they had operated in all their lives must have made it easier for women to write and to publish," "Women's Poetry and the Tudor–Stuart System of Gift Exchange," *Women, Writing, and the Reproduction of Culture*, eds. Mary E. Burke, Jane Donawerth, Linda L. Dove, and Karen Nelson (Syracuse: Syracuse University Press, 2000), 28. Though the system had declined by the eighteenth century, the New Year's date of "Poems Refering to the times" places this collection in the same tradition.

14 Ezell, *Patriarch's Wife*, 99–100.

15 Anyone outside the dominant political faction of the moment might find the possession of objectionable manuscripts dangerous. During the 1745 Jacobite rebellion, Edinburgh Jacobites surrounded the staunch Whig Alison Cockburn and threatened a search of her person because they suspected her of carrying Whig letters. Though she had no letters, she "had imprudently stowed in her pocket a parody on Prince Charlie's Proclamation, which she

had written with great conceit to the tune of 'Clout the Cauldron,' " but she
escaped without indignity. See Sarah Tytler and J. L. Watson, *The Songstresses
of Scotland*, 2 vols. (London: Strahan & Co., 1871), 1:201.

16 "Its most characteristic mode was the edition of one, copied by the writer for
private use into a personal miscellany or 'commonplace book'; however, this
was never an isolated activity since it always involved a transaction between
at least two individuals – the copyist and the provider of the exemplar," Love,
Scribal Publication, 79.

17 King analyzes the patch-work metaphor in two essays, "Galesia, Jane Barker,
and a Coming to Authorship," *Anxious Power: Reading, Writing, and Ambivalence
in Narrative by Women*, eds. Carol J. Singley and Susan Elizabeth Sweeney
(Albany: State University of New York Press, 1993), 91–104, and "Of Needles
and Pens and Women's Work," *Tulsa Studies in Women's Literature* 14 (1996),
77–93. In the essays she sees the metaphor as "a community of female
readers and writers" that ease Barker into authorship ("Needles and Pens,"
79). She also argues that the text/textile analogy makes women's writing
seem natural, as if it were another kind of women's work.

18 In *The Lining of the Patch-Work Screen*, the heroine's name is spelled "Galecia."
For consistency, I follow the spelling "Galesia" (Barker's spelling in *Bosvil
and Galesia* and *A Patch-Work Screen*) unless I refer to or quote from a specific
instance in *The Lining*.

19 For example, the commonplace book of Anne Milles, a contemporary of
Jane Barker shows these traits. MS W.a. 86, Folger Shakespeare Library.

20 In the manuscript, "Holy bretheren" is written in much larger letters for
emphasis, and an asterisk before the phrase signals the note "the sectarys,"
which appears at the foot of the page. A bracket in the margin signals the
triplet.

21 Jacqueline Pearson suggests that this story is adapted from Mary Pix's 1705
play *The Conquest of Spain*; "The History of *The History of the Nun*," *Rereading
Aphra Behn: History, Theory, and Criticism*, ed. Heidi Hutner (Charlottesville:
University Press of Virginia, 1993), 252, n. 20. Though it does resemble Pix's
play, Barker's plot is actually closer to Pix's source, William Rowley's *All's Lost
by Lust*. Significantly, both the Jacobite-inflected additions and the puzzling
inscriptions seem to be original to Barker.

22 Howard Erskine-Hill, "Literature and the Jacobite Cause: was there a
Rhetoric of Jacobitism?" *Ideology and Conspiracy: Aspects of Jacobitism, 1689–
1759*, ed. Eveline Cruickshanks (Edinburgh: John Donald Publishers, 1982),
49. Erskine-Hill states that the image was so used, though early on it was
reconfigured by Williamites. In this case, Barker's politics, and the combination of the image of rape and a usurper, makes the reference clear.

23 Annabel Patterson, *Censorship and Interpretation: the Conditions of Writing and
Reading in Early Modern England* (Madison: University of Wisconsin Press,
1984). Chapter 4, "The Royal Romance," is especially valuable for suggesting
interpretative strategies appropriate for Barker's fiction.

24 *The Lining of the Patch-Work Screen* (1726) contains a table of contents omitted in the Wilson edition.

25 After her death in 1732, two more editions of *The Entertaining Novels of Mrs. Jane Barker* (first printed in 1719 and consisting of *Bosvil and Galesia* and *Exilius*) were published in 1736 and 1743, but she did not profit from the printing of any other works during the rest of her life.

CHAPTER 8

Elizabeth Singer Rowe's tactical use of print
and manuscript

Kathryn R. King

Narratives of the emergence and development of print tend to be staunchly progressive. Print "rises" and "triumphs" over scribal modes of circulation and use; "rival" technologies "clash" and "collide," culminating at some point toward the end of the seventeenth century or by the middle of the next in the "ascendance" of the commercial press and the "decline" or "demise" of scribal culture.[1] The problem with the progressive narrative is not that its main storyline is untrue – few if any would deny that by the beginning of the eighteenth century the "printing press did finally, and unquestionably, prevail," as the editors of *English Manuscript Studies* put it.[2] The problem, for literary scholars at any rate, is that the assumptions embedded in the familiar agonistic metaphors of ascendancy, competition, and conquest tend to distort our understanding of actual writing and publishing practices during a time of transition. Metaphors such as these imply the existence of separate and opposed literary systems, when in fact the relation between manuscript and print, at least through the first half of the eighteenth century, is best understood in terms of coexistence, interpenetration and complex interplay.[3]

Though a growing body of work now urges recognition of this interpenetration, serious study of women's writing practices within the context of manuscript culture in the early modern period has been slow to get under way, for practical and theoretical reasons. To begin, manuscript study poses obvious problems of access. Publication pressures being what they are today, few scholars feel they have the time, resources, or even training to undertake such costly study. Add to this a theoretical climate that, until recently, did little to direct attention to female participation in manuscript-based literary culture. First-wave feminism assumed that women as a group were largely silenced during the early modern period and came into their own as writers only when they were able successfully to assume public roles in the marketplace of print. Indeed, according to earlier modes of feminist analysis, women's involvement in manuscript culture was less a phenomenon to be investigated than an example of female powerlessness, its very practice among purportedly timorous women evidence of patriarchal oppression.[4] Such models, as Margaret Ezell has argued with elegant clarity, made it difficult to recognize, much less appreciate, women's literary activities and achievements in the early modern period. Her insistence in *The Patriarch's Wife* (1987) and *Writing Women's Literary History* (1993) that women writers be studied in relation to the material practices of their own cultural and social setting, combined with ground-breaking methodical and conceptual work by Peter Beal, Harold Love, and others on seventeenth- century scribal culture more generally,[5] has already borne fruit in a number of individual studies, including important new assessments of the poet and dramatist Katherine Philips for example,[6] as well as in a broader recognition of the complex role played in the writing lives of early modern women by "scribal transmission," as it is coming to be known.

Accounts of women's writing during the half century or so after the death of Philips in 1664 continue, however, to assume and even emphasize a division of the female literary world into opposing camps – amateur manuscript writers *versus* print professionals – and then, more troubling still, to invest the categories in this polarized field with quasi-moralistic qualities. The chaste, decorous, respectable poetic amateurs of the Orinda tradition (Philips, Barker, Singer, Finch) are thus ranged in standard feminist literary histories like so many good girls against the transgressive, outspoken, and sexually self-displaying players of the emerging commercial print-world tradition (Behn, Manley, Haywood). One influential recent account, for example, portrays women writers as "forced into one of two classes": the first is the "shameless, crass, fallen woman" who competed with men in the new world of print; she stands in "stark contrast" to the second, the aristocrat who followed the "long-accepted practice" of "writing for herself and her circle and tastefully circulating manuscripts."[7] In fact the contrasts were never quite so stark, and many scholars have come to distrust such sharply drawn distinctions not only because they reproduce a good girl/bad girl split that turns the history of women's literary past into "a spectrum of virtue and vice," as Paula McDowell has put it,[8] but also because they oversimplify our understanding of literary culture at a time when manuscript and print presented not so much opposing as overlapping sets of publication possibilities.

In an effort to soften the edges of existing oppositions I offer an account of several passages in the literary career of Elizabeth Singer Rowe

(1674–1737), poet and devotional writer. Celebrated in the eighteenth century as the pious Mrs. Rowe, she has emerged in feminist scholarship as a leading example of a woman writer who achieved "commercial success without threat to the author's respectability."[9] She is regarded as one of the most "Orindan" of the early eighteenth-century women writers, a genteel manuscript poet *par excellence*. Her importance as a cultural phenomenon can hardly be overstated. She had a huge readership until well into the nineteenth century; was read closely by other poets, including Matthew Prior, Isaac Watts, Anne Finch, and Alexander Pope, the latter of whom responded to her celebrated elegy on the death of her husband in his *Eloisa to Abelard*;[10] and after her death was canonized, in both senses of the word, as a literary saint, earning the praise of Dr. Johnson among others.[11] As the sanctified and otherworldly Mrs. Rowe she was *the* exemplary woman writer in the Atlantic world and Germany as well, her works going into upwards of a hundred editions in English alone.[12] A full study of the sociocultural dynamics of the Mrs. Rowe phenomenon might tell us much about the culture that needed to make her a saint, while study of her texts and their reception would surely illuminate the strange and shifting relations among eros, piety, and the commerce of letters over the course of the eighteenth century. But such possibilities can only be touched on here. The present essay seeks instead to explore some of the ways her long writing life offers a rich study of the interplay of manuscript and print culture during the opening decades of the century.

The discussion that follows focuses on her passage into print on two widely separated occasions as each blurs in instructive ways the line between print and scribal transmission during this period of literary transition. My argument is that at crucial moments Elizabeth Singer Rowe was able to take advantage of the dual possibilities of manuscript and print to advance her literary ambitions, first as the Pindarical Lady of the periodical press, then as the quasi-aristocratic manuscript poet Philomela, and finally as the iconically pious Mrs. Rowe. The discussion begins with a look at her debut in the 1690s as a magazine poet in the *Athenian Mercury* (1691–97), drawing upon the fascinating but little studied "The Double Courtship" (1710), written by her promoter, former editor, and would-be lover, John Dunton. We turn next to a much later venture into print, the anonymous publication in 1728 of *Friendship in Death*, which I read against Mrs. Rowe's participation since the 1690s in elite manuscript circles centering on the Thynne family at Longleat, Wiltshire. This discussion draws largely on manuscript evidence, the primary source being correspondence and verse by Mrs. Rowe transcribed by her life-long friend the Countess of Hertford into a quarto letterbook now in the possession of the Duke of Northumberland and found in the library of Alnwick Castle (Alnwick MS 110). Although the existence of this letter-book (the Green Book, as it is sometimes called) has long been known, its contents remain little examined.[13] The 361 pages of correspondence and verse, including 159 numbered letters dating from 1697 onwards, spanning nearly four decades and reflecting the ongoing concerns of Mrs. Rowe's long writing life, provide a wealth of information about a provincial middle-class woman's entry into an aristocratic literary cul-ture and (more obliquely) her re-entry in the last decade of her life into the now well-established world of commercial print. Taken together the *Athenian Mercury* and Alnwick materials document in unusual detail a literary career shaped in response to the pressures and possibilities of two different but far from distinct literary environments, each providing different kinds of readers and recognitions, and each requiring different decorums and obligations. At virtually every stage in her career she can be seen to move between and exploit the resources of both cultures, negotiating a series of positions for herself in the early eighteenth-century literary world that drew in varying degrees upon traditional coterie lit-erary practices and the new forms of cultural authority offered by print.

I. THE BOOKSELLER AND THE PINDARICK LADY

The outlines of Mrs. Rowe's reputation as genteel manuscript poet can be discerned at least as early as the biographical notice in the official *Miscellaneous Works in Prose and Verse* (1739) published two years after her death. The notice draws upon the oft-intertwined myths of untutored genius and aristocratic benevolence to depict her as a poetic natural – she "could hardly write a familiar letter but it bore the stamp of the poet" – who was taken up by the local great folk and patronized by them for the rest of her life: she was the "favourite of persons so much superior to her in the outward distinctions of life" – that is, the Thynne family at Longleat – pleased for their part to cherish "such blooming worth."[14]

This fiction is remarkable for what it leaves out. At least two years before the Thynnes discovered her blooming worth, a teenaged Singer was blazing a very different path of recognition for herself as a mag-azine poet on the pages of the *Athenian Mercury*, becoming one of the earliest women writers to capitalize on the possibilities of the periodical press. The immensely successful *Athenian Mercury*, with its user-friendly question-and-answer format, was a new thing in late seventeenth-century English print culture: a publication which offered readers of all stripes and persuasions a rather easy avenue into print. Readers of any rank and region, including women and persons of middling and lower orders, were invited to submit questions, which meant that every reader was potentially a published writer. (Inevitably, the *Mercury* and its proprietor, the ebulliently populist John Dunton, met with reproach, anger, and ridicule from cultural conservatives.)[15] It remained for the young Elizabeth Singer, of a dissenting family in Somerset, to exploit the publication's potential as a venue for poetry. (She was not the first to submit verse. An admiring Jonathan Swift had earlier dispatched an ode for publication, to his subsequent disgust.)[16] By 1694, the year she is said to have come to the attention of the Thynnes, Singer had already established herself as the leading contributor of verse to the *Mercury*; and as the Pindarical Lady she had secured the enthusiastic attention of quite a different literary set – the men of the Athens, as Dunton and the so-called Athenian Society liked to style themselves. (We now know this "Society" to have consisted of Dunton, two men in his pay, and an advisor.) As will be seen, Mrs. Rowe would later have reason to regret that she had first come before the public in such company. It should come as no surprise, then, that the official life would seek to conceal its subject's early connection with Dunton, "Athens," and the *Mercury*, referring obliquely to this period as one that gave her "no little uneasiness in advanced life" and to her early verses as "juvenile follies" deserving of "perpetual oblivion."[17]

Literary scholars today often recur to the Dunton episode, in part because we relish the spectacle of immaculate piety bespattered and in part because the young Singer's relations with Dunton seem to offer a piquant illustration of female vulnerability at the hands of literary pimps, in Germaine Greer's phrase. Indeed, it is generally assumed that the Pindarical Lady was Dunton's creation, and Singer something of a victimized *naïf*.[18] The truth, as usual, is more complicated. To begin with, it was Singer who initiated the relationship with "Athens." As early as fall 1691, and no later than 1693, she sent poems and queries to the London address of the Athenian Society, concealing her actions from the eyes of her protective father ("Argus"). She is probably the young lady "*Poetically enclin'd*" whose queries were published 1 December 1691.[19] When the young lady, a fervid Williamite like Singer, sought the editors' opinion of her verses in praise of William at the Boyne (never apparently printed in the *Mercury*), Dunton responded with a show of gallantry: "Say, Dear unknown! *what is't that charms me so?/What secret*

Nectar through thy Lines does flow?/What Deathless Beauties *in thy Garden grow."* With this response to guide her, Elizabeth Singer developed for her appearances in the *Athenian Mercury* a teasing but deferential feminine persona such as masculine courtliness requires for its full exercise;[20] she must have quickly realized that printed displays of girlish femininity would go a long way toward seizing the means of seduction, to use Ballaster's witty formulation.[21] Her first certain appearance as a poet on the pages of the *Athenian Mercury* can be dated to 21 October 1693 (vol. 11, no. 30). The Athenian poem celebrating the poetic debut of the unknown "Bright Maid" begins with exclamatory iambic excitement –

> We yield! We yield! the *Palm*, bright *Maid*! be *thine*!
> How *vast* a Genius *sparkles* in each *Line*!
> How *Noble* All! how *Loyal*! how *Divine*!

– rises to "Thus sing, *Bright Maid*! thus and yet *louder* sing," and then falls with comic inevitability into praise of her body: "For sure a *Soul* so *fine* / Wou'd ne're possess a *Body* less *divine*."[22] The tone, bantering, avuncular and indulgent, typifies the welcome given the young woman who for her part was shrewd enough to lard her poetic offerings with admiring queries: "*Then tell, ye* Heirs *to ancient* Athens Fame / *Some way with more* Address *to hide my* Flame?" (They answer, predictably, "And can your *fatal Sex*, form'd to *deceive*, / Want *Arts* to make us what you please, believe?" [21 October 1693, vol. 11, no. 30].) Before long her verse was appearing regularly in the *Mercury*, and over the next two years she would contribute some two dozen poems – biblical paraphrases, pastorals, pindarics, occasional verse, and praise of the Athenians ("how shall I describe the matchless men?").[23] By May 1694 Dunton had dubbed her "the *Pindarical* Lady" (vol. 14, no. 3) – the classical sobriquet "Philomela," often misattributed to Dunton, would come later – and at the end of the year he dedicated the fifteenth volume to the Pindarical Lady, playing in the dedication upon the romance of their mutual anonymity ("*we fancy we neither are, nor ever shall be known to one another*").[24] The entire 18 June 1695 number is devoted to the poems of the "ingenious *Pindarick Lady*," "printed *Verbatim*, as we receiv'd 'em from her" (vol. 17, no. 23). Dunton later quotes her as assuring him that "all the Poems that I have, or shall for the future compose, are designed for the Gentlemen of the *Athenian Society*, to which 'tis suppos'd you belong."[25]

If Singer is ambitious to appear in print and Dunton to secure copy, the typological pas de deux they played out on the pages on the *Mercury* originated in an older world of amateur coterie practice. Margaret Ezell's discussion of the contemporaneous *Gentleman's Journal* (1692–94) helps bring this dimension of the episode into focus. She demonstrates that the interactive format of the *Journal*, a literary periodical produced by Peter Motteux, replicates in printed form the codes and conventions of amateur coterie practices. Her conclusion that Motteux's *Journal*, in its format and function, registers the transition from an "amateur coterie literary society to a commercial enterprise"[26] applies to the *Mercury* (1691–97) as well. Even more than Motteux, Dunton sought to collapse the distinction between manuscript and print cultures. A kind of print-world impresario, Dunton was endlessly inventive in devising strategies to encourage his readers to think of themselves as part of an extended print-world coterie, inviting them to interact with one another behind the cover of coterie sobriquets – famously in a "*Paper* War" between the sexes he sought to whip up in 1694.[27] In a sense, he adapted the conventions of masculine gallantry to the commercial print medium, as William Walsh did in 1691 when he likened printing a defense of women to "writing a Circular Love-Letter to all the fair Ladies in the Kingdom" and as Motteux did in 1693 when he averred that "a Dedication to the Fair, has much in it of a Declaration of Love."[28] Moreover in his relations with Singer, off the pages of the *Mercury* as well as on, Dunton seems to have regarded himself as engaged in the kind of amatory role-playing fashionable in amateur manuscript circles; Singer may have seen her approaches to the magazine as a kind of flirtation.[29] In any event, several of the poems printed in the *Mercury* and collected in *Poems On Several Occasions* (1696) mimic in their format the response pairings typical of manuscript collections. For example, "The WISH, in a POEM to the ATHENIANS" is followed in print by "The Athenians *Answer*," which begins in Dunton's courtliest manner, "Ah! Bright *Unknown!* you *know not what you ask!*"[30] In this episode, as in so many others in the writing and publishing careers of both Dunton and Singer, it is not easy to know where amateur manuscript culture leaves off and commercial print culture begins.

The line between manuscript and print blurs also in the so-called platonic correspondence that developed between Dunton and Singer off the pages of the *Mercury*. It is fitting that this "private" exchange began in a printed notice and survives today almost exclusively in typographical traces. 6 October 1694 (vol. 15, no. 10) Dunton inserted an advertisement directing the "Ingenious *Pindarick Lady* who formerly sent many *Poetical Questions* to the *Athenian Society*" to send the remainder of her poems to "our *Bookseller* at the *Raven* in *Jewen Street*," that is, to Dunton himself.

She did so, but failed to disclose her whereabouts, for 8 January 1695 (vol. 16, no. 7) a notice appeared asking for her address. She complied, and there began that platonic correspondence between Philaret and Cloris (as they styled themselves in this exchange) that culminated in a marriage proposal and furnished materials for one of Dunton's most outrageous pieces, the alternately hilarious and sinister "The Double Courtship," a rambling, sixty-one page rehearsal of his relationship with Singer and the eventual collapse of his platonic pretensions. (He was reduced, as he more than once put it – Dunton never said anything once – to "sighing and whining *and all but hanging* to enjoy her Person."[31]) He journeyed to Agford and proposed marriage, Singer refused him, and that was that. But cutting the print-world cord was not so easy. Two decades later, having consolidated her public identity as the pious Mrs. Rowe, she was still trying to disentangle herself from the bookseller's unwanted public attentions. In 1704 he had made her the subject of a dedication that ran to eleven pages;[32] in 1705 he celebrated the rich genius of "The Pindarick Lady in the West, alias *Philomela*, alias Madam *Singer*";[33] in 1710 he described her in the dedication to *Athenianism* as "the Pindaric Lady (Madam Singer)... to whose Platonic friendship my Six Hundred Projects owe their birth." The lead "project," "The Double Courtship," depicts Singer in terms she would hardly have appreciated: "As to her NECK and BREASTS, they are the best [formed?] that ever you saw, and of a dazling Whiteness, as well as her ARMS and HANDS: As to her BODY 'tis small and of a curious Shape, and is supported with handsome LEGGS, as I do believe (for I never saw 'em)."[34] He also threatened her with the publication of what he claimed were the five hundred letters that passed between them and then used the threat as an opportunity to make a portion of that correspondence public. "*Sir*," she writes in a letter which Dunton incorporates into the text, "*I am very sorry 'tis too late to have my* Character *rescu'd, but I beg you for the future to do nothing of that Nature without my Knowledge.*"[35] This is one of the several places in "The Double Courtship" where Singer is permitted a voice; ironically, she protests, futilely, against the very piece in which the letter is printed. The response which follows shows Dunton the publishing entrepreneur at his most brazen. He begins by brushing aside Singer's expressed wish for privacy as merely "her Great Humility," and then parlays an assurance that he will never print the letters she sent him – "(save under borrow'd Names)" – into an upper-case threat: he will never print them unless her protests force him to publish "our WHOLE CORRESPONDENCE," and then segues into an advertizing spot for the future work which, moments ago, he promised not to publish. These letters "cannot fail of affecting the most insensible Hearts with pleasing Agitations: so that if Novelty (or Variety either) have Charms, these five Hundred Letters can't miss of a kind Reception."[36]

This public retailing of a deeply unedifying episode must have caused Mrs. Rowe no little discomfort. In 1718, almost certainly at her request, one "J. W." issued what amounted to a gag order, warning Dunton in a letter never to name "Mrs. *Rowe*, nor Mrs. *Singer*, nor *Philomela*" in print again, informing him that the title "Pindarick Lady" is so "senseless and impertinent, that it would spoil the credit of any Author that should use [it]," and reminding him that, as "for Plato's Notions, and Platonic Love, those terms have been so justly exposed by the Spectator, and are so very ridiculous and unfashionable, that nothing of those chimeras and whimsies would sell in the genteel part of the world." Mrs. Rowe has "too just and modish a taste not to despise" his commercial trumpery.[37] For her part, Mrs. Rowe did her best to maintain a dignified silence on the subject of her dubious debut on the pages of the *Athenian Mercury*, in the understandable hope that the flirtatious self-displays and platonic foolery of the very young and socially unconnected Elizabeth Singer might be allowed to sink into perpetual oblivion.

II. PHILOMELA AND THE COUNTESS

In 1694, at roughly the same time that she began corresponding privately with Dunton, Singer entered into relations with the Thynne family at Longleat.[38] For the next year or two she maintained a double or rather triple identity: the Pindarical Lady for "Athens" and her magazine public, Cloris for her epistolary exchanges with Dunton / Philaret, and Philomela for the exclusive manuscript society in which her compositions now circulated. The 1696 collected volume, *Poems on Several Occasions*, is interesting in the present context chiefly for the mingling of literary relationships and environments suggested by the titles of its verses. Many belong to the Dunton/*Mercury* matrix – "*Platonick* Love," for example, of which Dunton later claimed he was the subject, and "*A Pindarick, to the* Athenian Society." Others reflect her new Thynne connections: "To my Lady CARTERET," "To the Honourable Mrs. E— Stretchy," "To Madam *S*— at the Court," and "The *Vision*. To *Theron*," the latter of which probably written to her patron Henry Thynne.[39] Within the next year or two Singer had successfully reinvented herself as Philomela, protégée of the local aristocracy, as materials dating from 1697 in Alnwick MS 110 make clear; hereafter, even when she ventured into print (as will be seen), she would seek primary recognition through manuscript exchange within an aristocratic literary milieu. Inserted among the letters are a number of complimentary verses written to solidify and sustain her relationship with the Thynnes – "On The Grove above the Gardens at Longleat," on a theme proposed by Lord Weymouth (MS 110, p. 22); an elegy on Henry Thynne (MS 110, p. 41); and a poem "To Cleone" (i.e. Grace Thynne), following which Singer has written, "Tis but just madam you should still be the subject of a muse that owes her improvement to your former encouragment" (MS 110, p. 44, p. 45).[40] The earliest letters, addressed to Grace Thynne, suggest that by 1697 Singer – Philomela as she now signs herself – was already a well-established member of a largely female scribal network that had its center in the aristocratic family at Longleat (and would come to include Anne Finch[41]), and that she had achieved fame locally, probably as a protégée of the Thynnes. Over the next decade some of her verses would be printed in the miscellanies, but she would send no compositions to the press until 1728 when, anonymously and with considerable effort to cover her tracks, she sought print-publication of her intensely pious and instructive *Letters from the Dead to the Living* (or *Friendship in Death*, as it is sometimes known), an episode to be taken up shortly.

Recent criticism tends to link Mrs. Rowe's retirement from the public arena in the post-Dunton years to changes in gender ideology, in particular the rise of an increasingly restrictive bourgeois feminine ideal that sanctioned piety and didacticism while inhibiting sexual and political expressiveness.[42] The transformation of the sprightly and publicly aspiring Elizabeth Singer into an other-worldly recluse of irreproachable purity is thought to demonstrate the "narrowing range of genres, public personae and ways of living open to women writers between the 1690s and the mid-eighteenth century," as Jeslyn Medoff has put it.[43] Doubtless there is truth in this gender-based explanatory model, but examination of Singer's self-fashioning as Philomela suggests that the damping effect of bourgeois femininity goes only so far in accounting for changes in her writing and publishing practices. Her turn to manuscript as her preferred medium of transmission, for example, would seem to reflect less the rise of the domestic ideal than an elevation in her social position. Through the offices of the Thynnes and their social ilk she had made the acquaintance of intellectuals and literati able to command greater cultural capital than could a middle-class London bookseller. They include Thomas Ken, the learned nonjuring Bishop of Bath and Wells who was part of the Longleat household and encouraged her biblical paraphrases, and the poets Matthew Prior and Isaac Watts, whom she met a few years later and with whom (as with Dunton) she also, apparently, entered into literary flirtations.[44] There was hardly place in this more rarefied social and literary milieu for a magazine poet and an uninhibited "platonic" friend-cum-bookseller. (Dunton alludes bitterly to his cast-off status when he later depicts Singer as having abandoned him for a set of "New Correspondents," naming Ken, Watts, and the reverend Henry Bowden, a local clergyman who also had Longleat connections.)[45] If the Pindarical Lady believed she had much to gain by a "platonic" friendship with Dunton, the better-connected Philomela knew otherwise. A client of the Thynnes, she could afford to set her sights higher, but she would have been acutely aware that her newly assumed social position was precarious. She had every reason to distance herself from Dunton, a man ridiculed in the hostile press for trafficking (in print) with chambermaids, oyster women, and the likes of Dorothy Tickleteat, the Islington milkmaid.[46] Tellingly, J. W.'s attempt to silence the bookseller expressed itself through insinuations of the latter's vulgarity: Dunton's self-promoting antics and exploded platonic notions provoke only laughter in "the genteel part of the world."[47] It was with the genteel world, and against the democratizing tendencies of the marketplace, that the reconstructed Philomela had cast her lot.

The Alnwick materials deserve closer scrutiny than I can give them here. They are, among other things, an invaluable source for study of a female manuscript culture that has much in common with the female world of love and ritual which flourished a century later in America, the latter analyzed by Carroll Smith-Rosenberg in a classic essay.[48] Throughout much of her life Elizabeth Singer Rowe took pleasure in verse exchange with men; indeed, in some of her moods she seems to have regarded verse writing as a form of flirtation. But the Alnwick letterbook consists entirely of letters and verse addressed to women, mostly Frances Thynne, later the Countess of Hertford, and her mother, the former Grace Strode ("Cleone"),[49] and these materials bring into view a strikingly homosocial feminine world. It is evident that manuscript exchange among women offered a refuge from the grossness and irreligion Mrs. Rowe expected to encounter as a matter of course in her quotidian dealings with men; it opened an imaginative space in which to spin out her well-known fantasies of love-after-death and pastoral egalitarianism without fear of check or the derision she routinely received (or imagined she did) from men.

In the nineties, for example, Henry Thynne had called her notions "fantastick & unreasonable";[50] Prior a few years later accused her of affecting the spleen ("your melancholly Gloom & unfrequented Shades, Dying Strains & complaining Lyres are sure Symptoms of a Person very far gone in that Distemper") and mocked her repeatedly ("Oh brave Mrs. Betty how d'y like me now?" he gibed after one particularly offensive thrust);[51] Lord Hertford was impatient with her earnest piousness ("I am afraid my Lord Hartford will be angry with me for turning y^r Mind to s^{ch} Serious Reflections," she writes[52]). Running like an anxious leitmotif through Mrs. Rowe's letters to the Countess (the latter's side of the correspondence has been lost) is a fear of derision should her letters come before Lord Hertford's eyes: "for ah! what height of virtue can stand the test of redicule."[53] In the preceding letter she declares concern for an unnamed woman whose private writings he had parodied. "I wish with all my soul she knew my Lord Hartford laughs at her," she writes. Though dismayed to think her own letters may suffer the same fate, she resolves with mock-bravado to suppress her anxiety (which she calls "modesty"): she will "stifle all those motions of modesty" and "go on through sense and nonsense, moral and immoral subjects to fill up my paper and defye any Peer in Great Brittain to imitate my stile."[54] She wished, it would seem, to screen the pious intimacies exchanged between women from the corrosive and potentially humiliating effects of exposure to male eyes.

It is hardly any wonder, then, that she was reluctant to go public with her later writings, many of them conceived within this protected female world of the imagination. Her apprehensions were shared by the (male) editor of a collection of posthumously published devotional meditations: he called it a "peece of nice and dangerous work" to recommend a book "wherein I knew some expressions would awaken the ridicule of the Age."[55] The breathless, excessively ardent style suitable to manuscript exchange among women was embarrassing when transferred into the public realm of print, as Mrs. Rowe knew all too well. She passed on two of her private meditations to the Countess "with the strongest injunctions" that they not be made public, "lest they be thought too rapturous," the Countess later reported.[56]

The print-publication in 1728 of *Friendship in Death in Twenty Letters from the Dead to the Living* shows Mrs. Rowe, in the last decade of her life, seeking to re-enter the marketplace of print from within the protected precincts of the feminine manuscript networks she had cultivated since the 1690s. Mrs. Rowe, like Frances Burney later in the century, went to

extraordinary lengths to conceal her authorship of her first volume of
prose fiction. She composed *Friendship in Death* in secret, according to
her brother-in-law and literary executor, Theophilus Rowe, and when
finished evidently got Theophilus to prepare a fair copy in his hand.
(Burney, it will be recalled, copied out the three volumes of *Evelina* in
a disguised hand in order to avoid detection by compositors familiar
with her handwriting.)[57] She then sent the manuscript to the poet and
Anglican divine Edward Young (1683–1765), the future author of *Night
Thoughts* (1742), addressing him in an unsigned dedication. Later she
was to remark of her ruse, "Dr. Young, I flatter myself, is in perfect
ignorance."[58] Since she and the Anglican clergyman moved in different
circles, she may have hoped the association of the printed volume with
his name would ensure her anonymity,[59] but Young was a shrewd choice
as an intermediary for other reasons. By 1728, as Dustin Griffin has
shown, he enjoyed the support of a network of well-connected friends
and distinguished Whig patrons, many with ties to the court. Two years
earlier he had received a royal pension and been named chaplain to the
Princess of Wales.[60] Mrs. Rowe showed more than a degree of savvy in
contriving that her prose fiction reach print under the auspices of a poet
and divine whose name would be likely to attract the notice of influential
patrons.

It is not, however, immediately clear why Mrs. Rowe worked so hard
to keep her hand hidden. *Letters from the Dead to the Living* is a work of
unassailable piety, after all, and was brought out in decorous anonymity.
A phrase in Theophilus Rowe's account of this episode may shed light on
the source of her misgivings. She hoped, he wrote, that "*all her acquaintance*
would imagine this piece to be written by some friend of that eminent
poet."[61] She did not, one might conclude from this, seek anonymity in
the public sphere so much as she aimed to protect her image as genteel
amateur within the circle of her own acquaintance, especially (we might
speculate) in the eyes of her aristocratic friend. This would explain the
uncharacteristic recourse to dissimulation in the letter in which Mrs.
Rowe tries to throw the Countess off the scent: "I have read the letters
y^r Las^p recomended to me" – *Friendship in Death*, that is; Lady Hertford
obviously had her suspicions – "& like them without exception on your
aprobation[.] that motive would tempt me to wish I had writt them if I
had the least ambition of being an author, but I need not justifye my self
so seriously on this subject."[62] This duplicity provoked the Countess's
anger. Mrs. Rowe's next letter begins, "If you will not let me write to
you I am resolv'd to write to my Lord Hartford & Lady Betty[.] I know

by my own heart you will not be angry with me in earnest."[63] She then apologizes for her artful concealment, confesses the pain caused by her violation of "the rules of Vertue & Friendship," and hopes that the "rest of the world" will continue ignorant of her authorship:

But not any of my Errors has given me so much uneasiness as speaking to y^u in my last in an artfull manner & using any sort of disguise[.] it has put me more in the spleen than I thought any misfortune could have done & I think (if I know my self) I w^d not be guilty of another Equivocation if I might gain the Empire of the World by it[.] I owe this Confession to the rules of Vertue & Friendship & now that my mind is at peace with it self I find nothing can escape the penetration of y^r Genius but I confess it would have been a pleasure to me to know y^r La^{ps} oppinion if you had not known the author and I hope the rest of the world will continue ignorant, except 2 or 3 who know my impertinent manner of thinking.[64]

The book is a "harmless folly," she continues, "& as all the events and Characters are fiction if it do's no body any good it will do them no hurt."[65] We would be wrong, I think, to characterize this as anxiety over a breach of feminine modesty or the uncertainties of her class position, although as a middle-class poet of dissenting background she must have felt the latter keenly enough. On a deeper level she seems to have re-garded this excursion into print as a kind of apostasy and to have feared that print-publication may have disrupted or weakened her link with the upper-class manuscript-based feminine literary culture that had sus-tained her since the regrettable Dunton days. In the next sentence she writes, "& I believe I shall content my self for the future wth copying the vanitys of my immagination for y^r Perusal only"[66] – as if by this implied promise to write solely for Lady Hertford she might not only shore up her relation with her patron-friend but also restore her connection with the intimate, emotionally uninhibited, female-centered world of manuscript exchange.

It is tempting to read Mrs. Rowe's next publishing venture, *Letters Moral and Entertaining* (Part I, 1729), as an attempt to reassert her connection with the Countess and her world. She prepared this epistolary collec-tion, a sequel of sorts to the exceedingly popular *Letters from the Dead to the Living*, in silent collaboration with Lady Hertford, whose contributions appear under the name of "Cleora." Ironically, this publication blurs the line between print and manuscript in ways oddly reminiscent of the *Athenian Mercury* affair. Helen Sard Hughes is uncertain whether Cleora's "Letters to the Author" were written for the volume or adapted from existing correspondence, but she finds that at least one of the "Letters to Cleora" was based upon an actual letter written by Mrs. Rowe to the Countess. The second letter in this group is "in large part a genuine letter" which can be found, with only a few minor variants, in Alnwick MS 110, although it was not included among the selections printed in the *Works*. Hughes calls attention to another letter, Cleora's Letter V on the death of "Lord—", that is, Heneage Finch, fourth earl of Winchilsea (1656–1727), which she strongly suspects is based on an actual letter. She concludes that "we can only guess" the extent to which "the correspondence between Cleora and the Author are derived entirely or in part from authentic letters."[67] In a sense it does not matter. Toward the end of her writing career as at its beginning Elizabeth Singer Rowe, like her old platonic bookseller-friend, can be seen using print alongside traditional scribal publication methods. Not only is this collection of fictionalized letters an adaptation to the marketplace of older forms of coterie epistolary exchange, as was also the case with the *Athenian Mercury*, but its author shows herself fully as willing as the print impresario himself to mingle public and private, fact and fiction, manuscript and print.

When Mrs. Rowe died in 1737 she left her papers in order. In a cabinet were found farewell letters to six of her friends, including the Countess of Hertford. One might have thought such letters too private to be deemed suitable for publication, but within two years all but one had appeared in print. These "private" letters, the last in a long series of letters from the dead to the living, seem in fact to have been conceived as part of a posthumous "good-death" print event staged by Mrs. Rowe at the end of her life from within the self-consciously elevating imaginative matrix constructed over four decades within a feminocentric world of loving manuscript exchange. "My Letters ought to be call'd Epistles from the Dead to the Living," wrote Mrs. Rowe in a letter the Countess dates to 1717.[68] In the case of Mrs. Rowe, the line separating life and death, like that separating print and manuscript, is not easily discerned.[69]

III. BEYOND TAXONOMIES

If this account of the writing life of Elizabeth Singer Rowe shows what might be gained by moving beyond the dichotomies that have framed much work on early modern women writers, it points toward other kinds of understandings as well. The story of the mechanical reproduction throughout Mrs. Rowe's lifetime of the verse and self-fashionings of the Pindarical Lady would seem to offer a striking illustration of the now familiar story of the hazards of print-publication during an age when the machinery of representation was largely in male hands. Loss of control over the social destinations of one's texts is, of course, an inescapable feature of print-publication. As Harold Love has written, the crucial moment in the publication process occurs when "the initiating agent," who may or may not be the author, "knowingly relinquishes control over the future social use of that text."[70] For women caught between the conventions of feminine "modesty" on the one hand and the potential for unchecked appropriation of their texts and image to sexualized ends on the other, the problem thus posed was acute. In Dunton's publications alone embarrassing images of the Pindarick Lady and Philomela and Madam Singer proliferate, traveling through new texts and destined for unknown readers in uncontrollable contexts. Her struggle to remove disavowed versions of her poetic self from circulation, to say nothing of references to her handsome if unespied "LEGGS," speaks of the dangers of print publication when the passage into print entailed surrender of one's texts to men who, gallantry and courtship postures notwithstanding, seldom hesitated to sexualize the women whose work they published. Her preference in the post-Dunton years for manuscript circulation, her participation in a separate feminocentric literary realm, and her extreme caution when she re-ventured into print during the final decade of her life suggest a calculated effort to manage the destination, reception, availability, and social uses of her texts.

It is certainly true that Elizabeth Singer Rowe wrote during a time when advances in the distribution of printed materials transformed relations among readers, writers, texts, and publishers, but the sharpness of these changes is easily exaggerated. We are reminded by the story of Mrs. Rowe's "bi-cultural" literary career that print capitalism did not so much replace scribal transmission as relegate the hand-written text to the cultural margins. Print was by no means the only game in town, but it attracted the major players; and though manuscript verse continued to possess considerable social prestige, it carried little cultural power. After her somewhat regrettable splash as the Pindarical Lady, Elizabeth Singer was happy to assume the more elegant role of Philomela and later that of the pious Mrs. Rowe, surfacing now and then in print miscellanies in appearances which hinted at her position within prestigious manuscript circles. But *Letters from the Dead to the Living* in 1728 marked a real shift. For perhaps the first time in her life Mrs. Rowe wrote deliberately and with full concentration *for* an unknown and impersonal audience that would read her work in print. *Letters from the Dead to the Living* is in effect a strong acknowledgment of the new cultural authority of print. This prose fiction was not a bid for fame or public recognition, but a platform from which to be heard by large numbers. Readers today might be baffled to account for the appeal of what a modern critic calls "a deadening book ... full of the most explicit and tedious moralizing,"[71] but its meditations on the shifting and porous boundaries between life and death obviously resonated for her contemporaries: even Dr. Johnson found in it much to praise. Her decision in the last decade of her life to re-enter the commercial world of print, even at some risk to her carefully groomed status as a genteel amateur, is a measure of her determination to advance her religious views.

One of the most insistent needs of feminist literary history is to construct a theoretical framework that accounts for the complexity and variousness of women's writing in early print culture without recourse to moralized dichotomous models. The usual division of the field of women's writing into decorous manuscript poets and transgressive print-performers seriously narrows what we are prepared to see and discuss when we read the works of early modern women. The example of Elizabeth Singer Rowe suggests some directions for rethinking our approaches to other women writers during this period. We need, it seems to me, to determine more precisely the spectrum of publication possibilities available to women across various class positions at any given moment and also to identify the cultural forces that interact to move writers toward one or another of those possibilities. The attractions of scribal transmission, with its aristocratic, socially privileged, intrinsically conservative appeal to men and women alike, and its special appeals to women in particular, might be regarded as a centripetal force tending at any moment to encourage confinement within socially prestigious, relatively controllable, but increasingly marginal forms of manuscript exchange. The attractions of print publication, with its potential for reaching a large audience of unknown and otherwise unreachable readers, might then be thought of as a centrifugal force, pressing women writers outward from traditional scribal circles to seek new forms of cultural authority associated with the medium of print. The task, then, would be to identify and describe these forces as they interact with gender and class (but also religion, region, family, and so on) to enable a range of writing strategies on the part of particular women. Such a shift in focus would at once render our moralized taxonomies obsolete and reinsert women writers into the web of textual and human relationships from which oppositional models too often remove them.

NOTES

Research for this paper was supported by a Newberry Library/NEH Fellowship and a grant from the University of Montevallo. For permission to publish materials from the Alnwick MSS I am grateful to the Duke of Northumberland. I would like to thank Faye Massey for heroic measures in securing interlibrary loan materials, and Peter Beal for advice and counsel of various sorts.

1 Alvin Kernan, for example, in his influential *Samuel Johnson and the Impact of Print* (Princeton: Princeton University Press, 1987), 8, is able to invoke a point in the eighteenth century when "print destroyed the old oral and manuscript culture."

2 Peter Beal and Jeremy Griffiths, Preface, *English Manuscript Studies 1100–1700* (1989), 1:viii.

3 The interpenetration of print and manuscript cultures in the previous century is usefully discussed by Margaret W. Ferguson, "Renaissance Concepts of the 'Woman Writer,'" *Women and Literature in Britain 1500–1700*, ed. Helen Wilcox (Cambridge: Cambridge University Press, 1996), esp. 156–63. She writes: "the existence of manuscript publication, and its use by both men and women, creates an interesting border territory on various ideological maps" (161). See also in the same collection Elizabeth H. Hageman, "Women's Poetry in Early Modern Britain," 190–208.

4 An illustration may be found in the introduction to *British Women Poets 1660–1800: an Anthology*, ed. Joyce Fullard (Troy: Whitston, 1990). "When women were bold enough to defy convention and publish their work, it was seldom viewed seriously or evaluated fairly, and for this reason many chose to circulate their poems only in manuscript among a limited circle of friends and family" (3).

5 Margaret J. M. Ezell, *The Patriarch's Wife: Literary Evidence and the History of the Family* (Chapel Hill: University of North Carolina Press, 1987); *Writing Women's Literary History* (Baltimore: Johns Hopkins University Press, 1993). For manuscript exchange and circulation in the seventeenth century, see also Peter Beal, *Index of English Literary Manuscripts, 1450–1700*, 4 vols. (London: Bowker and Mansell, 1980–93); Mary Hobbs, *Early Seventeenth-Century Verse Miscellany Manuscripts* (Aldershot: Scolar, 1992); Harold Love, *Scribal Publication in Seventeenth-Century England* (Oxford: Clarendon Press, 1993); Arthur Marotti, *Manuscript, Print and the English Renaissance Lyric* (Ithaca: Cornell University Press, 1995); H. R. Woudhuysen, *Sir Philip Sidney and the Circulation*

of Manuscripts 1558–1640 (Oxford: Clarendon Press, 1996); Peter Beal, *In Praise of Scribes: Manuscripts and their Makers in Seventeenth-Century England* (Oxford: Clarendon Press, 1998).

6 Elaine Hobby, *Virtue of Necessity: English Women's Writing 1649–1688* (Ann Arbor: University of Michigan Press, 1989), 128–42, was one of the first to propose Philips as a publicly aspiring poet within a manuscript-based courtly literary context. For a valuable recent discussion see Beal, *In Praise of Scribes*, chapter 5.

7 Paula R. Backscheider, *Spectacular Politics: Theatrical Power and Mass Culture in Early Modern England* (Baltimore: Johns Hopkins University Press, 1993), 81.

8 Paula McDowell, "Consuming Women: the Life of the 'Literary Lady' as Popular Culture in Eighteenth-Century England," *Genre* 26 (1993), 235. McDowell is one of several recent critics to challenge the oppositional model, on the grounds that it flattens difference as it sets up polarities. Carol Barash, *English Women's Poetry, 1649–1714: Politics, Community, and Linguistic Authority* (Oxford: Clarendon Press, 1996) seeks to undo what she does not hesitate to call the "false opposition" between Philips and Behn (5, note 8).

9 Cheryl Turner, *Living by the Pen: Women Writers in the Eighteenth Century* (London and New York: Routledge, 1992), 48.

10 For a general account of Rowe's reputation and literary relations, see Henry F. Stecher, *Elizabeth Singer Rowe, the Poetess of Frome: a Study in Eighteenth-Century English Pietism* (Bern and Frankfurt: Herbert Lang and Peter Lang, 1973). Rowe's elegy on her husband Thomas, "Upon the Death of her Husband. By Mrs. Elizabeth Singer," was included as an appendix in the 1720 edition of *Eloisa to Abelard*; for the relation of these two works, see Madeleine Forell Marshall (ed.), *The Poetry of Elizabeth Singer Rowe (1674–1737)* (Lewiston: Edwin Mellen Press, 1987), 24–28. For Rowe's relations with Finch, see Barbara McGovern, *Anne Finch and Her Poetry: a Critical Biography* (Athens and London: University of Georgia Press, 1992), 117–19.

11 Mrs. Rowe's "posthumous life" as a saintly "textual product" is discussed by Marlene R. Hans, "The Pious Mrs. Rowe," *English Studies* 76 (1995), 34–51. Hans concludes that the culture "needed a female writer who was completely pure, chaste, and devoted, a woman who was all soul" and in the pious Mrs. Rowe found "the most fitting repository for this image" (35).

12 Stecher, *Elizabeth Singer Rowe*, identifies some ninety editions of her work to 1840, not including printings of single poems. Marshall, *Poetry of Elizabeth Singer Rowe*, records some additional publications (10, note 6).

13 Helen Sard Hughes examined Alnwick MS 110 as part of her research for *The Gentle Hertford: her Life and Letters* (New York: Macmillan, 1940), chapter 5, and "Elizabeth Rowe and the Countess of Hertford," *PMLA* 59 (1944), 726–46, but her handling of the manuscript evidence is not always reliable and most of her quotations come from the correspondence printed in *The Miscellaneous Works in Prose and Verse of Mrs. Elizabeth Rowe*, 2 vols., ed. Theophilus Rowe (London: Hett and Dodsley, 1739), with no indication that the printed letters are greatly altered from the manuscript sources. The changes include

slight verbal variations, often in the interest of elegance; omissions ranging from names to substantial passages; transpositions of material – indeed,
many of the printed letters are composites of two or more letters in Alnwick
110 arranged without regard to chronology. The editing of Mrs. Rowe's
correspondence deserves a study in itself.

14 Rowe, *Miscellaneous Works*, xv, xvii.

15 Hostility to the democratizing tendencies of Dunton's periodical is expressed
by the rival *London Mercury* when it describes the *Athenian Mercury* as filled
"with Impertinent Questions of Apprentices and Chamber-maids" and its
female correspondents as ranging from "the Lady in her cock'd Commode,
to the Oyster-wench in her lawful Occupation at the Tavern-Door" (vol. 1,
no. 1). For the *Athenian Mercury* as subversive of class distinctions, see Kathryn
Shevelow, *Women and Print Culture: the Construction of Femininity in the Early
Periodical* (London and New York: Routledge, 1989), 74–78, and *passim*.

16 For a brief account, see Stephen Parks, *John Dunton and the English Book Trade:
a Study of his Career with a Checklist of his Publications* (New York: Garland, 1976),
90–92. For the cultural significance of Dunton's life and writing, see J. Paul
Hunter, "The Insistent I," *Novel* 13 (1979), 19–37, and *Before Novels: the Cultural
Contexts of Eighteenth-Century English Fiction* (New York: W. W. Norton, 1990),
99–106. For the importance of the *Athenian Mercury* and "Athenianism" in
Dunton's journalistic career, see Gilbert D. McEwen, *The Oracle of the Coffee
House: John Dunton's Athenian Mercury* (San Marino: Huntington Library, 1972).

17 Rowe, *Miscellaneous Works*, xvi, li.

18 "Dunton was the archetypical literary pimp. The extent to which
'Philomela,' Dunton's 'Pindarical Lady,' was Dunton's invention rather
than the authentic voice of Elizabeth Singer ... cannot now be known,"
Germaine Greer, Introduction, *Kissing the Rod: an Anthology of Seventeenth-
Century Women's Verse*, eds. Germaine Greer, Susan Hastings, Jeslyn Medoff,
and Melinda Sansone (New York: Farrar Straus Giroux: Noonday Press,
1988), 27. Hans, "The Pious Mrs. Rowe," 36, observes that her personae
"were to a large extent the creations of the men who patronized and published her work, Elizabeth Singer, or 'Philomela', of John Dunton, and
Elizabeth Rowe of her brother-in-law Theophilus Rowe." The charge of
male image-fashioning is largely unwarranted in the case of Theophilus
Rowe: the Mrs. Rowe that emerges from the official *Miscellaneous Works in
Prose and Verse* is in large measure the creation of Lady Hertford, who silently
assisted Theophilus when he turned to her in paroxysms of editorial inadequacy. For the making of the official volume, see Hughes, "Elizabeth Rowe,"
739–46. The case of Dunton is less clear since the Pindarical Lady must be
seen as the product of a collaboration between publisher and poet. As for
her poetic name "Philomela," it does not appear in the *Mercury* until 10
June 1697 when Dunton inserts an advertisement for poems "by *Philomela*,
the most Ingenious *Pindarick* Lady." That the classical sobriquet is not mentioned by Dunton until after Singer stopped writing for the *Mercury*, and
that he nowhere takes credit for bestowing it upon her, argue strongly for

the name's originating elsewhere, almost certainly in her exchanges with the Thynnes.

19 *Athenian Mercury*, vol. 5, no. 1, question 5. Singer's association with Dunton and the *Mercury* is often dated from 21 October 1693, when several poems known to be written by her first appeared in print. Stecher, *Elizabeth Singer Rowe*, 38, and McEwen, *Oracle of the Coffee House*, 106, date it from 1 December 1691, identifying the "late Famous *Pastoral Poem*" there mentioned as Singer's "Upon King William's passing the Boyn," first printed in 1696. Because a number of significant details of the Singer poem do fit the Athenian description, I am inclined to accept the 1691 date, although it is not easy to explain why another two years would pass before any of her verse was printed.

20 Sometimes she gives the impression of bright earnestness keen to secure the approval of learned men – "*What Books of Poetry wou'd you Advise one that's Young, and extreamly delights in it, to read, both Divine and other?*" (24 October 1693; vol. 12, no. 1, question 4) – and sometimes of giddy impetuousness: "let the world think me *inspir'd, or mad,* / I'le surely write whilst paper's to be had" ("To one that perswades me to leave the Muses," 18 June 1695; vol. 17, no. 23).

21 Ros Ballaster, "Seizing the Means of Seduction: Fiction and Feminine Identity in Aphra Behn and Delarivier Manley," *Women, Writing, History 1640–1740*, eds. Isobel Grundy and Susan Wiseman (Athens: University of Georgia Press, 1992), 93–108.

22 For a witty examination of the dynamics of praise in male commendatory verse, see Joanna Lipking, "Fair Originals: Women Poets in Male Commendatory Poems," *Eighteenth-Century Life*, n.s. 12 (1988), 58–72.

23 A detailed account of the *Mercury* episode is provided by Stecher, *Elizabeth Singer Rowe*, 37–57. The quote is from "*A Pindarick, to the* Athenian Society" (9 July 1695; vol. 17, no. 29).

24 The dedication to volume 15 (4 September–15 December 1694) begins, "You have so often Oblig'd our *Mercury*, and the World, by your Ingenious Questions, that we think our selves bound both in Gratitude and Interest, to Dedicate this Volume to your self" (italics reversed).

25 Dunton, "The Double Courtship," *Athenianism: or, the New Projects of Mr. John Dunton* (London: John Morphew, 1710), 3, italics reversed.

26 Margaret J. M. Ezell, "The *Gentleman's Journal* and the Commercialization of Restoration Coterie Literary Practices," *Modern Philology* 89 (1992), 324.

27 10 November 1694 (vol. 15, no. 20) Dunton inserted a "Proposal to all Ingenious Ladies" challenging them to contribute copy to the *Mercury* in a (paper) battle of the sexes: "The Lady who first made the CHALLENGE gives publick Notice of it in this Paper, in hopes that the Witty CLEONTA, the Learned ARTEMISA, and the PINDARICK LADY . . . will come in *Volunteers* to this LITTERAL WAR, in which all the *Dresses, Customs, Honours and Priviledges*, &c. belonging to the Fair Sex, will be vigorously attackt." Three days later Dunton placed a notice promising that the names of all ladies agreeing to engage in the challenge shall be "inserted . . . from time to time, as they

come to hand." *The Challenge* was published in 1697, with a preface signed "Philaret," Dunton's coterie name. See Parks, *John Dunton*, 320–21.

28 William Walsh, *A Dialogue Concerning Women, Being a Defence of the Sex. Written to Eugenia* (London: R. Bentley and J. Tonson, 1691), 2; Peter Motteux, Dedication "To the Fair Sex," *The Gentleman's Journal: or The Monthly Miscellany*, October 1693, 323. The number was devoted to pieces by women.

29 A similar relationship may have developed in the 1680s between Jane Barker and her bookseller, Benjamin Crayle. In a group of poems by Crayle included by him in the second part of *Poetical Recreations*, a miscellany of poems by Barker and others, he addressed her as "Cosmelia," the object of his secret passion.

30 Elizabeth Singer, *Poems On Several Occasions. Written by Philomela* (London: Dunton, 1696), 2:1–5. Other pairings include "*The Vanity of the World, In a* Poem *to the* Athenians" and "The Athenians *Answer*" (*POSO*, 1:33–35); "A Pindarick POEM on HABBAKUK" and "The ATHENIANS To the Compiler of the Pindarick *now Recited.*" (*POSO*, 1:18–26); "A Poetical Question *concerning the* Jacobites, *sent to the* Athenians" and "The *Athenians* Answer" (*POSO*, 1:27–30).

31 Dunton, "Double," 13.

32 Dedication, *The Athenian Spy: Discovering the Secret Letters which were Sent to the Athenian Society by the most Ingenious Ladies of the Three Kingdoms . . .* (London: R. Halsey, 1704).

33 J. B. Nichols (ed.), *The Life and Errors of John Dunton, Citizen of London*, 2 vols. (London: J. Nichols and Bentley, 1818), 1:185.

34 Dunton, "Double," 48. It is characteristic of Dunton, whose self-plagiarizing prose often induces a sense of déja-vu in the dedicated reader, that earlier he used a version of the same passage to describe a Mrs. Edwards in *Some Account of My Conversation in Ireland. In a Letter to an Honourable Lady. With Her Answer to it.* Bound with *The Dublin Scuffle* (London: for the Author, 1699), 360–61 [misnumbered 344–45].

35 Ibid., 23.

36 Ibid., 23–24.

37 The letter, dated 5 November 1718, is reprinted in Nichols, *The Life and Errors of John Dunton*, xxx. The original is in the Bodleian, MS Rawlinson D. 72, fol. 119.

38 The 1694 date comes from her biographer's statement that she "was not then twenty" when she came into the Thynne orbit, Rowe, *Miscellaneous Works*, xvii.

39 Prior uses the name of Theron to invoke the liberality of his patron in a 1694 letter to the Earl of Dorset, echoing a usage of Cowley. See Historical Manuscripts Commission, *Calendar of the Manuscripts of the Marquis of Bath Preserved at Longleat. Wiltshire.* (Hereford: His Majesty's Stationery Office, 1908), 3:21.

40 Anne Finch also addressed Grace Thynne as Cleone. See McGovern, *Anne Finch*, 113.

180 *Kathryn R. King*

41 Alnwick MS 110, 78: Singer asks the recipient to pass on her thanks to Mrs. Finch for letting her have the copy of "The Storm." McGovern, *Anne Finch*, 118–19, offers an account.

42 Standard accounts are by Jane Spencer, *The Rise of the Woman Novelist: from Aphra Behn to Jane Austen* (Oxford: Blackwell, 1986) and Janet Todd, *The Sign of Angellica: Women, Writing and Fiction, 1660–1800* (London: Virago, 1989).

43 Jeslyn Medoff, "The Daughters of Behn and the Problem of Reputation," *Women, Writing, History 1640–1740*, eds. Isobel Grundy and Susan Wiseman (Athens: University of Georgia Press, 1992), 49.

44 Nine letters from Prior to Singer (her side of the correspondence has disappeared), preserved at Longleat, are printed with useful commentary in H. Bunker Wright, "Matthew Prior and Elizabeth Singer," *Philological Quarterly* 24 (1945), 71–82. For her relationship with Watts, see Stecher, *Elizabeth Singer Rowe*, 88–105.

45 Dunton, "Double," 58, 48–49.

46 Starting as early as 1692 Dunton's detractors portrayed him as vulgar and his publications, the *Mercury* especially, as threatening to class distinctions. See, in addition to Shevelow (note 15 above), McEwen, *Oracle of the Coffee House*, 76–84.

47 Nichols, *Life and Errors*, xxix.

48 Carroll Smith-Rosenberg, "The Female World of Love and Ritual: Relations Between Women in Nineteenth-Century America," *Disorderly Conduct: Visions of Gender in Victorian America* (New York: Knopf, 1985).

49 Grace Strode was a wealthy heiress, the daughter of Sir George Strode of Leweston, Dorset; she married Henry Thynne in 1695. The marriage licence was applied for 29 April 1695; her fortune was reported to be £20,000. See G. E. Cokayne, *The Complete Peerage of England, Scotland, Ireland, Great Britain and the United Kingdom, Extant, Extinct or Dormant*, 14 vols. (London: St. Catherine's Press, 1910–59), 12:Part 2, 588.

50 MS 110, 14.

51 Prior to Singer, 25 November 1703 and 15 February 1703/4. Printed in Wright, "Matthew Prior," 77, 78.

52 MS 110, 17.

53 MS 110, 119.

54 MS 110, 118.

55 Letter from Isaac Watts to Benjamin Colman, 31 May 1738; quoted in Stecher, *Elizabeth Singer Rowe*, 92–93. According to Stecher, 96, Watts's preface to *Devout Exercises of the Heart* (1737), a collection of devotional meditations, "was an attempt to apologize to the 'polite world' for the excessive ardor that marked both his own and Mrs. Rowe's writings."

56 Stecher, *Elizabeth Rowe*, 96.

57 Frances Burney, *Memoirs of Dr. Burney* (Philadelphia: Key and Biddle; Boston: Allen and Ticknor, 1833), 120–23.

58 Hughes, "Elizabeth Rowe," 734.

59 "The author of these Letters is above any View of Interest, and can have no Prospect of Reputation, resolving to be concealed," unsigned Dedication to Dr. Young, *Friendship in Death, in Twenty Letters from the Dead to the Living*, 3rd edn. (London: T. Worrall, 1733).

60 Dustin H. Griffin, *Literary Patronage in England, 1650–1800* (Cambridge: Cambridge University Press, 1996), 155–58.

61 Rowe, *Works*, 1:lxx; emphasis mine.

62 Alnwick MS 110, 195.

63 Ibid., 196.

64 Ibid., 197.

65 Ibid., 197–98.

66 Ibid., 198.

67 Hughes, "Elizabeth Rowe," 735, 736.

68 Alnwick MS 110, 64.

69 For posthumous publication in the context of manuscript culture more generally, see Margaret Ezell's essay in this volume.

70 Love, *Scribal Publication*, 39.

71 John J. Richetti, *Popular Fiction Before Richardson: Narrative Patterns 1700–1739* (Oxford: Clarendon Press, 1992), 245.

CHAPTER 9

Lady Mary Wortley Montagu and her daughter: the changing use of manuscripts

Isobel Grundy

Lady Mary Pierrepont (later Wortley Montagu) was just the kind of person one might expect to get involved in coterie writing and exchange of manuscripts. Not only was she a nobleman's daughter, but her father (Marquess of Dorchester while she was growing up, later Duke of Kingston) was one of the select list of potential patrons who read the youthful Alexander Pope's eclogues in manuscript. He was a member, too, of the Kit-Kat Club, and introduced his eldest daughter there at the age of eight as a potential toast. She later believed that this experience had given her an incurable addiction to admiration and flattery: flattery not from just anybody, but from poets and leaders of men.[1] By the time she reached her teens she was serious about her writing; and she lived to fullfil the promise of her juvenilia.

During her self-imposed apprenticeship she wrote poems, a prose-and-poetry romance (following Aphra Behn), and a brief epistolary novel; she collected her work successively in two nicely bound and carefully copied albums whose title-pages go some way towards imitating print.[2] She seemed to be in training as one of the great ladies on their secluded estates whom Virginia Woolf writes of in *A Room of One's Own*, but also in training to be more professional than those noblewomen whom Woolf sees as a dead end for the growth of women's writing, no matter how admirable and fascinating in themselves.

The child Lady Mary was well-versed both in the classical background and in the latest literary trends. She used her manuscript albums (which were clearly cherished possessions) to construct herself as an author: the individualist, self-centered, exceptionally well-read young poet who is a recognizable feature of any number of literary traditions; not unlike that young Pope who sent his eclogues round among her father's friends. But there was another side to this writing. On the covers of her albums and on spare pages at the back she listed the fictional characters in plays and romances she had read (placing the female characters first).[3]

Among these lists are jottings which bear witness to a more sociable, less intellectually strenuous aspect of life: drawings of hearts, diamonds, clubs, and spades; the name of a sister, Lady Frances Pierrepont, and of a friend, Sarah Chiswell.

There may have been some overlap between the life of a young lady and the life of a young poet. Mentors who are audible in Lady Mary's early poetry include – along with Cowley, Katherine Philips, Behn, and Dryden – a number of living gentlemen-poets (including those who, like Congreve and Samuel Garth, may have toasted her in her childhood). The poems themselves show that the young writer experienced one intense literary friendship, and it is possible that those whose names appear on her volumes (and perhaps others in her circle) were also her readers. A few years after writing her juvenile albums she was exchanging books and printed lampoons with the older, married Frances Hewet and with her own contemporary Mary Banks. The latter also sent her manuscripts: some by the yet-unpublished poet Mary Molesworth Monck and her relations. Lady Mary seems to have kept copies of some of these, and she supplied Banks with a letter written in Italian, to send to Monck as her own.[4] All this is suggestive; but the direct participation of anyone else in her early writings remains a speculation.

It is much more surprising to learn that Lady Mary's daughter, another Mary Wortley Montagu, was a highly accomplished poet during her teenage years. Young Mary was an only daughter whose brother (five years the elder of the two) was away first at school and then banished for misdeeds to the other side of the world. But she enjoyed the company of contemporaries in her extended family: girl cousins (whose brothers were largely absent) and her mother's two much younger half-sisters. These upper-class adolescents led busy social lives, and no evidence has been found that any of them kept up her literary pursuits beyond the early days of marriage. Lady Mary, indeed, virtually apologized to her daughter years later for not having given her a learned education (citing as her reason the fact that young Mary, as an heiress, was expected to marry well). But though the young Mary Wortley Montagu was not a scholar like her mother, she nevertheless took the lead in the poetry-writing of her circle, and between them these girls produced a book of poems no less remarkable than those of the girl Lady Mary.[5]

These two collections, of Lady Mary's writing done at Thoresby Hall, Nottinghamshire, in 1704–05, and of her young relatives' writing done in or near London in the 1730s, contrast with each other in many ways: in period, in setting (isolated rural estate versus sophisticated urban and suburban milieu), in ideology, in the balance of subject-matter between poetic models and life experience, in being chiefly individual and chiefly collaborative, and in Lady Mary's overt literary ambitions, which her daughter's generation did not share. Between them they cover a wide range of the possibilities open to family coterie writing. A comparison of the two should prove illuminating.

For Lady Mary Pierrepont, literature was in the family. She later prided herself on the brain power of her great-grandfather "Wise" William Pierrepont. Until she was ten she attended church in a space dominated by a lengthy and remarkable epitaph to her grandfather Robert Pierrepont, written mostly in latter-day metaphysical verse, which may be the work of her grandmother. Another church where she worshipped contains an epitaph to the satirist John Oldham, erected by Oldham's patron, her uncle. Her father's library, the site of her self-education, contained a relatively high proportion of works by women, a large number of which celebrated female achievement (not all of it by saints and martyrs). Whether or not these had been acquired by female ancestors, they offered a range of role models, and help to account for the intense high-mindedness which Lady Mary later identified as the leading characteristic of her upbringing.[6]

What she says of that upbringing is somewhat confusing, especially since most of her forays into autobiography were conducted under the cloak of fiction. She had a pious governess who tried without lasting success to prime her with superstitious religiosity. But also she was taught to adhere to what she calls "old Whiggism," to despise distinctions of rank, and to believe poverty a sign of virtue. This does not sound like the teaching of the governess, and it sounds downright unacceptable to her father. It may have had something to do with two liberal and learned bishops, Burnet and Tenison, who directed (but to what extent it is impossible to tell) the young Lady Mary in her studies.[7] Her teenage writing, therefore, was encompassed by contraries.

She addressed her earlier volume ("Poems Letters Novels Songs etc") "to the fair hands of the beauteous Hermensilda by her most obedient Strephon"; yet her title-page explanation and justification for its acknowledged faults begins, "1. I am a Woman." She writes of the poet as "haughty in rags and proudly poor," and as despising a lord;[8] yet the poets of her first-hand acquaintance were suave and well-dressed, and included not only friends of the lord her father, but lords in their own right, like Lansdowne and John Sheffield Duke of Buckingham. Her models in poetry were seventeenth century or classical; yet here and there, in a reference to the pleasures of "dear London," the contemporary and the non-pastoral creep in.[9]

If her literary activity was less of a solitary affair than (in her own later account of it) her self-education was, then the circle of friends for whom she wrote was an interestingly mixed assemblage of bright young women whose fathers were peers, gentry, estate agents, and attorneys. But she does not choose her topics from the lives of these young women, or the marriage-market experience which was looming ever closer for them. The dominant mode of her writings is fictive: the developed narratives, in prose and in prose-and-verse, of Indamora and of Strephon; briefer poetic narratives, some of them from Ovid or Virgil; epistolary poems which, like dramatic monologues, communicate the situation of their protagonists as a backdrop to their feelings. Even the poems which one may suspect of telling an autobiographical story tell it under the guise of the love of Clarinda for Hermensilda. Love in these poems is either classical-heroic or courtly-pastoral. It involves the swearing of vows, the exchange of hearts, the writing of names on the barks of trees. Marriage (the actual prospect of Lady Mary and her putative audience) appears in these volumes only in contexts safely removed by history or fantasy. In "The Adventurer," which is part-satirical, wholly allegorical, and centered on a male protagonist, marriage is an "Old Ruinous Palace," the abode of "Discord, Strife and uneasyness."[10]

The poems of the younger generation lack the self-consciously literary cast of Lady Mary's: the range of bookish allusion, the assumed preference of country to town life and of pastoral values to contemporary ones, the switch of gender identity to encompass the coveted role of poet. They are more concentratedly social. The album containing them incorporates the work of a whole circle of poets (though the youngest, Mary Wortley Montagu, is the dominant voice); members of this circle address each other as confidantes, and deal almost exclusively with their own affairs. They too write under pastoral names, but unlike Lady Mary's their pseudonyms imply no fictive identities. They write as themselves.

Both generations of girl-poets are interested first and foremost in love-situations. But where Lady Mary writes of Alexander and Roxana, Julia and Ovid (as well as others who *might* be actual acquaintances), her daughter writes entirely about herself and her circle. The volume turns on the courtship of her cousin Lady Frances Pierrepont ("Melantha") by a young man, "Melanthus," who in life was one Philip Meadows, whom Lady Mary (her niece's guardian) suspected of being a fortune-hunter. The social customs surrounding marriage (dowries, legal settlements, family endorsement), which are almost absent from Lady Mary's volumes, stand at the center of this one; but they are treated in language very different from the sober lawyers' prose in which they are generally encountered (and which Lady Mary approximated in her courtship correspondence, written some years after her juvenilia).

Comparison of the two collections reflects the lower educational attainment of the second generation, but does not suggest that this was either imposed or resented. It was simply the absence of something exceptional. Lady Mary made her original writing share its space with lists of books and their characters which are those of a polymath in the making: from Scudéry, from Ovid's *espistles* (presumably the *Heroides* in English translation), from "a Tartarian Hystory," and from innumerable plays.[11] Evidently her reading and her writing went together. Names of characters in her poems – Orinda, Ardelia, Silvianetta, Belvidera – are borrowed from the literary world, either from the pseudonyms of established women writers, or from names of fictional characters.

In the later collection, too, the names are literary, with their roots in romance. "Sylvia" (*nom de plume* of Lady Mary's daughter, the future Countess of Bute) suggests a denizen of the green natural world, while "Melantha" is the name of a character in Eliza Haywood's first novel, *Love in Excess*.[12] Haywood as source does not suggest the bookishness implied by the use of Katherine Philips or Madeleine de Scudéry. But the younger generation's narrower reading is balanced by a greater sophistication in social experience. In the fashionable world, it seems, young women have become a constituency with their own standards and attitudes. These include an open and candid antagonism toward the older generation, a solidarity in teenage rebellion which sounds positively twentieth-century. Whereas just one poem by Lady Mary ("'Twas folly made mee fondly write") *implies* a clash with censorious elders over the indulgence of "love and wit," in poem after poem her daughter and her niece explicitly depict their female elders as quadrille-playing "beldames," "old Matrons as grave as a cat." And whereas the child Lady Mary was a penitent sinner ("I own I tre[s]pass'd wickedly in rhime"), the next generation is irrepressible: "When age has furrow'd every feature / Then like them we'll vent our Satyr. / We've time enough for growing wise."[13]

One way to express the difference between the collections would be to say the following. Lady Mary stands revealed in her juvenile albums as an exceptional individual – in her solemnity, her moral idealism, her mastery of the various discourses of poetry, her protean role-playing – as someone at odds with the norms of her early-Queen-Anne culture. Her daughter and her friends are much better adjusted. The imaginative life revealed in their poetry comes not from their reading but from their daily occupations, a round of pleasure-seeking with the ultimate aim of husband-hunting. Their poetic personae are endearingly light-hearted, flippant and giggling. Apart from the astonishing fact of their writing, they were probably not very different from other upper-class female adolescents of their generation all over Britain.

This point of comparison can be developed by looking at the trespass which is highlighted in each collection: two very different infringements. Lady Mary's albums encapsulate clues to a story they do not quite tell: of her being detected in writing and ordered to desist. The experience is rendered with strong emotion but with a degree of abstraction which makes it impossible to tell exactly what was seen as reprehensible about her writing. The force of her sorrow and repentance suggests a more charged situation than a casual reprimand delivered to a child, and speaks the language of mature experience even while someone unnamed is denying her right to either experience or maturity.

The complete poem goes like this.

> 'Twas folly made mee fondly write
> (For what [have] I to doe with Love and wit?)
> I own I tre[s]pass'd wickedly in Rhime
> But oh my Punishment exceeds my crime.
> My Folies tho' on parchment writt
> I soon might burn and then forget,
> But if I Now both burn and blot
> (By mee) the[y] cannot bee forgot.

The physical appearance of this poem explains a good deal about it. It was added later to a page already pretty well filled, in Lady Mary's first album, alongside twenty stubs of pages cut out of the volume and another entirely obliterated by heavy scribbling. It is a fair assumption that this poem, more than most of her juvenilia, deals with direct experience: its author has indeed burned and blotted. (But she did not stop writing; she defiantly transcribed most of the surviving poems from her first, defaced album into a second, whose title-page imitates a published "Complete Works.")

Her crime, then, was to write: to be the exceptional person she was. The linking of love and wit may simply reflect her poems' choice of love as their subject matter (including the love affairs of Alexander, Julius Caesar, and the protagonist of Virgil's eclogue ten). Or it may reflect the poet's thwarted love for Hermensilda. This love, which informs several poems, seems to be a poetic rendering of Lady Mary's feeling for Jane Smith, whose father was Speaker of the House of Commons. It takes up many pages in the second album, and may well (judging from the title-page of the first) have done the same there. It is not likely to have been a fully developed lesbian affair (though that possibility cannot be ruled out); but it certainly involved strong feeling, role-playing, and poetic expression.

Lady Mary was detected in something – whether writing or writing *and* loving – which her elders severely blamed. She felt scarred and victimized. While her family probably saw the whole matter as something childish and forgettable, she internalized their blame, wrote of it obliquely, could not forget it. Her niece Lady Frances Pierrepont, at the other extreme in relationship between ego and super-ego, made herself the talk of the town as an unmarried girl by an unsanctioned love affair and an elopement which dictated the whole course of her future life. But her poetic comments on these actions after the event, and the more detailed comment and narrative of her cousin Mary Wortley Montagu while the story unrolled, express no self-blame and no self-consciousness. To both of them this remains a romantic story; Lady Frances's action is supported and endorsed, albeit with some soul-searching, by her contemporaries; it is something that only beldames would gripe at. Her infraction of social codes is far more serious than was the one recorded in her aunt's poems, but in her own writing circle it is taken far more lightly.

In each of these collections of writing, then, some defiance of convention and authority was central. Lady Mary's seems to have been an attempt to choose, with the aid of poetry, a style of life which was in some way derived from the world of poetry, and conceived as fundamentally different from the one mapped out for her by social expectation. She failed, and the whole matter, rebellion and recantation, remained unknown outside her family; her account of it is half fictional and only half explained. Her niece and daughter rebelled more flatly and sweepingly, in private actions which would inevitably become public; but their defiance of convention was itself a convention. Elopements, though against the rules, were happening every day. *Vers de société* knew how to handle them, and society itself knew how to respond, and how to place the blame. Their own account of the affair, in its closing stages, seems designed to counter these public voices.

What in Lady Mary's, or Strephon's, "Poems Letters Novels Songs etc" can have proved so shocking? It bears the dates of "1704" and "1705" on its title-page and cover, claims to have been composed at fourteen, and has been mutilated in the manner already described. Its surviving contents live up to the title-page designation: poems, the verse-and-prose romance "The Adventurer," and the novel "Indamora." For her other, apparently later volume, Lady Mary chose a title sounding less like a miscellany and more like a definitive collection. Her first choice for the title of this second volume was the classical and dignified "Opera," but she crossed this out and opted for "The Entire Works of Clarinda / London." The longer works from the Strephon volume reappear here, revised in detail but not in overall plan. Some poems are repeated; others may be either new or restored from the censored pages of the other volume. Except for the pair of poems about the crisis with Hermensilda (which bear exact dates in May 1705) the contents of these two volumes seem innocuous enough. It may well have been the very fact of writing which was regarded by authority as transgression.[14]

Circumstantial evidence shows that the untitled volume compiled by the next generation opens in 1733, almost thirty years after the first. The album used would have been less expensive to buy than Lady Mary's, and though it is nicely and neatly produced it makes no attempt to imitate print. It mixes several handwritings, of which the first and most frequent is that of "Sylvia," Lady Mary's daughter. Next (in sequence and in frequency) comes "Melantha," who is Lady Frances Pierrepont, the heiress daughter of Lady Mary's dead brother, who was now living under her aunt's guardianship. Later in the volume, other contributors join in, calling themselves Timandra, Evadne, and Eurilla.[15] The collection opens with an exchange between Sylvia and Melantha. The former (anticipating Frances Greville's famous poem by some years) voices her disdain for love and her preference for friendship, even for "Cold Indiference," and Melantha rallies to the defense of love, from the position of one who knows it at first hand: "I return a passion / And meet an equall flame." Melantha's flame is to be the central motif of the volume, whose transgressiveness is therefore built into its fabric.

The central story is skillfully introduced. Melantha's lover is marked as hers by the name "Melanthus"; but sometimes in the sequence he is called "Phil," to fix him in the actual world beyond the poems, where Philip Meadows assiduously courted Lady Frances Pierrepont, caused her to turn down the family-approved suitors who offered themselves, and eloped with her the day after she turned twenty-one. The poems credit her with agency and with tactical deception: "Tho' she with Cold Indiference put him by / Her eyes did plainly give her Tongue the Lye." For the real-life status of marriage as financial transaction, the young poets employ a romantic or pastoral vocabulary reminiscent of Lady Mary: Melanthus "had not wealth for her relations pride"; those relations would rather see her "great in misery" than "poor and blest." Led by her brother, they apply emotional blackmail, threatening rejection if she will not comply with their wishes and marry someone called Clitophon. (In life this was John Spencer, a grandson of Sarah, Duchess of Marlborough.) Melantha, facing the dilemma of losing her brother or her lover, resolves to do "what I think is right."[16] She dreams of love in a cottage; she worries about Melanthus's capacity to remain faithful through trials. For a while she thinks she could submit, marry Clitophon, and love Melanthus platonically; then she realizes she could not.

Around the central thread of Melantha's courtship there cluster a number of other love-situations. The collection's various subject-matter thus parallels its composition among many collaborative hands. Sylvia and Melantha often compose together: they speak jointly in a poem which they wrote to go "in a book entitle'd the Platonick Lover's (Lent us by Timandra)," and antiphonally in a pastoral dialogue pitting country against town, love against indifference (as if each of them had chosen to speak in one of two conflicting voices of the young Lady Mary). Sylvia alone wrote "A Fable" about a country squire humanized by love.

It is the subordinate writers who come closest to anything resembling social critique. Eurilla contributes a poem on the cause of unhappy marriages: she lays these disasters at the feet of Avarice, not Hymen. That is, through the poetic terms at her disposal she argues that not marriage itself, but the social conventions surrounding it for her generation and her class, are to blame. Timandra chooses the dream vision form for a cautious tribute to Melantha's illicit suitor, a poem which praises him for qualities which it recognizes he might have lacked. While *this* young man has all the virtues without the seal of family approval, it implies that other illicit suitors might be different.

Lady Mary's youthful poems relate to seventeenth-century pastoral poetry and French romance. The literary progenitors of Sylvia's and Melantha's verses are closer to home: the *vers de société* which were common in this culture.[17] Their collection includes poems which comment *à clef* on others' love-affairs, and *bouts rimés* (created by means of a parlor-game of filling in lines of verse to incorporate a pre-set list of rhyme-words). At the same time these poems seem to inhabit the world of the new novel: not that of Richardson or of either Fielding (who had not yet arrived on the scene), nor yet of Defoe (who came from, and wrote of, a different rank from these young writers), but of Eliza Haywood, Mary Davys, and Jane Barker. Like these young poets, the novelists pit love against one form or another of power or convention; they too satirize the social or fashionable world which is unworthy of their heroines. But none of these fiction-writers deals with quite this combination of ideal-istic youth and cynical age: in this the young people of the Pierrepont family anticipate the novel of the 1740s.

Lady Mary employs a moral standpoint from literary tradition for her early criticism of the materialism and snobbery of her own class. She laments the passing of that golden age when "There was no giveing Rich, nor begging poor, / In Common all enjoy'd an equall store."[18] Characters in her poems who are not modeled on historical or allegorical figures are young ladies responding with ecstasy to the beauties of nature, abjuring "th'inconstant Town," or playing the role of muse to poets or painters: young ladies, in short, from between the covers of books. In her daughter's poems, such young ladies are much more worldly. They dance, they hunt, they flirt, they go in water parties on the Thames, they play games which circle round the all-pervasive theme of courtship. They criticize their society strictly from an angle dictated by their gender and class position in it: their wished-for reforms are those concerning social liberty and marriage choice.

To Lady Mary it was natural to put her narratives in the past tense. Even an epiphany of a moment (when Belvidera on the banks of the Severn drinks in the beauties of the scene around her and abjures London life) is rendered in the past. The "Now" of " 'Twas folly made mee fondly write" is unusual. Melantha and Sylvia, on the other hand, typically write to the moment, like Pamela or like Boswell; and like those indefatigable scribblers they sometimes seem to live to write.[19] On the occasion of a visit to the opera (which they hope, like Lady Mary before them, to use as a rendezvous) each dashes off one stanza beforehand and another afterwards to express her anxious feelings.

The ideal of conduct marked out in Lady Mary's juvenilia is that of heroic fiction: of works like Biondi's *Eromena*, translated into English in 1632, in which she marked with a star an account of a heroine's intellec-tual aspirations and strict moral self-scrutiny: her "vigilancy to accuse and correct her selfe, if her perfections could have been capable of the least error."[20] To her niece and daughter love rather than intellect, and teenage-romantic rather than heroic love, was the source of perfection; self-scrutiny and self-accusation were not on the agenda.

Lady Mary at fourteen or fifteen is already a feminist-in-training. When she imitates Virgil's tenth eclogue (a typical representation of mag-nanimously forgiving masculine grief in response to perfidious female infidelity) she swaps his gender roles to present an injured woman and fickle man. (She might have learned this exchange from Behn, who had swapped gender roles in imitating an ode by Horace.)[21] On the fairly conventional topic of a woman's lament that her lover has to leave her to go to war, she suggests that her speaker longs to share her lover's adventures as much as she longs to keep him with her. He has glory in prospect; she has not. She concludes, "what my Soul wou'd doe, my Fate denies, / And I can kill with nothing but my Eyes."[22]

Killing with their eyes seems enough to satisfy the poets of the next generation. They delight in drawing the attention of "many a teddy Lad." (A marginal note explains that "teddy" means clever; it clearly means desirable too.)[23] Though the volume begins with Sylvia's abjuring love, she is later attracted, for a while, to Sylvander. Whenever she sees him, "My heart begins strongly to move. / It is not at the Sight of a he, / I believe it is being in love." With reluctance, with some regret for her lost feelings of serene indifference, with cries of "alack and a [sic] welladay," she accepts that love has infiltrated her heart.[24] All this is rendered with verisimilitude rather than with attention to the requirements of romance. Particularly striking as an example of realism is the fact that when Sylvia discovers Sylvander's infidelity (not with a new great love, but with a series of flirtations) she fights a brief, fierce struggle with her feelings and overcomes them. It is not that she scorns love to pursue the masculine phantoms of literary or poetic glory, but that in the arena of love she is non-heroic, sensible, and self-protective. On every point except that of refusing to know or to name her own feelings, she behaves as the conduct-books would wish. Though she and Melantha decry the behavior of (older) women, neither aspires to widen or to change the female role available to them. The avarice which causes unhappy marriages appears to Eurilla to be personal vice, not the inbuilt tendency of society to commodify women in the shape of their marriage portions.

Each collection of poems provides glimpses of a wider world. The War of the Spanish Succession impinges on Lady Mary's poems with images of demobilized soldiers: the "tatter'd red coat begging in the street" is treated by others with pitying scorn at best; but he himself, even in beggary, is proud of his honorable scars. This image comes from a poem of Augustan survey, a search through every walk of life to see who is, or might be, happy; it concludes with a pious swerve away from the world towards "Heaven's unknown and unimmagin'd bliss."[25] Sylvia and Melantha, growing up under the long-lived sway of Robert Walpole, had no wars to write about. Sylvia, however, wrote a rollicking song on the elections of 1734, in which her father was considered by his own party and local supporters to have struggled gallantly to throw a temporary spoke into the wheel of the Walpole electioneering machine. Sylvia subscribes to neither side ideologically: instead, she frowns on politics, which distract "youngsters" from love: "The Men ought to Lose our affection / Who leave the dear Town / And range up and down / For the sake of a filthy Election."[26]

The younger generation is amazingly accomplished, although one of them, Evadne, chose to begin her earliest contribution to the volume by conventionally bewailing her lack of talent. It would be hard to say which was the more promising embryo poet at the age of fifteen: Lady Mary as Strephon or Clarinda, or her daughter as Sylvia (even if one discounts Sylvia's various co-writers as outclassed by the competition). The difference is not in accomplishment, but in the seriousness of Lady Mary's literary ambitions.

Lady Mary, choosing her fictional identity first as Strephon and then as Clarinda, seems to have followed consciously and purposefully in the footsteps of Behn and Philips, of Cowley in *The Mistress* and Waller in his Myra poems. In her miniature imitation of the adult genre of gendered humble apology she achieves a *tour de force* of compression, and like her begging redcoat she leaves no doubt that her assumed humility cloaks very real pride.

I Question not but here is very manny faults, but if any reasonable person considers three things they will forgive them.

1. I am a Woman
2. without any advantage of Education
3. all these was wrote by me at the age of 14.

Sylvia, Melantha, and the others do not address "any reasonable person" but exclusively each other.

The themes of Lady Mary's juvenile poems can be traced in her later life, and – for she is more interesting as a writer even than as she is as a woman – in her works. The circle of friends who can be glimpsed as clustered around her juvenilia foreshadow groupings later in her life. At fifteen or so Lady Mary seems to have read Astell; her friends may have read her too. Later Montagu and Astell were to compose poems of trenchant social critique on opposite sides of a single sheet of paper; and Astell was to add her unpublished introduction to share the slow progress towards publication of Montagu's Embassy Letters.[27] Meanwhile Lady Mary's poems to and about Hermensilda laid the foundations for her powerful poetic avowals of love for Francesco Algarotti. Her courtship novel "Indamora to Lindamira," even though it rewards its heroine's virtue with a happy ending, was nevertheless a trial run for her fictions of unrewarded virtue: "Louisa," "Mademoiselle de Condé," and "Princess Docile".[28] The imitations of Ovid and Virgil were similarly prototypes of her later mock-imitations. Her youthful dreams about a flight from society to "some close obscure retreat" may be read as a foretaste either of her many plans for retirement (the idyll of life at Naples which she proposed in her courtship letters, the successive retreats which she actually constructed at Constantinople and Twickenham, at Avignon and Gottolengo) or of the recurrent, fruitful tension in her writings between the desire for society and the desire for solitude.

So far as is known, the other collection had no such far-reaching literary consequences. Its immediate practical consequences may well have included the first opening of a rift between Lady Mary and her beloved daughter, a rift which took more than a decade to heal. For the poems undoubtedly facilitated the courtship and elopement which they delineate. This collection shows art as not merely intertwined with life but as actively shaping it.

The poems' account is essentially factual. Lady Frances Pierrepont had a fortune of £20,000 to come to her at her marriage. Following the successive deaths of her father, mother, grandfather, and great-aunt, she was under Lady Mary's care. She was courted by the impecunious and "teddy" (in both senses) Philip Meadows. Her elder brother the second Duke of Kingston, who came of age around the time that the earliest poems were being written in the volume,[29] wanted her to marry John Spencer. Spencer was a younger brother, but his family connections were stellar, beginning with his grandmother Sarah Duchess of Marlborough. Though Sarah had formerly doted on this grandson, she had recently become disenchanted with him; he was no longer the focus of her formidable matchmaking tendencies. Lady Mary had recently written in strong terms against mercenary marriages.[30] It seems the oppressor of Lady Frances was her brother (as the poems explicitly state), not an alliance of older women (as they indirectly seem to imply).

The poems record and heroicize the actual episode of Lady Frances's resistance to marrying Spencer. By early August 1733 it was publicly known that her resistance had proved successful. The "censorious part of the town" (said her uncle Lord Gower) were reporting that she had set her heart on Meadows; Lady Strafford thought their love-affair had "gon to farr to be prevented." Lady Frances continued to make herself a mark for gossip (by fainting at a ball, for instance) when Lady Mary took her niece and daughter to the races at Lichfield in Staffordshire.[31] From there they went on to Gower's estate at Trentham, and from there to Thoresby Hall, the site of Lady Mary's long-ago adolescent writings, now owned by Melantha's brother, the Duke of Kingston. Sylvia's and Melantha's poems describe only some of these events, and their handling stands midway between the high-flown tone in which they originally introduced the love of Melantha and Melanthus, and the gossipy letters of bystanders. The visit to Thoresby, for instance, appears in the album not as an obstacle for Melantha's love to surmount, but as an occasion for sardonic reportage of the irresponsibly flirtatious behavior (towards third parties) of the two mentors, Lady Mary and the Duke of Kingston.

In October the duke left England for France, resigning the care of his sister (and presumably the direction of her marriage) to Lady Mary. "Clitophon," already out of the picture, married someone else in February 1734. Next month the unfortunate Princess Anne married the deformed but properly Protestant Prince of Orange; among her white-clad attendants to the altar were Lady Frances Pierrepont (Melantha) and her near-contemporary aunt Lady Caroline Pierrepont (probably the Evadne of the poems).[32] Next month again Lady Frances celebrated her twenty-first birthday.

On 23 April 1734, the day after she came of age, she and "Sylvia" attended the opera at Lincoln's Inn Fields. At least once before, as their verses record, they had gone to the opera together with their minds on meeting young men. Indeed, it may have been that earlier occasion, indelibly associated with love by means of the poems written about it, which inspired their present plan. They sat in a box, near "Melanthus" in another box. After the first act they stepped out, on the grounds that Lady Frances felt ill again. When Meadows too left (after a discreet pause) "[m]ost people guessed what they were about," according to Mary Pendarves (later Mary Delany).

For Melantha the immediate future held a wedding (after some weeks which were no doubt filled with financial negotiations not unlike those which follow Lydia's elopement in *Pride and Prejudice*) and, seven months later, the birth of her first child.[33] Neither the sexual activity which must almost certainly have occurred before the elopement, nor the business dealings which followed it, appear in the poems: they were topics which the genre could not encompass. Society (typified by the very different viewpoints of Mary Pendarves and John, Lord Hervey) was generally unsympathetic and censorious towards Lady Frances.[34] Mary Wortley Montagu the younger sorely missed her companionship (as she eloquently explained in a poem beginning "How Tedious is Life now Melantha is gone"). Mary Wortley Montagu the elder seems to have retained for years some bitterness over these events. Something of Rochefoucauldian pleasure in the misfortunes of others sounds in her expressions of pity for Lady Frances Meadows in the 1740s and 50s, when the whole Meadows family was living as poor dependents of Lady Frances's brother the duke, with an obligation to behave nicely to his reigning mistress.[35]

Meanwhile it was left to the manuscript album to assert the happiness of the ending. Sylvia contributed poems of warmest good wishes, and transcribed responses from Melantha which are vibrant with love and happiness. Her husband, the former Melanthus, has borne out those "Indications of the Noblest Mind" which she had long since read in him; he "allways has Deserv'd / The Love which I so Resolute preserv'd."[36] She depicts her married life as an ecstatic version of the traditional love in a cottage. The volume ends like a novel, with a triumphant narrative closure which is foreign to the collection format of Lady Mary's juvenile albums.

A different ending, skeptical if not cynical, was written outside the bounds of the volume. It seems that young Mary showed her mother the latest poems from the married Lady Frances, and that Lady Mary responded, as was a habit with her in topical verses, not by inventing words but adapting the pre-existing words of others.[37] One of her refashioned comments is a version of a seventeenth-century epigram, spoken by a rejected to a successful suitor. In the present case it would be spoken by John Spencer to Philip Meadows, and it warns him not to boast of a conquest which does him no credit. "No wonder that her Heart was lost / Whose senses first were gone . . . Her loving thee is not the Cause; / But Sign that she is mad."

Her other, longer poem has a more complicated provenance. Someone (perhaps one Mary Wortley Montagu or the other; perhaps someone unconnected with either of them) had adapted Nicholas Rowe's popular "Colin's Complaint" and entitled the new version "Melinda's Complaint." Lady Mary kept a copy of this, and adapted it further to her niece's situation as "Melantha's Complaint." The opinions she wrote for her niece are the very opposite of those which Melantha expressed for herself about her marriage. In Lady Mary's version the new bride wishes the elopement undone, partly because (how unlike the pastoral companions of Lady Mary's youth!) she regrets losing the pleasures of the town, but more because the very object of her choice, the company of her dear Phil, has now become loathsome to her: "Whatever a Lover may boast /A Husband is what one may hate." Her only solace now is to dream of the town.[38] Lady Mary is surely the author: the astringency is typical of her, while nothing suggests that Sylvia would snub her cousin like this.

In a twist which gives a backward look at Lady Mary's own juvenile poems, Sylvia and Melantha's volume has had its final pages cut out. The vandal (almost certainly contemporary) was probably not Lady Mary. Her feelings about the volume must have been mixed, since it so vividly demonstrates her daughter's accomplishment while revealing attitudes which she most probably deplored. She would not have felt, like her own elders, that the act of writing was in itself transgressive. It is hard to see how, while letting the volume as a whole stand, she could yet find something particular to delete. A possible, though entirely speculative, explanation would be that she got hold of the volume and violated its tone by inserting her own crushing conclusion. The coauthors would then have had no recourse but to erase this contribution from a hostile older voice. The early history of this volume, like that of its predecessors, remains undeciphered.

Both volumes testify to the remarkable technical virtuosity, near-professional confidence, and individual style that can be reached in poetry by talented youngsters. But as well as marking poetry's educative potential they point to its potential for socially deviant self-expression. Here two generations of adolescents, the nascent writer and merely intelligent and high-spirited future wives and mothers, found in poetry both an agenda and a voice for their rebellion.

The volumes also provide a substantial footnote to social history. It seems that during the thirty years separating these two manuscripts, in one family at least, the influence of Renaissance pastoralism and near-chivalric idealism reached its furthest verge of influence, and retired. Society became more class-bound but also more oriented towards a public world of expense and entertainment, in which young women saw themselves as a group apart from adults, with a developing teenage counter-culture which is highly literate though far from literary. The remarkable thing is that they remain so well able to command a confident, varied speaking voice in poetry, and that their resistance to the norms of (older) society is so spirited and so witty. At a moment when conduct-book culture was gathering power, these young women deployed their own literary resources for mental independence and imaginative self-realization. They apparently did not aspire to be learned ladies; their exchanges of poetry were a living element in their own kind of popular culture.

NOTES

1 Wharncliffe MS M 506, Sheffield Central Library.
2 Lady Mary Wortley Montagu, *Essays and Poems and Simplicity a Comedy*, eds. Robert Halsband and Isobel Grundy (Oxford: Clarendon Press, 1977, revised edn. 1993), 9.
3 Harrowby Manuscripts Trust, Sandon Hall, Stafford, 250, 251. I have written about these works in Isobel Grundy, "'The Entire Works of Clarinda': Unpublished Juvenile Verse by Lady Mary Wortley Montagu," *Yearbook of English Studies* 7(1977), 91–107.
4 I owe this point to Carolyn Creed.
5 Isobel Grundy, *Lady Mary Wortley Montagu: Comet of the Enlightenment* (Oxford: Clarendon Press, 1999), 24. Manuscripts by Mary Monck or her circle are extant in Harrowby MSS 81.
6 Grundy, *Lady Mary Wortley Montagu*, 3, 10–11, 15–16.
7 Ibid., 87–8, 8.
8 Harrowby 250, 5.
9 Harrowby 251, 29.
10 Ibid., 2.
11 By Beaumont and Fletcher, Dryden, Behn, Congreve, Corneille, Molière, and a dozen more.
12 Haywood's Melantha, a capricious and likable coquette, bobs up again after every misfortune. The end of part 2 finds her (in a parallel probably closer than any intended when the name was selected for Lady Frances Pierrepont) married at last, and enjoying "the good fortune not to be suspected by her husband, though she brought him a child in seven months after the wedding," Eliza Haywood, *Love in Excess; Or, The Fatal Enquiry*, ed. David Oakleaf (Peterborough: Broadview Press, 1994), 116, 132–33, 177.

13 Harrowby 250, 5; Wharncliffe MS M 506, 3–4.

14 Harrowby MSS 250, 251. 31–32 (20 and 26 May 1705).

15 Wharncliffe, 68.

16 Wharncliffe, 1–2, 5–7. Lord Hervey had reported in 1731 a rumour about Meadows being about to marry a widow (Ilchester 105).

17 Lady Mary collected a couple of such volumes. Harrowby MSS 81, 255.

18 Harrowby 251, 25–26.

19 The Pamela on whom Evadne wrote "Verses" cares only for dress; she is nothing like Richardson's yet-to-be-created heroine. Wharncliffe, 8–12 [sic: pages misnumbered], 14–18, 20–21, 28, 47.

20 Page 12 of a volume now at Sandon Hall.

21 Montagu later reversed the genders in the same ode in the same way: "The 5th Ode of Horace imitated," Montagu, *Essays*, 302.

22 Harrowby 251, 30.

23 The marginal definition of "teddy" reads "clever" (presumably from some actual Edward – probably not "Sylvia's" banished brother). But this definition shares with other explications of nonce-words in these poems a deliberate air of misrepresentation or mystification. To "becalm" is "another word for sweat"; "a Phil" is "a dangerous person": surely these are oblique gestures against adult standards or decrees. "Teddy" was perhaps designed to assimilate the cleverness valued by mothers with the sexiness valued by daughters.

24 Wharncliffe, 12–13, 21.

25 Harrowby 250, 5.

26 Wharncliffe, 58.

27 Grundy, *Lady Mary Wortley Montagu*, 240–41, 200–01.

28 Ibid.

29 On 3 April 1733.

30 Montagu, *Essays*, 271–72.

31 Gower to Essex, 7 August 1733 (BL 27732. 218); Lady Strafford and someone else to Lady Huntingdon, 26 August, 23 September (Hastings, 17, 18).

32 Spencer married Georgiana Carteret on 14 February. The Prince of Orange married Princess Anne on 17 March.

33 A marriage settlement was drawn up (BL Egerton MS 3660. 95). The wedding took place on 14 May and the birth on either 14 or 17 December (newspapers; Cokayne).

34 Hervey to Henry Fox, 11 May 1734, BL Additional MS 51410; Delany to Ann Granville, 27 April (1:461–62).

35 Marie Thérèse de La Touche; then Elizabeth Chudleigh; perhaps Frances Anne, *née* Hawes, Lady Vane (Egmont, *Diary*, 2:381; Chudleigh, *Avantures*, 36–37, 41, 79, 124–27; Ilchester, 256, 258). All this paid off in the end: the duke was never legally married, and his estate devolved on Lady Frances's second son, bringing a title in its train.

36 Timandra voiced admiration, but no desire to follow suit (Wharncliffe, 69–71, 73–74, 75–76).

37 Both these adapted poems are probably, not certainly, by her.
38 The original of Montagu's "Supposed to be wrote from J[ohn] Sp[encer] to Ph[ilip] M[eadows] on his marriage" has been variously ascribed, Grundy, *Lady Mary Wortley Montagu*, 314–15. "Melinda's Complaint" is in Harrowby 255, 58–9 and other copies. Scholarly opinion has wavered as to whether to attribute the "Melantha" version to Lady Mary: it is given in her *Works* (5:220–23), but omitted from her *Essays*. The Harrowby Manuscripts contain a complete copy in Lady Bute's hand and only an incomplete one in hers (81, 55, 168–69). But in the light of this poem's occasion (only recently investigated) Lady Mary is the likelier author.

CHAPTER 10

Suppression and censorship in late manuscript culture: Frances Burney's unperformed The Witlings

George Justice

SEE last advance, with bashful grace,
    Downcast eye, and blushing cheek,
Timid air, and beauteous face,
    Anville, – whom the Graces seek,

Though ev'ry beauty is her own,
    And though her mind each virtue fills,
Anville, – to her power unknown,
    Artless strikes, – unconscious kills.[1]

When the eponymous heroine of Frances Burney's *Evelina* enters the pump room at Bristol Hot Wells in Volume III of the novel, she is greeted by "a party of young men" who follow her and whisper phrases from a set of verses in praise or blame of the season's young women. These verses, penned by the impoverished poet Macartney, have been circulating in manuscript. Evelina's tormentor, Sir Clement Willoughby, forces her to read the portion of the poem devoted to her own charms by handing her his own copy of the lines. Evelina is pictured in the verse with "downcast eye, and blushing cheek." The perusal of the poem has for Evelina "the power of rouge," says her protector, the satirical Mrs. Selwyn. The circulated verses, which accurately if intrusively describe her, cause great embarrassment – her representation is out of her own control.[2] The limited circulation of the verses mirrors Sir Clement's insistence on inappropriately private conversation with Evelina. As Evelina herself has noted, she has "an aversion the most sincere to all mysteries, all private actions."[3]

This moment in *Evelina* exemplifies Burney's understanding and representation of manuscript circulation. My essay argues that Burney's turn toward a skillful manipulation of the possibilities for authorship in the public world of print-publication stems from a distrust of – and a bad experience with – coteries as a network for publishing writing. While many literary women of her day affiliated themselves with discrete

groups of women or men and women, Burney eventually chose to stake
out an independent position that eschewed the controls imposed by literary communities, preferring to try her luck with the world at large, the
"public" she refers to in the Preface to *Evelina*. For Burney as well as for
other pioneering women of the late eighteenth century a turn toward the
literary marketplace of print represented an assertion of independence.
The version of literary authorship which she pursued over the course of
her career was constructed specifically in opposition to the constricting
and now anachronistic process of manuscript production and distribution. Ultimately, Burney stood for a professionalism that would serve her
fiscal and artistic ambitions. Professional authorship allowed the public to
have access to her writings while it preserved her sense of privacy. In contrast, a private means of literary distribution results in public humiliation.
Burney is thus a prominent writer whose career helped to create (rather
than merely reflect) "the triumph of print." She was a woman author
who shaped the literary history that is occasionally described as "male."

Scribal publication – or, at least, the circulation of manuscripts as the
primary mode of distribution of some literary works – was alive and well
at the end of the eighteenth century. Such a reality belies the truism that
the "rise" of print publication in the seventeenth and eighteenth centuries
spelled the end for a rich and complex literary culture of manuscript circulation. Like "patronage," which underwent alteration of form rather
than extinction during the long eighteenth century,[4] manuscript circulation remained important even when print and performance seemed to
render it obsolete. Writers and patrons passed along unprinted writing
for a number of purposes: to receive suggestions for refinement before
publication; to puff works that would eventually be printed and sold; and
to publish manuscript writings whose purpose and meaning worked in
synch with the mechanism of scribal publication.[5] Diaries and journals
of the time abound with verses written and circulated for private purposes of friendship or rivalry. As the Advertisement to Hannah More's
"Bas Bleu: or, Conversation" of 1786 makes clear, the same mode of
manuscripts circulating out of control which induced Pope to revise and
publish the *Rape of the Lock* could force the less disingenuous More to
print the "correct" copy of a poem. The potential of print to fix and
protect an author's work through relative uniformity of appearance and
copyright law could be a last resort rather than a final aim. More writes:

The slight performance . . . was never intended to appear in print: It is, in
general, too local, and too personal for publication; and was only written with

a wish to amuse the amiable Lady to whom it is addressed [Mrs. Vesey], and a few partial friends. But copies having been multiplied, far beyond the intention of the Author, she has been advised to publish it, lest it should steal into the world in a state of still greater imperfection; though she is almost ashamed to take refuge in so hackneyed an apology, however true.

Margaret J. M. Ezell has shown that such claims by authors can be conventional rather than disingenuous. She comments on manuscript culture in the seventeenth century:

[S]elf-deprecation and the repeated insistence on lack of financial motive were at least partially literary conventions . . . rather than a strictly personal revelation. The harshest and most frequent criticism, whether by men or by women, is directed at the "gainsayer," the person who writes for personal profit and glory.[6]

Harold Love has looked in detail at the continued use and transformation of manuscript culture in *Scribal Publication in Seventeenth-Century England*. His description of "The Ambiguous Triumph of Print" characterizes the literary culture that Burney contributed to with her novels – and her plays. Hannah More herself was an unconventional and innovative writer, despite her conservative politics. Increasingly, gestures toward manuscript publication become merely conventional. 1800 is not the point at which the professional writer becomes fully glorified as a creative genius – that she or he has inhabited Foucault's "author function." Neither have all women writers uniformly desired a hearing in the public marketplace of print (let alone overcome the real social restrictions placed upon professional writing, especially for the theater).[7] Burney pioneers the shifts in literary culture towards simultaneously creative and profit-making authorship.

Unlike some of the writers who turned to professionalism from need in the eighteenth century, Burney made her initial forays into writing for publication and performance from a kind of compulsion. Like Alexander Pope, who aspired to the status of a gentleman even as he dirtied his hands in the literary marketplace of the day,[8] Burney wished to profit economically and achieve literary glory from a market she nominally disdained to enter. In the *Epistle to Arbuthnot*, Pope wrote, "I lisp'd in numbers, for the numbers came." As Burney writes of herself in the third person in the *Memoirs of Doctor Burney* in 1832, "At eight years of age she was ignorant of the letters of the alphabet; though at ten, she began scribbling, almost incessantly, little works of invention; but always in private; and in scrawling letters, illegible, save to herself."[9]

Burney's mentor, and her father's friend, Samuel "Daddy" Crisp played into this, pushing Burney to think of herself as a creative genius rather than an artisan. And he used Alexander Pope as the proper example. In response to a letter in which Burney complained about the "hard fagging" of trying to produce a work within the year, he said, "It was not *hard Fagging* that produced such a work as Evelina!—it was the Ebullition of true Sterling Genius! you wrote it, because you could not help it! leave *Fagging*, & Labour, to him

> —who high in Drury Lane,
> Lull'd by soft Zephyrs thro the broken pane,
> Rhymes ere he wakes, & prints before Term Ends,
> *Compell'd by Hunger & request of Friends*

Tis not sitting down to a Desk with Pen, Ink & Paper, that will command Inspiration."[10] Alexander Pope, rather than any of the amateur male or female writers with whom Burney came into contact, presents the most compelling ancestor for the shaping of her authorial career.

Burney's social and professional lives depended upon a clear demarcation between her public, professional life and her private life as a woman. In lines often quoted with puzzlement or disbelief by critics, Burney wrote upon having her hopes for *The Witlings* dashed: "I would a thousand times rather forfeit my character as a *Writer*, than risk ridicule or censure as a *Female*."[11] As a play written for profit as well as artistic satisfaction, *The Witlings* should eventually have been performed and published. Burney circulated the manuscript of the play in order to receive advice – the use of "scribal publication" that has remained potent, at least until the advent of electronic communication. Burney's circulation of her manuscript concluded with what Margaret Anne Doody has called the "censorship" of the play. I wish to discuss here not only the process leading to this suppression, but its implications for understanding the role of gender in manuscript, performance, and print in the eighteenth century.

The story of the composition and subsequent suppression of Burney's *The Witlings* has been well told by Doody in Chapter Three of *Frances Burney: the Life in the Works*, and there is no need to duplicate in detail her narrative, which derives for the most part from Burney's Journals, but includes as well letters of Dr. Burney and an unpublished letter of Burney's sister, Susanna, recounting the reading of the play on 2 August 1779. Most of the story can be traced in the new edition of Burney's *Early Journals and Letters* edited by Lars E. Troide, although some of Burney's continued correspondence on the play must be read in earlier editions of Burney's *Journals* until Troide's edition is complete.

In brief, after the phenomenal success of *Evelina*, Burney was pushed towards a number of literary coteries: the Streatham circle presided over by Hester Thrale; the group of men surrounding Samuel Johnson, Sir Joshua Reynolds, her father Dr. Charles Burney, and others; and the bluestocking circle of women prominent in literary affairs, presided over at this point by Elizabeth Montagu, "queen of the blues." In addition to these gatherings, Burney had an intense literary friendship with Crisp, who acted as an informal literary advisor. At Streatham she was encouraged by Arthur Murphy and Richard Brinsley Sheridan to try her hand at writing a play. In relatively short order, she came up with *The Witlings*, which was understood by its manuscript readers as a satire upon Montagu and the Bluestockings. Eventually, her father and Crisp discouraged Burney, "censoring" her, despite the praise provided by Sheridan and Murphy. Manuscript circulation killed the play. Indeed, I argue that the moments in *The Witlings* in which characters pursue the late eighteenth-century version of scribal publication seem to mark such publication as repressive or amateurish. The play's meaning coheres with its own history in a way certainly not intended by its author.

The Witlings has two main plots. One concerns the sentimental love story involving Beaufort and Cecilia, an orphaned heiress. The other concerns Beaufort's aunt, Lady Smatter, the character who Dr. Burney feared would be associated with Elizabeth Montagu. Lady Smatter heads up the "Esprit Club" and is its resident bad critic. The club's other chief members are Lady Smatter's rival, the trite Mrs. Sapient, and Mr. Dabler, the coterie's bad amateur poet. (We are first introduced to Dabler in Act One by reputation as one who "makes verses upon [Cecilia]."[12]) Also present are Beaufort's slow stepfather, Mr. Codger, and his hyperactive stepbrother Jack. The action of the play is predicated upon an external disaster: Cecilia's guardian – who happens also to manage her inheritance – goes bankrupt. Cecilia is thrown to the mercy of the snobbish and unfeeling Lady Smatter and is banished temporarily to the house of Mrs. Voluble, who also rents a room to Mr. Dabler. While the Club meeting continues in satirized fashion, Mr. Censor goes to Cecilia in the place of his friend Beaufort. Cecilia refuses to listen to him (a somewhat irritating aspect of the plot) and confusion ensues. It turns out that the only way to break Lady Smatter's snobbish resolution to part her nephew from his now penniless love is for Censor to destroy the Esprit Club's literary pretensions. First, he humiliates Dabler by proving his aspirations to poetry to be completely false. (He does so through appropriating one of Dabler's manuscript verses.) Then he threatens Lady Smatter with a series of cutting lampoons which he has written and distributed through manuscript (and the high spirits of Jack). At the end of the play, Censor follows up by providing Cecilia with a portion of £5,000 so that she need not marry Beaufort without self-sufficiency.

Like Hester Thrale, modern critics such as Margaret Doody and Clayton J. Delery (who has edited the play for Colleagues Press) attribute Dr. Burney's suppression of the play to the insult Lady Smatter would give to Elizabeth Montagu. Thrale wrote in her journal that she, like Arthur Murphy, "like[d] it very well for my own part, though none of the scribbling Ladies have a Right to admire its general Tendency."[13] Thrale's footnote to the passage reads: "[Burney's] confidential friend Mr Crisp advised her against bringing it on, for fear of displeasing the female Wits – a formidable Body, & called by those who ridicule them, the *Blue Stocking Club*." Dr. Burney and Crisp apparently understood that the play's strengths consisted of its effective satire, and they feared the result of Frances Burney's giving offense when she was just rising in the literary world. For the play to be successful, it *had* to give offense. Dr. Burney's advice was equivocal. An increase in international tension has, he suggests, made people leery of spending money on the theater, and while he suggests to his daughter that "Many Scenes & Characters might otherwise be preserved," he primarily suggests that she turn from the stage to the writing of novels, in which "there is no danger – & in that, *no times* can affect ye."[14]

In the next year, however, Crisp rejected Burney's offer to revise the play "to entirely omit all mention of the club"; "to curtail the parts of Smatter and Dabbler as much as possible"; and "to change the nature of Beaufort's connexions with Lady Smatter, in order to obviate the unlucky resemblance the adopted nephew bears to our female pride of literature."[15] Crisp responded, "What you mean to leave out – the club and the larger share of Smatter and Dabbler – seems to have been the main subject of the play."[16] Following her father's lead, Crisp pushed Burney toward the form of the novel, which better fit his expectations of propriety and in which her satirical impulses might be diffused. He wished for her to carve out an autonomous position within her literary culture, a position dependent only upon her own genius. The cultural life of the country, her mentors suggested, demanded that as a woman she rely on herself, and the best way for a writer to rely on herself was to pursue the writing of fiction.

Even if in her career as an author Burney was able to pursue a high degree of autonomy, she was seen as part of a competitive marketplace for writing. She had been encouraged even from the beginning of her stay with the Thrales at Streatham to think of Elizabeth Montagu as a rival. *The Witlings*, therefore, might be seen as the product of a directly competitive literary world which her father wanted to draw her away from. Burney had left for her first visit in August 1778, shortly after the publication of *Evelina*. In mid September, Hester Thrale revealed that Montagu was to visit the next day:

Mrs. T To morrow, Sir, Mrs. Montagu Dines here! & then you will have Talk enough.

Dr. Johnson began to see-saw, with a Countenance strongly expressive of *inward fun*, – &, after enjoying it some Time in silence, he suddenly, & with great animation, turned to me, & cried *"Down* with her, Burney! – *down* with her! – spare her not! attack her, fight her, & *down* with her at once! – *You* are a *rising* Wit, – *she* is at the *Top*, – & when *I* was beginning the World, & was nothing & nobody, the Joy of my Life was to fire at all the established Wits! – & then, every body loved to hallow me on; – but there is no Game *now*, & *now*, every body would be glad to see me *conquered*: but *then*, when I was *new*, – to vanquish the Great ones was all the delight of my poor little dear soul! – So at her, Burney! – at her, & *down* with her."

O how we all hollow'd! By the way, I must tell you that Mrs. Montagu is in very great estimation here, even with Dr. Johnson himself, when others do not praise her *improperly*: Mrs. Thrale ranks her as the *first of Women*, in the Literary way.[17]

Johnson assumes that the literary world into which he sees Burney entering operates according to rules shared with the world of writing as it existed at the beginning of his career. This is a *competitive* world, even if competition does not preclude admiration and respect. "O how we all hollow'd" signals Burney's genuine excitement – provoked probably by Johnson's admiration as well as by pride in her own potential for achievement. The competitive vision of women's literary production varies from the picture provided by Sylvia Harcstarck Myers in *The Bluestocking Circle: Women, Friendship, and the Life of the Mind in Eighteenth-Century England*. Influenced by second-wave feminist criticism, Myers recreates the relationships shared among Montagu and other women of letters, underscoring the friendship and shared support in the "circle" of the Bluestockings. It is true that in contrast to the model of competitive authorship promoted by Johnson, Burney herself had hoped for no envy, no enmity to arise from her authorship of *Evelina*. "All *Authorship Contention* I shudder to think of!"[18] Myers thus includes Burney as a second-generation Bluestocking, ending her introduction by quoting Thrale's lines attributing the suppression of *The Witlings* to the offense it would give to Montagu. In general, Myers emphasizes the importance of the closed circle of the coterie to women's literary production in the eighteenth century.

Third-wave feminist criticism has allowed us to complicate our understanding of eighteenth-century female authorship. Myers's own account includes the minor and major rifts that developed between the "members" of this informal literary club. The renewed interest readers have taken in eighteenth-century women's writings has given us a more complete picture of the range of careers followed by women, including Eliza Haywood, Elizabeth Griffith, Frances Brooke, Frances Sheridan, and Charlotte Lennox, whose *Female Quixote* Thrale saw as inferior only to the novels of Rousseau and Richardson.[19] Some of these women wrote professionally during the heyday of the Bluestockings without being admitted into their privileged circles. It is now useful, I think, to acknowledge that all women writers were not members of a team. Issues of social class and literary generation as well as gender must come under consideration for an understanding of the literary politics informing *The Witlings*.[20]

Indeed, Montagu did not think highly of Burney's *Evelina*. A footnote on the page of Thrale's journals that includes her approbation of *The Female Quixote* quotes from a letter from Montagu. Thrale comments: "Mrs. Montagu cannot bear Evelina – let not that be published – her Silver Smiths are Pewterers, She says, & her Captains Boatswains. The Attorney General says you must all have commended it out of a joke, My Master laughs to see me Down among the dead Men & I am happy to see him laugh."[21] Whether or not Montagu's opinion was ever "published" to Burney, it is not far fetched to imagine that Burney might have become aware of its content. Throughout her acquaintance with Montagu, Burney maintained an ambivalence, praising her knowledge and her understanding, while describing gatherings of the Bluestockings in potentially satirical terms.

The play itself was read in manuscript by Dr. Burney to his gathered family. The letter from Burney's sister Susanna describes the moment in which the manuscript for *The Witlings* was turned into private performance:

The Witlings – "Good" s^d. M^r. Crisp – "Good – I like the Name" – the Dramatis Personae too pleased him, & the name of *Codger* occasion'd a general Grin . . . the Milliners Scene & indeed all the first act diverted us *extremely* all round – "It's *funny* – it's *funny* indeed" s^d. M^r. C. who you know does not love to throw away praise – the Second Act I think much improved, & its being more compressed than when I first heard it gives to the whole more *Zest* – it did not flag at all in the reading. – The 3^d. is charming – & they all went off wth. great spirit . . . the fourth act was upon the whole that wch. seemed least to exhilarate or interest the audience, tho' Charlotte laugh'd till she was almost black in the face at Codger's part, as I had done before her – The fifth was more generally felt – but to own the truth it did not meet all the advantages one could wish – My Father's voice, sight, & lungs were tired . . . & being entirely unacquainted wth. what was coming not withstanding all his good intentions, he did not always give the Expression you meant to be given – Yet he exerted himself . . . to give it force and Spirit – & except this Act, I believe only yourself w^d. have read the play better.

For my own part the Serious part seem'd even to improve upon me by this 2^d. hearing, & made me for to cry in 2 or 3 places – I wish there was more of this Sort – so does my Father – so, I believe, does M^r. Crisp – however their sentiments you are to hear fully from themselves, wch. will make me the less eager to write them – Codger & Jack too seem Characters which divert every body, & w^d. yet more I sh^d. imagine in a public Representation. (92)

Although only one manuscript copy of *The Witlings* survives, it is clear from Susanna Burney's letter that she had collaborated with Burney on an earlier version of the play.[22] Her father, however, was reading the play for the first time. Burney collaborated with readers on other works as well, the best-documented example being *Camilla*, which benefited from suggestions provided by her husband and sister before publication, and which was affected by the strictures of critics after.

Although only the one copy remains, it would be inaccurate to think of the play as intended for limited readership or for private performance. Much work has recently been done on closet drama in the late eighteenth and early nineteenth centuries, usefully attempting to overturn notions that public performance should take precedence over the private productions of theatrical works.[23] Women's writing has been shown to overturn an eighteenth-century distinction between public and private spheres. As noted above, however, Burney's writings consistently attempt to differentiate between the public and the private. *The Witlings* is not closet drama, but a play suppressed by the private reading/performance described in Susanna Burney's letter.

As Doody argues, the pseudo-bluestockings in Burney's play are consumed by the same cultural transformations that allowed for the judicial decision in Donaldson v. Becket in 1774, which, as Mark Rose has shown, relied upon allied notions of property, originality, authorship, and aesthetics.[24] Doody draws our attention to the Esprit Club's reliance upon an emergent notion of "originality" in *The Witlings*.

We see clearly that in this vulgar little set, the "'Sprit Party," are victims of a social and intellectual change which not only requires a higher level of culture in well-to-do persons than formerly, but also demands (as it still demands) that new vague something we call "originality." It is that modern, ur-Romantic quality that is pursued so heartily by Mrs. Sapient (in opinions), Dabler (in poems), and Lady Smatter (in criticism). (It is an irony that Dr. Burney in effect accused Frances Burney, who had her own originality, of plagiarizing – that must have hurt.)[25]

In Doody's reading, Burney implicates herself in her play's satire: Mr. Dabler himself possesses traits of his author, and we can recall the preface to *Evelina* which expresses an ambivalence about the possibility and necessity of originality in literary composition.[26]

Judy Simons has observed that in the conclusion of the play "the power of the printed word is nicely proved indomitable."[27] In contrast, I would emphasize the ways in which the play employs and attacks the distribution of literature through manuscript circulation. The printed word never appears directly in the play. While Censor turns out to be no more of a modern *author* than Dabler, he does exhibit genuine skill as a versifier. Burney understands authorship to be based on a contradictory convergence of (low) economic status and (polite) social class. Like Sir Benjamin Backbite's manuscript effusions in Sheridan's *School for Scandal*, Censor's lampoons are inappropriate for a polite world. Because Censor has no personal need to write, his skill comes across as unattractive, although necessary in the play's outdated world of scribal publication. Like the Reverend Marchmont in Burney's third novel, *Camilla* (1796), Mr. Censor is a gentleman of independent means who represents an anachronistic ideal of amateur authorship, indeed of participation in circles of scribal publication as explained by Love. He is intelligent and disinterested, and he produces the directly satiric "lampoons" singled out by Love as characteristic of manuscript culture. (Unlike Sir Benjamin's, however, Censor's lampoons are understood as fair in the context of the play.)

Like Censor, the Esprit Club occupies the amateur end of the world of literary production. Unlike Burney's novels, Mr. Dabler's poems, Lady Smatter's criticism, and Mrs. Sapient's opinions had no value – either monetary or cultural – in the literary marketplace. Their target audience and means of production both remain in the world of the Club, a world as confining as the ideological pressures that Barbara Darby focuses on in her important analysis of *The Witlings*. The play does not include any examples of professional writing; indeed none of Burney's literary works includes a character who successfully pursues a career of selling writing. In her literary works, if not in her life, the best writers are those with independent economic status and judicious temperament.

Barbara Darby's otherwise sensitive reading of the play as a literary text and a performance piece thus oversimplifies the representation of social class in *The Witlings* by suggesting that somehow there is an alliance between the working class and women on the one hand and between moneyed privilege and men on the other. The central character in her analysis, as in the play, is Mr. Censor. In seeing the play into an attack upon Censor, Darby makes it sympathetic to the working class represented by Mrs. Wheedle and Mrs. Voluble and their various assistants. Darby suggests that these apparently downtrodden characters understand the impossibility of genuine independence in the world. According to Darby, these characters are subtly preferred in the play to Beaufort and Censor, who represent male class privilege. Darby's understanding of the play would fit with a version of Burney's biography that demonizes Dr. Burney and Samuel Crisp as the censors who prevent Burney from pursuing her dramatic ambitions. "*The Witlings* depicts the triumph of censorship and subjugation over independence, and it is women who are publicly censored or confined financially, physically, and intellectually."[28]

I would argue, on the other hand, that Mr. Censor's brand of censorship and independence are allied – if somewhat incoherently – in *The Witlings*. For Burney, gender politics and class politics operate independently of each other; moreover, one's identity, either in terms of class or gender, alone provides little in terms of the evaluation of character. The play certainly focuses on the issues of gender and independence, as Darby shows. However, it is as concerned with *literary* politics as gender or class politics. In the print culture of late eighteenth-century England, a culture simultaneously debased and elevated by its reliance upon the supply and demand of readers, writers, and booksellers meeting venally in a literary marketplace, the only genuine alternatives faced by characters of polite status are the useless and self-absorbed exercises of Mr. Dabler and the Esprit Club and the censorious austerity of Mr. Censor. The professional authorship assumed by Burney herself is nowhere present in the play, perhaps because Burney herself had not yet fully realized it. Her subsequent career in writing novels (and plays) served to carve out a niche for the independent female author of polite standing. Professional authorship thus provides a way out of the restrictions of class and gender illustrated in her writings. Thus, her class and gender politics in her literary works can by themselves remain relatively conventional, relatively conservative, while her own life and career blazed new trails.[29]

As Doody points out, the play's opening setting in a milliner's shop is most unusual for an eighteenth-century play, and it signals Burney's interest in and sympathy for the position of women who must work for a living. Nevertheless, Mrs. Wheedle lives up to her name, continually manipulating and lying to her clients. In the beginning of Act I an otherwise unidentified "Young Woman" enters and asks Mrs. Wheedle politely to examine her wares: "If you please, ma'am, I should be glad to look at some Ribbons." Mrs. Wheedle answers, "We'll shew you some presently" (1.30–32), but Mrs. Voluble enters immediately. Mrs. Wheedle offers her a chair and proceeds to enter into a gossipy conversation. Eventually the Young Woman says, "I wish Somebody would shew me some Ribbons, I have waited this half Hour," whereupon Mrs. Wheedle remembers her business: "O, ay, I forgot; do shew this young Gentlewoman some Ribbons. (*in a low voice*) Take last year's. You shall see some just out of the loom" (1.67–71). No stage direction is provided, but we might assume that the Young Woman is led away by one of Mrs. Wheedle's employees to survey old merchandise. The Young Woman is never seen again; the only purpose she serves is to show the manipulation involved in Mrs. Wheedle's business. As Darby shows, all of the satirized characters in the play are dependent upon each other. Darby suggests therefore that somehow these characters are admirable, and their understanding of social complexity undercuts the play's ostensible theme of "self-sufficiency." Censor, whose material generosity and creative power force the apparently happy ending to the play, is a confiner rather than a liberator; freedom and independence are impossible in the world of *The Witlings*.

Doody provides a more nuanced reading both of "self-sufficiency" and of the character of Censor, whom she calls "ambiguously seen throughout."[30] For Doody, Censor represents the failure of literary culture:

[Censor] succeeds in "censoring" Lady Smatter's conduct, but only by proving himself a Witling of sorts, composing verses for his own purposes – and his verses will have to be suppressed, or censored too, after this private hearing. Literary satire, Burney suggests in her satiric play, has little power . . . [31]

This is an astute analysis, and I agree that Censor cannot provide a model for modern literary authorship as Burney understands it. Rather, Censor is the mechanism through which the failure of scribal publication is revealed to the audience of the play. Burney's representation of scribal publication, in its debased form as the late eighteenth-century coterie, centers on the Esprit Club.

The Esprit Club in the play is itself based upon a contradiction in its status. While Censor is a private individual who only *threatens* to enter the public arena, the Club is a properly private venue that aspires to public attention. When in Act II Cecilia declines to enter more fully into the life of the Club by saying, "My pursuits, whatever they might be, are too unimportant to be made public," Lady Smatter replies, echoing the language of originality that she perpetually misuses:

Well to be sure, we are all Born with sentiments of our own, as I read in a Book I can't just now recollect the name of . . . for, I declare, if my pursuits were not made public, I should not have any at all, for where can be the pleasure of reading Books, and studying authors, if one is not to have the credit of talking of them? (II.18–25)

Indeed, she and Dabler confuse the proper roles of the public and private spheres throughout the play: "Oh," she exclaims, also in Act II, "how little does the world suspect, when we are figuring in all the brilliancy of Conversation, the private hardships, and secret labours of a Belle Esprit!" (II.63). Act II sets up the mechanism of scribal publication that the play attacks. Lady Smatter tells Dabler that she has "had the pleasure of seeing something of yours this morning" (II.166–67). Dabler affects "alarm," and complains that "people are so little delicate in taking Copies of my foolish manuscripts, that I protest I go into no House without the fear of meeting something of my own" (II.170–72). Lady Smatter suggests that the memory of a poet should be short, "that his Works may be original," attributing the comment to "Pope or Swift." Dabler reads out his "Epigram upon that very Subject," insisting, however, that his readers "don't get it by Heart," after Codger claims to want to copy it "in my own Hand" the better to appreciate Dabler's talent.

As Doody suggests, Dabler can be seen as a self-deprecating representation of Burney herself. First, he damns himself ironically, when his own ironic self-deprecation becomes truth: "my Writings are mere trifles, and I believe the World would be never the worse, if they were all committed to the flames" (II.222–24). (Beaufort drives the double irony home by telling the audience in an aside, "I would I could try the experiment" [II.225].) Later in the play we will see the boxes of "miniscrips" Dabler keeps in his room, emphasizing the ephemerality of non-published work. Next, Dabler appropriates the notion of natural scribbling to describe himself: "I have indeed . . . some little facility in Stringing Rhymes, but I should suppose there's nothing very extraordinary in that: every body, I believe, has some little Talent, – mine happens to be for Poetry, but it's all a chance! nobody can chuse for himself, and really, to be candid, I don't know if some other things are not of equal importance" (II.232–37). (Here we can recall that Burney herself at age fifteen had "made over to a bonfire . . . her whole stock of prose goods and chattels; with the sincere intention to extinguish for ever in their ashes her scribbling propensity.")[32]

The act continues with Dabler believing that the stupid Codger is a connoisseur who can appreciate Dabler's poetic abilities. Dabler boasts more about his "surprising" facility for versifying, contrasting it with his having been "hard Worked" during charade season when he had to search the dictionary for words with double meanings! Dabler's informal versifying and his method of distributing verse parody the scribal publication of the seventeenth century as outlined by Love. Practically begging Codger to read his work over, Dabler says, "Dear Sir, such trifles as these are hardly worth your serious study; however, if you'll promise not to take a Copy, I think I'll venture to trust you with the manuscript, – but you must be sure not to shew it to a single Soul, – and pray take great care of it" (II.322–25). Codger declines the invitation, upon which Dabler says in an aside, "what a tasteless old Dolt" (II.330).

After Jack reveals the bankruptcy of Cecilia's guardian (prompting Dabler to imagine that he will write a "pretty good Elegy" which "nobody will read with dry eyes" [II.493–99]), Act III moves the action to Mrs. Voluble's house, and we see Dabler in the act of composition. He labors for terrible rhymes, turning to Bysshe's *The Art of English Poetry* for aid. Mrs. Voluble interrupts him just as he thinks he is "upon the point of making as good a Poem as any in the Language" (III.298–99). And he deludes himself into thinking that Censor will approve of his Epigram, which he digs up from the mass of his papers. As with circulation through scribal publication, the method through which Dabler will provide his poem to Censor is anonymous. He will "pass it off for some Dead Poet's" (III.306) although Pope is not good enough for him. Dabler regales Mrs. Voluble with an awful song "*on a young lady blinded by Lightning*" which Mrs. Voluble calls "the prettiest, most moving thing I ever heard in my life" (III.331–39). Mrs. Voluble's approval of the poem follows a pattern set up by *Evelina* as well as the action of *The Witlings*: the mingling of the classes produces promiscuous results. In her first novel, the mixing of the Branghtons with Sir Clement or with Lord Orville produces moments of the most extreme pain for Evelina. Here, the mixing reveals the failure of a private literary culture that pretends to a dignity it cannot attain. The failure of this culture manifests itself in the broken circulation of Dabler's "miniscrips." After Dabler leaves Mrs. Voluble in his room alone to leave for "'*Sprit* Night," she rummages through his papers, sharing such poems as "*A Dialogue between a Tear and a Sigh*" and "*Elegy on the Slaughter of a Lamb*" with her apprentice, Miss Jenny.

Lady Smatter has given Censor a "paper" providing him with information on Cecilia's whereabouts. Censor has refused to give the paper to Beaufort. When he meets Cecilia in Mrs. Voluble's house, she refuses to take a "paper" from him that seems to contain money to tide her over. Everywhere in the play the circulation of information is interrupted by the foolishness of the characters. Act IV – the act that Susanna felt lagged behind the others – continues the play's representation of coterie publication. The Esprit Club meets, and Dabler begins with the recitation of his self-absorbed lines celebrating his fellow members (anticipating Hannah More's lines on the Bluestockings?):

> On a certain Party of Beaux Esprits
> Learning, here, doth pitch her Tent,
>   Science, here, her Seeds doth Scatter;
> Learning, in form of Sapient,
>   Science, in guise of heavn'ly Smatter.
>
> (IV.29–33)

Both women praise Dabler to his face, but sneer in asides that he has overestimated the talents of the other. Censor's arrival on the matter of Cecilia's "business" (which Smatter opposes to the Esprit Club's "Region of Fancy and Felicity" [IV.205]) offers Dabler the opportunity of circulating his verses under pretense that he only has a copy of them, that he did not write them himself. Censor displays his disapprobation of these verses, and Dabler, who has pretended that they are the work of John Gay, "walks aside and writes in his Tablets," claiming that he will turn it into a Lampoon and drop it off at Stapletons', a club Sabor has identified only through a letter of Horace Walpole's. Dabler is following the customs of scribal publication which, as Love points out, often relies on the coffeehouse or club as a site of distribution for manuscripts.

At this point Censor begins to humiliate the members of the club to their faces. He says, for example, that "the principle maxim of the learned members is That no one shall listen to what is said by his neighbor" (IV.322–23). Lady Smatter challenges Dabler to compose an

"Extempore," which, as Sandra Sherman has pointed out, reveals the deficiencies in Dabler's participation in modern culture.[33] Dabler prevaricates until he can take the opportunity to consult one of his manuscript poems, carried about his person in a manner similar to that described by Love. The stage direction states that Dabler drops the manuscript when intending to replace it in his pocket. Censor continues to call Dabler's bluff, giving him a number of topics upon which Dabler might create verses. Finally, Censor asks Dabler to compose an "Epigram on slander," which Dabler wishes to change to fashion. Censor can take his own slanderous story away from this incident; he tells Jack in a whisper meant to be overheard by all, "This anecdote will *Tell* as well without the Verses as with them" (IV.453–55).

Because Dabler has invested his entire image, he is "ruined" by his inability to compose verses extemporaneously. He pretends that he has composed the verses, but that Censor's earlier refusal to hear them has disqualified Censor from hearing them now. Dabler leaves in a huff. Censor quotes from the *Epistle to Arbuthnot* – "Glad of a Quarrel strait he shuts the Door" – and picks up the manuscript of the verse Dabler had claimed to compose on the spot (IV.547). Despite his having told Jack that the anecdote alone would sufficiently condemn Dabler, the manuscript proof of his inability to write seems crucial.

Act V takes place back at the house of Mrs. Voluble. When Mrs. Sapient arrives, Mrs. Voluble defends her gentility as a landlady – and then offers to show Mrs. Sapient up to Dabler's room to have a look at his poems. There is "a matter of an hundred of his *miniscrips*" (V.384–85) on his table. Mrs. Sapient particularly wants to know about Dabler's love poems – it turns out that he is an object of desire for both Mrs. Sapient and Lady Smatter, injecting a note of self-interest into the proceedings of the Esprit Club which, like the Bluestockings described by Myers, pretends to operate through a disinterestedness grounded in the appreciation of culture. Sapient says, "And now perhaps I may discover whether any of his private Papers contain my name" (V.394–95). Dabler, however, returns unexpectedly, forcing Sapient to hide in the closet. Dabler misses the song to Cleora that Voluble had taken from his room to peruse, but she covers by telling him that Sapient is hiding in the closet – and that she "admires Mr. Dabler" (V.469).

Beaufort and Cecilia – whose misunderstanding has been a merely artificial aspect of the plot – make up, but the opposition of Lady Smatter to their marriage still must be overcome. Censor's entrance at V.645 sets the comic ending of the play in motion. He does so, however, through

peculiarly cruel means. Love explains the shift from scribal publication
to print publication through a turn from the direct lampoon of the late
seventeenth century to the irony favored by poets of the eighteenth. As the
anachronism he is, Censor turns to the lampoon to bully Lady Smatter
into submission. Censor *reads* a copy of a manuscript lampoon he claims
to have picked up at the coffeehouse (although he wrote it himself):

> Yes, Smatter is the Muse's Friend,
> She knows to censure or commend;
> And has of Faith and Truth such store
> She'll ne'er desert you – till you're poor.
> (v.661–64)

Dabler calls this "poor stuff" and defends Lady Smatter – until Censor
produces the paper, the "miniscrip," from which Dabler had taken his
supposedly extemporaneous verses on dinner: "your reputation is now
wholly in my power, and I can instantly blast it, alike with respect to
Poetry and to Veracity" (v.676–78).

Smatter suspects that the lampoons were authored by Censor, but he
shows her the manuscripts in another's handwriting, seemingly proving
that they are by another. Burney then includes another extended lampoon, which Censor pretends to have found on the other side of the
paper. This lampoon somewhat cruelly attacks her for her age:

> Were madness stinted to Moorfields
> The World elsewhere would be much thinner;
> To Time now Smatter's Beauty yields –
> She fain in Wit would be a Winner.
> At Thirty she began to read,
> At Forty, it is said, could spell,
> At Fifty, 'twas by all agreed
> A common School Girl she'd excell.
> Such wonders did the World presage
> From Blossoms which such Fruit invited,
> When Avarice, – the vice of Age, –
> Stept in, – and all expectance blighted.
> (v.694–719)

Jack enters singing a ballad which he claims to have taken "from a man
who was carrying it to the Printers" (v.806).

> I call not to Swains to attend to my Song;
> Nor call I to Damsels, so tender and young;
> To Critics and Pedants, and Doctors I clatter,

For who else will heed what becomes of poor Smatter.
   with a down, down, derry down.
This lady with Study has muddled her head;
Sans meaning she talk'd, and Sans knowledge she read,
And gulp'd such a Dose of incongruous matter
That Bedlam must soon hold the Carcase of Smatter.
   with a down, down, derry down.
She thought Wealth esteem'd by the foolish alone,
So, shunning offence, never offer'd her own;
And when her Young Friend dire misfortune did batter,
Too wise to relieve her was kind Lady Smatter.
   with a down, down, derry down.
Her Nephew she never corrupted with pelf,
Holding Starving a Virtue – for all but herself
Of Gold was her Goblet, of Silver, Her platter
To shew how such Ore was degraded by Smatter.
   with a down, down, derry down.
A Club she supported of Witlings and Fools,
Who, but for her Dinners, had scoff'd at her rules;
The reason, if any she had, these did shatter
Of poor empty-Headed, and little-Soul'd Smatter.
   with a down, down, derry down.   (v.772–803)

Censor admits that he is the writer; when Lady Smatter resists him, even though Dabler has been forced to concur with Censor, he threatens to "drop Lampoons in every Coffee-House, Compose Daily Epigrams for all the Papers, Send libels to every corner of the Town, Make all the Ballad Singers resound your Deeds, And treat the Patagonian Theatre with a Poppet to represent you" (v.832–40). Smatter bursts into tears, and Censor follows up with:

But, if you relent, – I will burn all I have written, and forget all I have planned; Lampoons shall give place to panegyric, and libels, to Songs of Triumph; the liberality of your Soul, and the depth of your knowledge shall be recorded by the Muses, and echoed by the whole Nation. (v.844–48)

Censor has won the day for the marriage of Beaufort and Cecilia. He punctuates Act v by giving Cecilia an order for £5,000, which will provide her with a portion. "Dwells Benevolence in so rugged a Garb? – Oh Mr. Censor," exclaims Cecilia (v.901). The play ends with the discovery of Mrs. Sapient in the closet and the hope on Censor's part that "these Witlings will demolish their Club" (v.944).

The play thus exposes the contradictions inherent in the anachronistic system of scribal publication: the coterie of the Esprit Club, which playgoing audiences would likely have associated with the Bluestocking circle, is condemned as an inappropriate site for the production and publication of poetry and criticism. However, the play's comic denouement is predicated upon Censor's *use* of the medium of scribal publication in a seemingly authentic seventeenth-century mode. The culture of scribal publication, which encouraged lampoons and the direct satirical attacks made possible by manuscript circulation, has the potential to harm women even more than men. As Dabler awkwardly stammers, "we men do not suffer in the World by Lampoons as the poor Ladies do; – they, indeed, may be quite – quite ruined by them" (v.741–43). There is no answer provided by the play to the difficulties faced by talented writers in a developing print culture. That *The Witlings* takes recourse in an outdated manuscript culture underscores the impossibility that a writer like Burney could achieve satisfaction in her literary culture – until, that is, Burney herself pioneered a kind of professional literary authorship open to women with her writing and publication of *Camilla*. The play itself, as a piece of literature intended to make money for its author in a public performance, would seem to present an answer, but the history of its suppression only emphasizes the bind in which Burney was placed. *The Witlings* is a conservative play that mixes social and literary classes only to separate them. The play's satiric hero is someone whose literary production is based on an attack on literary culture. Dabler hopes at the end that the Club will disintegrate; its very existence seems to trouble the properly ordered world of literature. Censor's quotation of Pope's *Epistle to Arbuthnot* signals that he, like Pope, must stand alone against a multitude of scribblers.

Burney's play, then, works according to the logic of print as Harold Love interprets it from both Ong's and Kernan's application of the ideas of McLuhan. Love explains the prominence of irony in the eighteenth century as a result of authors' embracing of the possibilities of print. The play as a literary artifact refutes, therefore, the manuscript culture it represents. To the audience, at least, characters like Smatter and Dabler damn themselves through Burney's *ironic* presentation of their speeches and their literary culture more broadly. Censor's asides, however, pointing the audience to Smatter's and Dabler's stupidity, shows that irony alone still won't do. Like others of Burney's characters who resort to direct means of cleansing the *private* sphere of cant – one can think of the cruel violence of Captain Mirvan in *Evelina*, the more measured satire of Gosport in *Cecilia*, or the reserved privacy of Marchmont in *Camilla* – Censor is, again, portrayed "ambiguously." His distasteful lampoons are tactically necessarily. Censor need not, however, escape the restrictive structure of private literary culture in his authorial endeavors. He is a man of genuine intellectual and financial independence, and thus unavailable as a cultural model to others not in his position.

The Witlings is thus primarily concerned with labeling as anachronistic the still powerful manuscript culture of the late eighteenth century. Contemporary print culture is present only in its conspicuous absence and, at this point in Burney's career, does not represent an obvious alternative for the publication of writing. That Dr. Burney and Samuel Crisp were able to induce Burney to give the play up represents the material repercussions of the situation Burney wished to attack. Private literary production leads to censorious suppression or laughable self-indulgence. Evelina's preference had been for open, public declarations. But, as the play shows, women faced particular difficulties when publicity equaled exposure. Burney would eventually be able to accomplish "self-dependence," as Beaufort eulogizes it at the end of the play, only through an authorship centered on novels, which, like print culture more generally, are nowhere to be seen in *The Witlings*.

NOTES

1 Frances Burney, *Evelina* (New York: Norton, 1998), 275.
2 As many commentators have noted, embarrassment is a key issue in *Evelina*. See, most recently, William Gilperin, "The Radical Work of Frances Burney's London," *Eighteenth-Century Life* 20 (1996), 37–48.
3 Burney, *Evelina*, 216.
4 See, most recently, Dustin H. Griffin, *Literary Patronage in England, 1650–1800* (Cambridge: Cambridge University Press, 1996).
5 For puffery, see Margaret M. Smith, "Prepublication Circulation of Literary Texts: the Case of James Macpherson's Ossianic Verses," *Yale University Library Gazette* 64 (1990), 132–57.
6 Margaret J. M. Ezell, *The Patriarch's Wife: Literary Evidence and the History of the Family* (Chapel Hill: University of North Carolina Press, 1987), 89.
7 See Harold Love, *Scribal Publication in Seventeenth-Century England* (Oxford: Clarendon Press, 1993) especially Part II, Chapter 7.
8 See David Foxon and James McLaverty, *Pope and the Early Eighteenth-Century Book Trade* (Oxford: Clarendon Press, 1991).
9 Frances Burney, *Memoirs of Doctor Burney* (London: Edward Moxon, 1832) 2:124.
10 Frances Burney, *The Early Journals and Letters of Fanny Burney*, eds. Lars E. Troide, *et al.* (Kingston: McGill-Queen's University Press, 1988–94) 3:352.
11 Ibid., 3:212.

12 Frances Burney, *The Witlings*, in *Complete Plays*, ed. Peter Sabor, 2 vols. (Montreal & Kingston: McGill-Queens University Press, 1995), vol. 1, 1.50. Further references to the play will be to this edition, and will be cited in the text by act and line number.

13 Hester Lynch Thrale, *Thraliana: the Diary of Mrs. Hester Lynch Thrale (Later Mrs. Piozzi)*, ed. Katharine C. Balderston (Oxford: Clarendon Press, 1951), 1:381.

14 *The Letters of Dr Charles Burney*, ed. Alvaro Ribeiro, S J (Oxford: Clarendon Press, 1991), 1:280–1.

15 Frances Burney, *Diary and Letters of Madame D'Arblay* (London: Henry Colburn, 1842), 1:294–5.

16 Ibid., 1:300.

17 Ibid., 3:150–51.

18 Ibid., 3:399.

19 Thrale, *Thraliana*, 1:329.

20 Use of the word "generation" might cause problems, especially because eighteenth-century culture could oppose women's reproduction and literary production. Nevertheless, there is no word that captures the chronological and psychological position of a writer like Burney in the eighteenth century. Burney's struggle against immediate ancestors – the novelists she cites in the Preface to *Evelina* and the Bluestockings who set some of the possibilities for the culture of feminine genteel writing – informs career and aesthetic choices that she made.

21 Thrale, *Thraliana*, 1:329.

22 See Clayton, J. Delery, ed., *The Witlings* (East Lansing: Colleagues Press, 1995), 21–22, for a description of the manuscript.

23 See, particularly, Catherine B. Burroughs, *Closet Stages: Joanna Baillie and the Theater Theory of British Romantic Women Writers* (Philadelphia: University of Pennsylvania Press, 1997), esp. 1–26.

24 See Mark Rose, *Authors and Owners: the Invention of Copyright* (Cambridge: Harvard University Press, 1993).

25 Margaret Anne Doody, *Frances Burney: the Life in the Works* (New Brunswick: Rutgers University Press, 1988), 81.

26 "To avoid what is common, without adopting what is unnatural, must limit the ambition of the vulgar herd of authors: however zealous, therefore, my veneration of the great writers I have mentioned . . . I yet presume not to attempt pursuing the same ground which they have tracked; whence, though they may have cleared the weeds, they have also culled the flowers, and though they have rendered the path plain, they have left it barren . . . I have, therefore, only to entreat that what I have ventured to say in regard to imitation, may be understood, as it is meant, in a general sense, and not be imputed to an opinion of my own originality, which I have not the vanity, the folly, or the blindness, to entertain," Burney, *Evelina*, 7.

27 Judy Simons, *Fanny Burney* (London: Macmillan, 1987) 121.

28 Barbara Darby, *Frances Burney, Dramatist* (Lexington: University Press of Kentucky, 1997), 22.

29 Burney's "feminism" and the implicit political leanings of her writings have been the subject of much recent criticism. Kristina Straub, *Divided Fictions: Fanny Burney and Feminine Strategy* (Lexington: University Press of Kentucky, 1987) and Marilyn Butler, *Jane Austen and the War of Ideas* (Oxford: Clarendon Press, 1975) remain to me convincing in their portrayals of Burney's politics. See, however, Julia Epstein, *The Iron Pen: Frances Burney and the Politics of Women's Writing* (Bristol: Bristol Classical Press, 1989) for a strongly argued case that Burney's writings are radical in their implications.

30 Doody, *Frances Burney*, 90.

31 Ibid., 90.

32 Burney, *Memoirs of Dr. Charles Burney*, 2:125.

33 Sandra Sherman, "'Does Your Ladyship Mean an Extempore?': Wit, Leisure, and the Mode of Production in Frances Burney's *The Witlings*," *Centennial Review* 40 (1996), 401–28.

Bibliography

PRIMARY SOURCES

Alnwick Castle, Alnwick, MS 110.

Aubrey, John. *Aubrey's Brief Lives*. Edited by Oliver Lawson Dick. London: Secker and Warburg, 1949.

Ballard, George. *Memoirs of Several Ladies of Great Britain*. Edited by Ruth Perry. Detroit: Wayne State University Press, 1985.

Barker, Jane. "A Collection of Poems Refering to the Times; since the Kings Accession to the Crown. Occasionally writ according to the circumstance of time and place" (1700/01). British Library Add. MS 21,621.

A Patch-Work Screen for the Ladies; Or Love and Virtue Recommended: In a Collection of Instructive Novels. London: E. Curll, 1723.

The Lining of the Patch-Work Screen; Designed for the Farther Entertainment of the Ladies. London: A. Bettesworth, 1726.

The Galesia Trilogy and Selected Manuscript Poems of Jane Barker. Edited by Carol Shiner Wilson. Oxford University Press, 1997.

Bèze, Theodore. *The Psalmes of David, Truly Opened and Explaned by Paraphrasis*. Translated by Anthony Gilby. London, 1581. *STC* 2034.

Bodenham, John. *Bel-vedére or the Garden of the Muses*. [Edited by], A. M. [unday?]. London, 1600.

Bowack, John. *The Second Part of the Antiquities of Middlesex*. London, 1706.

Calendar of the Manuscripts of the Marquis of Bath Preserved at Longleat, Wiltshire. Historical Manuscripts Commission. Hereford: His Majesty's Stationery Office, 1908.

Burney, Charles. *The Letters of Dr. Charles Burney*. Edited by Alvaro Ribeiro, S. J. Oxford: Clarendon Press, 1991.

Burney, Frances. *Evelina*. New York: Norton, 1998.

Memoirs of Doctor Burney. 3 vols. London: Edward Moxon, 1832.

Complete Plays. Edited by Peter Sabor. 2 vols. Montreal & Kingston: McGill-Queen's University Press, 1995.

Diary and Letters of Madame D'Arblay. Vol. 1 (1778–80). London: Henry Colburn, 1842.

The Early Journals and Letters of Fanny Burney. 3 vols. Edited by Lars E. Troide *et al*. Kingston: McGill-Queen's University Press, 1988–94.

The Witlings. Edited by Clayton J. Delery. East Lansing: Colleagues Press, 1995.

Calvin, John. *The Institution of Christian Religion*. Translated by Thomas Norton. London, 1578. STC 4418.

The Psalmes of David and Others. With J. Calvins Commentaries. Translated by Arthur Golding. London, 1571. STC 4395.

Calendar of the Manuscripts of the Marquis of Bath Preserved at Longleat. Wiltshire. Historical Manuscripts Commission. Hereford: His Majesty's Stationary Office, 1908.

Carleton, Dudley. *Dudley Carleton to John Chamberlain 1603–1624: Jacobean Letters*. Edited by Maurice Lee. New Brunswick: Rutgers University Press, 1972.

"D. Philippus Sidnaenus. Silva," Exequiae.

Chudleigh. *Les Avantures trop amoureuses, ou Elisabeth Chudleigh*. 1776.

Cleveland, John. *J. Cleaveland* [sic] *Revived*. London, 1659.

Cocks, Roger. *Hebdomada Sacra: a Weekes Devotion: Or, Seven Poeticall Meditations, Vpon the Second Chapter of St. Matthewes Gospell*. London, 1630.

An Answer to a Book Set Forth By Sir Edward Peyton, Knight and Baronet, Carrying this Title, A Discourse Concerning the Fitnesse of the Posture, Necessary to be Used, in Taking the Bread and Wine at the Sacrament. London, 1642.

Collins, An. *Divine Songs and Meditacions*. London, 1653.

Cope, Esther S. (ed.). *Prophetic Writings of Lady Eleanor Davies*. Oxford: Oxford University Press, 1995.

Crum, Margaret (ed.). *The Poems of Henry King*. Oxford: Clarendon Press, 1965.

Daniel, Samuel. *Delia and Rosamond Augment. Edited by Cleopatra*. London, 1594.

Davison, Francis. *Davison's Poetical Rapsody*. Edited by A. H. Bullen. London: George Bell and Sons, 1890.

Delery, Clayton J. (ed.). "Introduction," *The Witlings* (East Lansing: Colleagues Press, 1955), 21–22.

Davies, John of Hereford. *The Muses Sacrifice, or Divine Meditations*. London: George Norton, 1612.

The Writing Schoolemaster or the Anatomie of Faire Writing. 1636. Amsterdam: Walter J. Johnson, 1976.

De Beer, E. S. (ed.). *The Correspondence of John Locke*. 8 vols. Oxford: Clarendon Press, 1976–1993.

Delany, Mary. *The Autobiography and Correspondence of Mary Granville, Mrs. Delany*. [1st–2nd Series.] Edited by Lady Llanover. London: R. Bentley, 1861, 1862.

Dickenson, John. *Arisbas, Euphues amidst his Slumbers: Or Cupids Journey to Hell*. London, 1594.

Donne, John. *The Complete English Poems*. Edited by A. J. Smith. London: Penguin, 1971.

Drayton, Michael. *The Works of Michael Drayton*. Edited by J. William Hebel. Introductions, Notes and Variant Readings. Edited by Kathleen Tillotson and Bernard Newdigate. Oxford: Basil Blackwell, 1931.

Dunton, John. *The Athenian Spy: Discovering the Secret Letters which were Sent to the Athenian Society by the most Ingenious Ladies of the Three Kingdoms* . . . London: R. Halsey, 1704.

Athenianism: or, the New Projects of Mr. John Dunton. London: John Morphew, 1710.

The Life and Errors of John Dunton, Citizen of London. Edited by J. B. Nichols. 2 vols. London: J. Nichols and Bentley, 1818.

Egmont, John Perceval, Earl of. *Diary.* London: Historical Manuscripts Commission, 1920–23.

Englands Helicon 1600. Edited by Hyder Edward Rollins. Cambridge: Harvard University Press, 1935.

Epitaphia in Mortem Nobilissimi et Fortissimi Viri D. Philippi Sidneii Equitis. Edited by Georgius Benedicti (Werteloo). Leiden and Louvain: J. Paedts, 1587.

Exequiae Illustrissimi Equitis, D. Philippi Sidnaei, Gratissimae Memoriae ac Nomini Impensae. Edited by William Gager. Oxford, 1587.

Florio, John, trans. *The Essayes or Morall, Politike and Millitarie Discourses of Michel de Montaigne.* London: Edward Blount, 1603.

Freeman, Sir George. *The Golden Remains of Sir George Freeman.* London, 1682.

Gethin, Lady Grace. *Misery's Virtue's Whet-stone.* London, 1699.

Grosart, Alexander B. (ed.). *The Lismore Papers (First Series), viz., Autobiographical Notes, Remembrances and Diaries of Sir Richard Boyle, First and "Great" Earl of Cork,* 5 vols. Private Circulation Only, 1886.

Halkett, Anne. Halkett MSS, The National Library of Scotland, MS 6495.

Harington Sir John of Kelston. Letter to Lucy, Countess of Bedford, 19 December 1600. Inner Temple Petyt MS 538.43.14, fol. 303v.

"Treatise on Play," *Nugae antiquae: being a Miscellaneous Collection of Original Papers in Prose and Verse; Written in the Reigns of Henry VIII, Queen Mary, Elizabeth, King James, etc. A New, Corrected and Enlarged Edition, in 3 vols.* Edited by Henry Harington (London: J. Dodsley and T. Shrimpton, 1779).

The Letters and Epigrams of Sir John Harington. Edited by Norman Egbert McClure. Philadelphia: University of Pennsylvania Press, 1930.

Nugae Antiquae: being a Miscellaneous Collection of Original Papers in Prose and Verse; Written in the Reigns of Henry VIII, Queen Mary, Elizabeth, King James, &c. A New, Corrected, and Enlarged Edition, in 3 vols. Edited by Henry Harington. London: J. Dodsley and T. Shrimpton, 1779.

Harrowby Manuscripts Trust, Sandon Hall, Stafford.

Hastings Manuscripts. London: Historical Manuscripts Commission, 1934

Haywood, Eliza. *Love in Excess; Or, The Fatal Enquiry.* Edited by David Oakleaf. Peterborough: Broadview Press, 1994.

Hunnis, William. *Seven Sobs of a Sorrowfull Soule for Sinne: Comprehending those seven Psalmes of the Princelie Prophet DAVID, commonlie called Poenitentiall.* London, 1589.

Seven Sobs of a Sorrowfull Soule for Sinne. London, 1583. *STC* 13975.

Certayne Psalmes Chosen out of the Psalter of David, and Drawen Furth into Englysh Meter. London, 1550. *STC* 2727.

Jonson, Ben. *The Complete Poems*. Edited by George Parfitt. Harmondsworth: Penguin Books, 1975; rpt. 1980.

   Poems. Edited by Ian Donaldson. London: Oxford University Press, 1975.

   Works. Edited by C. H. Herford and P. and E. Simpson. 11 vols. Oxford: Oxford University Press, 1925–52.

Kastner, L. E. (ed.). *The Poetical Works of William Drummond of Hawthornden*. 2 vols. Manchester: Manchester University Press, 1913.

Killigrew, Anne. *Poems*, 1686.

Klene, Jean (ed.). *The Southwell-Sibthorpe Commonplace Book: Folger MS V.b.198*. Tempe, AZ: Renaissance English Text Society, 1997.

Lanyer, Aemilia. *The Poems of Aemilia Lanyer: Salve Deus Rex Judaeorum*. Edited by Susanne Woods. New York: Oxford University Press, 1993.

Lewis, Thomas Taylor (ed.). *Letters of the Lady Brilliana Harley*. London: Camden Society, 1854.

Lloyd, John of New College, Oxford (ed.). *Peplus, Illustrissimi viri D. Philippi Sidnaei Supremis Honoribus Dicatus*. Oxford, 1587.

Lodge, John, and Mervyn Archdall. *The Peerage of Ireland; or, a Genealogical History of the Present Nobility of that Kingdom*. 7 vols. Dublin: J. Moore, 1789.

Loomis, Catherine (ed.). "Elizabeth Southwell's Manuscript Account of the Death of Queen Elizabeth [with text]," *English Literary Renaissance* 26 (1996): 482–509.

Lovelace, Richard. *The Poems of Richard Lovelace*. Edited by C. H. Wilkinson. Oxford: Clarendon Press, 1953.

Mahaffy, Robert Pentland (ed.). *Calendar of the State Papers Relating to Ireland, of the Reign of Charles I, 1625–1632*. London: HMSO, 1900.

Marshall, Madeleine Forell (ed.). *The Poetry of Elizabeth Singer Rowe (1674–1737)*. Lewiston/Queenston: The Edwin Mellen Press, 1987.

Matthews, John, and George F. Matthews. *Abstracts of Probate Acts in the Prerogative Court of Canterbury*. London: Chancery Lane [1902].

McClure, Norman Egbert (ed.). *The Letters of John Chamberlain*. 2 vols. Philadelphia: American Philosophical Society, 1939.

Moffet, Thomas. *Nobilis or a View of the Life and Death of a Sidney and Lessus Lugubri*. Edited by Virgil B. Heltzel and Hoyt H. Hudson. San Marino: Huntington Library, 1940.

   The Silkewormes and their Flies: Lively Described in Verse, by T. M. a Countrie Farmar, and an apprentice in Physicke. London, 1599.

Mollineaux, Mary. *Fruits of Retirement*. London, 1702.

Monck, Mary. *Marinda*. London, 1716.

Montagu, Lady Mary Wortley. *Works*. Edited by James Dallaway. London: Phillips, 1803.

   Essays and Poems and Simplicity a Comedy. Edited by Robert Halsband and Isobel Grundy. Oxford: Clarendon Press, 1977. Revised edition, 1993.

   Romance Writings. Edited by Isobel Grundy. Oxford: Clarendon Press, 1996.

Morton, Richard (ed.). *Poems by Mrs. Anne Killigrew*. Gainesville, FL: Scholar's Facsimiles and Reprints, 1967.

Motteux, Peter. *The Gentleman's Journal: or The Monthly Miscellany.* October, 1693.

Neville, Alexander (ed.). *Academiae Cantabrigiensis Lacrymae Tumulo Nobilissimi Equitis, D. Philippi Sidneii Sacratae.* 1587.

Nichols, J. B. (ed.). *The Life and Errors of John Dunton, Citizen of London.* 2 vols. London: J. Nichols and Bentley, 1818.

Osborne, Francis. *Historical Memoires on the Reigns of Queen Elizabeth and King James.* London, 1683.

Parker, Matthew. *The Whole Psalter translated into English Metre.* London, 1567. *STC* 2729.

 The Whole Psalter translated into English Metre, which Contayneth an Hundreth and Fifty Psalmes. London, 1575.

Peacham, Henry. *The Complete Gentleman.* 1622. *STC* 19502.

Polwhele, Richard. *The History of Devonshire in Three Volumes* [1797 and 1806]. London: Kohler & Coombes, 1977.

Prince, John. *Danmonii Orientales Illustres: Or, the Worthies of Devon.* Exeter, 1701.

Rowe, Elizabeth. *Friendship in Death, in Twenty Letters from the Dead to the Living.* 3rd edition. London: T. Worrall, 1733.

 The Miscellaneous Works in Prose and Verse of Mrs. Elizabeth Rowe. Edited by Theophilus Rowe. London: Hett and Dodsley, 1739.

Rudick, Michael (ed.). *The Poems of Sir Walter Ralegh: A Historical Edition.* Tempe, AZ: Renaissance English Text Society, 1999.

Savage, James E. (ed.). *The "Conceited Newe" of Sir Thomas Overbury and His Friends. A Facsimile Reproduction of the Ninth Impression of 1616 of Sir Thomas Ouerbury His Wife.* Gainesville, FL: Scholars' Facsimiles, 1968.

S.C. *The Life of Lady Halket* [sic]. Edinburgh, 1701.

Seager, Francis. *Certayne Psalmes Select out of the Psalter of David and Drawen into Englyshe Metre.* London, 1553. *STC* 2728.

Sidney, Mary. *The Collected Works of Mary Sidney Herbert, Countess of Pembroke.* Edited by Margaret P. Hannay, Noel J. Kinnamon, and Michael G. Brennan. 2 vols. Oxford: Clarendon Press, 1998.

 A Discourse of Life and Death. Written in French by Ph. Mornay. Antonius, A Tragedie written also in French by Ro. Garnier. Both done in English by the Countesse of Pembroke. London: William Ponsonby, 1592.

Sidney, Philip. *An Apologie for Poetrie. Written by the Right Noble, Vertuous and Learned, Sir Philip Sidney, Knight.* London: Henry Olney, 1595.

 The Countesse of Pembrokes Arcadia. Written by Sir Philip Sidney Knight. Now since the first edition augmented and edited. London: William Ponsonby, 1593.

 The Countess of Pembrokes Arcadia. [The Old Arcadia]. Edited by Jean Robertson. Oxford: Clarendon Press, 1973.

 The Countess of Pembrokes Arcadia. [The New Arcadia]. Edited by Victor Skretkowicz. Oxford: Clarendon Press, 1987.

 Miscellaneous Prose of Sir Philip Sidney. Edited by Katherine Duncan-Jones and Jan Van Dorsten. Oxford: Clarendon Press, 1973.

The Poems of Sir Philip Sidney. Edited by William A. Ringler, Jr. Oxford: Clarendon Press, 1962.

Syr P. S. His Astrophel and Stella. London: Thomas Newman, 1591.

Sidney, Philip, and Mary Sidney Herbert, Countess of Pembroke. *The Psalms of Sir Philip Sidney and the Countess of Pembroke*. Edited by J. C. A. Rathmell. New York: New York University Press, 1963.

Sidney, Robert. *The Poems of Robert Sidney*. Edited by P. J. Croft. Oxford: Clarendon Press, 1984.

Singer, Elizabeth. *Poems On Several Occasions. Written by Philomela*. London: Dunton, 1696.

Sternhold, Thomas, John Hopkins, *et al*. *The Whole Booke of Psalmes. Collected into English meter*, by Tho. Sternhold, Joh. Hopkins, and others. London, 1569. *STC* 2440.

Suckling, Sir John. *Fragmenta Aurea. A collection of all the Incomparable Peeces written by Sir John Suckling*. London, 1646.

Sullivan, Ernest W. (ed.). *The First and Second Dalhousie Manuscripts: Poems and Prose*. Facsimile edn. Columbia: University of Missouri Press, 1988.

The Swedish Intelligencer. The Third Part. London, 1633.

Surrey, Henry Howard, Earl of. *The Poems of Henry Howard, Earl of Surrey*. Edited by Frederick Morgan Padelford. Seattle: University of Washington Press, 1928.

Sylvester, Josuah, trans. *Bartas: His Devine Weekes and Workes*. London: Humfrey Lownes, 1605.

Lachrimæ Lachrimarum. 1613. STC 23578.

The Divine Weeks and Works of Guillaume de Saluste Sieur du Bartas. Edited by Susan Snyder. Oxford: Clarendon Press, 1979.

Thrale, Hester Lynch. *Thraliana: the Diary of Mrs. Hester Lynch Thrale (Later Mrs. Piozzi)*. Edited by Katharine C. Balderston. 2 vols. Oxford: Clarendon Press, 1951.

Tyler, Margaret, trans. *The First Part of the Mirrour of Princely deeds and Knighthood...Nowe newly translated out of Spanish into our vulgar English tongue, by M. T.* London: Thomas East, 1578.

Vivian, J. L. (ed.). *The Visitations of the County of Devon, Comprising the Herald's Visitations of 1531, 1564 and 1620*. Exeter, 1889–95.

Walsh, William. *A Dialogue Concerning Women, Being a Defence of the Sex. Written to Eugenia*. London: R. Bentley and J. Tonson, 1691.

Wharncliffe MS M 506, Sheffield Central Library.

Whyte, Rowland. Letter to Robert Sidney, 14 January 1598. De L'Isle and Dudley MS U1475 C12/121.

Wither, George. *Abuses Stript, and Whipt* 1613. *STC* 25891.

A Preparation to the Psalter. London, 1619. *STC* 25914.

The Schollers Purgatory. London, 1624.

Wroth, Mary Sidney. *The First Part of The Countess of Montgomery's Urania by Lady Mary Wroth*. Edited by Josephine A. Roberts. Binghamton: MRTS/RETS, 1995.

Lady Mary Wroth's "Love's Victory": the Penshurst Manuscript. Edited by Michael
  G. Brennan. London: The Roxburghe Club, 1988.
The Poems of Lady Mary Wroth. Edited by Josephine A. Roberts. Baton Rouge:
  Louisiana State University Press, 1983.
Lady Mary Wroth: Poems. A Modernized Edition. Edited by R. E. Pritchard. Keele:
  Keele University Press, 1996.

SECONDARY SOURCES

Adamson, J. H. and H. F. Folland. *The Shepherd of the Ocean: an Account of Sir Walter
  Ralegh and His Times.* London: The Bodley Head, 1969.
Alexander, Gavin, "Constant Works: a Framework for Reading Mary Wroth."
  Sidney Newsletter & Journal 14.2 (1996): 5–32.
  "Five Responses to Sir Philip Sidney 1586–1628." Ph.D. thesis, University of
  Cambridge, 1996.
  "A New Manuscript of the Sidney Psalms: a Preliminary Report." *Sidney
  Journal* 20 (2000).
Attridge, Derek. *Well-Weighed Syllables: Elizabethan Verse in Classical Meters.*
  Cambridge: Cambridge University Press, 1974.
Austern, Linda. " 'For Music is the Handmaid of the Lord': the Psalm Tradi-
  tion and Women's Musical Performance in Late Renaissance England."
  Paper read at the annual meeting of the Renaissance Society of America,
  University of Maryland, March 1998.
Backscheider, Paula R. *Spectacular Politics: Theatrical Power and Mass Culture in Early
  Modern England.* Baltimore: Johns Hopkins University Press, 1993.
Baker-Smith, Dominic. " 'Great Expectation': Sidney's Death and the Poets." In
  Sir Philip Sidney: 1586 and the Creation of a Legend. Edited by Jan Van Dorsten,
  Dominic Baker-Smith and Arthur F. Kinney. Leiden: J. J. Brill and Leiden
  University Press, 1986, 83–103.
Ballaster, Ros. "Seizing the Means of Seduction: Fiction and Feminine Identity
  in Aphra Behn and Delarivier Manley." In *Women, Writing, History 1640–
  1740.* Edited by Isobel Grundy and Susan Wiseman. Athens: University of
  Georgia Press, 1992, 93–108.
Barash, Carol. *English Women's Poetry, 1649–1714: Politics, Community, and Linguistic
  Authority.* Oxford: Clarendon Press, 1996.
Baron, Helen. "Mary (Howard) Fitzroy's Hand in the Devonshire Manuscript."
  Review of English Studies, n.s. 45 (1994): 318–335.
Beal, Peter. *In Praise of Scribes: Manuscripts and their Makers in Seventeenth-Century
  England.* Oxford: Clarendon, 1998.
  Index of English Literary Manuscripts, 1450–1700. 4 vols. London: Bowker and
  Mansell, 1980–93.
Beal, Peter, and Griffiths, Jeremy. *English Manuscript Studies 1100–1700.* Vol. 1
  (1989).
Beilin, Elaine. *Redeeming Eve: Women Writers of the English Renaissance.* Princeton:
  Princeton University Press, 1987.

Blain, Virginia, Isobel Grundy, and Patricia Clements (eds.). *The Feminist Companion to Literature in English*. New Haven: Yale University Press, 1990.

Bland, Mark. "The Appearance of the Text in Early Modern England." *Text* 11 (1998): 14–17.

Bradshaw, Brendan, J. C. Simms, and C. J. Woods. "Bishops of the Church of Ireland from 1534." In *A New History of Ireland*. Edited by T. W. Moody, F. X. Martin, and F. J. Byrne. Oxford: Clarendon Press, 1984.

Brennan, Michael G. "The Badminton Manuscript of Sir Richard Barckley's *A Discourse of the Felicitie of Man* (1598)." *EMS* 6 (1996): 70–92.

"The Date of the Countess of Pembroke's Translation of the Psalms." *RES* 33 (1982): 434–36.

"'First rais' de by thy blest hand, and what is mine/inspird by thee': the 'Sidney Psalter' and the Countess of Pembroke's completion of the Sidneian Psalms." *Sidney Newsletter & Journal*, 14.1 (1996): 37–44.

"Licensing the Sidney Psalms for the Press in the 1640s." *N&Q* 31 (1984): 304–05.

Literary Patronage in the English Renaissance: the Pembroke Family. London: Routledge, 1988.

"Sir Robert Sidney and Sir John Harington of Kelston." *N&Q* 34 (1987): 232–37.

"William Ponsonby: Elizabethan Stationer." *Analytical and Enumerative Bibliography* 7 (1983): 91–111.

Brown, Nancy Pollard. "Paperchase: the Dissemination of Catholic Texts in Elizabethan England." *English Manuscript Studies 1100–1700* 1 (1989): 120–43.

Burke, Bernard. *The General Armory of England, Scotland, Ireland and Wales*. London, 1884.

Burke, Victoria E. "Women and Early Seventeenth-Century Manuscript Culture: Four Miscellanies." *The Seventeenth Century* 12 (1997): 135–150.

Burroughs, Catherine B. *Closet Stages: Joanna Baillie and the Theater Theory of British Romantic Women Writers*. Philadelphia: University of Pennsylvania Press, 1997.

Butler, Marilyn. *Jane Austen and the War of Ideas*. Oxford: Clarendon Press, 1975.

Butler, Martin. "Jonson's Folio and the Politics of Patronage." *Criticism* 35 (1993): 377–90.

Carlson, David R. *English Humanist Books: Writers and Patrons, Manuscript and Print, 1475–1525*. Toronto: University of Toronto Press, 1993.

Cavanaugh, Jean C. "The Library of Lady Southwell and Captain Sibthorpe." *Studies in Bibliography* 20 (1967): 243–54.

Charles, Amy M. *A Life of George Herbert*. Ithaca: Cornell University Press, 1977.

Child, Elizabeth. "'To Sing the Town': Women, Place and Print Culture in Eighteenth-Century Bath." *Studies in Eighteenth-Century Culture* 28 (1999): 155–72.

Clarke, Elizabeth. "'A Heart terrifying Sorrow': The Deaths of Children in Women's Manuscript Writing." In *Representations of Deaths of Children*. Edited by Gillian Avery and Kimberley Reynolds. London: Macmillan, 1999.

Cokayne, G. E. *The Complete Peerage of England, Scotland, Ireland, Great Britain and the United Kingdom, Extant, Extinct or Dormant.* 13 vols. London: St. Catherine's Press, 1910–59.

Cope, Esther S. *Handmaid of the Holy Spirit: Dame Eleanor Davies, Never Soe Mad A Ladie.* Ann Arbor: University of Michigan Press, 1992.

Crane, Mary Thomas. *Framing Authority: Sayings, Self, and Society in Sixteenth-Century England.* Princeton: Princeton University Press, 1993.

Crawford, Patricia. "Women's Published Writings 1600–1700." In *Women in English Society 1500–1800.* Edited by Mary Prior. London: Methuen, 1985.

Croiset Van Uchelen, Anthony R. A. "Dutch Writing-Masters and the 'Prix de la Plume Couronee.'" *Quaerendo* 6 (1976).

Dalton, Charles. *Life and Times of General Sir Edward Cecil.* 2 vols. London, 1885.

Darby, Barbara. *Frances Burney, Dramatist.* Lexington: University Press of Kentucky, 1997.

Darling, John Lindsay. *St. Multose Church, Kinsale.* Cork, 1895.

Davis, Joel. "Stoicism and Gender: the Conditions of the Literary Quarrel between Fulke Greville and the Countess of Pembroke." Papers read at the Medieval Congress, Kalamazoo, Michigan, Part 1 in 1999 and Part 2 in 2000.

De Ricci, Seymour, and W. J. Wilson. *Census of Medieval and Renaissance Manuscripts in the United States and Canada.* 2 vols. New York: H. W. Wilson, 1935.

Doelman, Jim. "A Seventeenth-Century Publication of Three of Sir Philip Sidney's Psalms." *N&Q* 38 (1991), 162–63.

Doody, Margaret Anne. *Frances Burney: the Life in the Works* (New Brunswick: Rutgers University Press, 1988).

Donawerth, Jane. "Women's Poetry and the Tudor-Stuart System of Gift Exchange." In *Women, Writing, and the Reproduction of Culture in Tudor and Stuart Britain.* Edited by Mary E. Burke, Jane Donawerth, Linda L. Dove, and Karen Nelson. Syracuse: Syracuse University Press, 2000, 13–18.

Dove, Linda L. "Composing (to) a Man of Letters: Lady Anne Southwell's Acrostic to Francis Quarles." *ANQ* 11 (1998): 12–17.

Dubrow, Heather. *Echoes of Desire: English Petrarchism and its Counterdiscourses.* Ithaca: Cornell University Press, 1995.

Duncan-Jones, Katherine. Review of *The Poems of Lady Mary Wroth*, edited by Josephine A. Roberts. *RES* n.s. 36 (1985): 565–66.

Sir Philip Sidney: Courtier Poet. New Haven: Yale University Press, 1991.

Epstein, Julia. *The Iron Pen: Frances Burney and the Politics of Women's Writing.* Bristol: Bristol Classical Press, 1989.

Erskine-Hill, Howard. "Literature and the Jacobite Cause: was there a Rhetoric of Jacobitism?" In *Ideology and Conspiracy: Aspects of Jacobitism, 1689–1759.* Edited by Eveline Cruickshanks. Edinburgh: John Donald Publishers, 1982.

Evans, Robert C. *Ben Jonson and the Poetics of Patronage.* Lewisburg: Bucknell University Press, 1989.

Ezell, Margaret J. M. "The Myth of Judith Shakespeare: Creating the Canon of Women's Literature." *New Literary History* 21 (1990): 579–92.

The Patriarch's Wife: Literary Evidence and the History of the Family. Chapel Hill: University of North Carolina Press, 1987.

Writing Women's Literary History. Baltimore: Johns Hopkins University Press, 1993.

"Elizabeth Delaval's Spiritual Heroine: Thoughts on Redefining Manuscript Texts by Early Women Writers." *English Manuscript Studies 1100–1700* 3 (1992): 216–237.

Social Authorship and the Advent of Print. Baltimore: Johns Hopkins University Press, 1999.

"The *Gentleman's Journal* and the Commercialization of Restoration Coterie Literary Practices." *Modern Philology* 89 (1992): 323–40.

Ferguson, Margaret W. "Renaissance Concepts of the 'Woman Writer.'" In *Women and Literature in Britain 1500–1700.* Edited by Helen Wilcox. Cambridge: Cambridge University Press, 1996, 143–168.

Fisken, Beth Wynne. "'To the Angell spirit...': Mary Sidney's Entry into the 'World of Words.'" In *The Renaissance Englishwoman in Print: Counterbalancing the Canon.* Edited by Anne M. Haselkorn and Betty S. Travitsky. Amherst: University of Massachusetts Press, 1990, 265–66.

Fleay, Frederick G. *Biographical Chronicle of the English Drama 1559–1642.* 2 vols. London: Reeves and Turner, 1891.

Forman, Valerie. "Contested Narratives: Historical Writing and the Genealogy of 'Women' in Marguerite de Navarre's *The Heptameron.*" Paper presented at the Shakespeare Association of America conference, Cleveland, March 1998.

Foucault, Michel. "What is an Author?" In *The Foucault Reader.* Edited by Paul Rabinow. New York: Pantheon Books, 1984, 101–20.

Foxon, David, and James McLaverty. *Pope and the Early Eighteenth-Century Book Trade.* Oxford: Clarendon Press, 1991.

Fullard, Joyce. *British Women Poets 1600–1800: an Anthology.* Troy: Whitston, 1990.

Gilperin, William. "The Radical Work of Frances Burney's London." *Eighteenth-Century Life* 20 (1996): 37–48.

Goldberg, Jonathan. *Desiring Women Writing: English Renaissance Examples.* Stanford: Stanford University Press, 1997.

Writing Matter: from the Hands of the English Renaissance. Stanford: Stanford University Press, 1990.

Goreau, Angeline. *The Whole Duty of a Woman: Female Writers in Seventeenth-Century England.* Garden City: Dial Press, 1985.

Greene, Roland. *Post-Petrarchism: Origins and Innovations of the Western Lyric Sequence.* Princeton: Princeton University Press, 1991.

Greer, Germaine, Susan Hastings, Jeslyn Medoff, and Melinda Sansone (eds.). *Kissing the Rod: an Anthology of Seventeenth-Century Women's Verse.* London: Virago Press, 1988.

Griffin, Dustin H. *Literary Patronage in England, 1650–1800.* Cambridge: Cambridge University Press, 1996.

Grimaldi, David A. *Amber: Window to the Past*. New York: American Museum of Natural History, 1996.

Grundy, Isobel. " 'The Entire Works of Clarinda': Unpublished Juvenile Verse by Lady Mary Wortley Montagu." *Yearbook of English Studies*, 7 (1977): 91–107.

Lady Mary Wortley Montagu: Comet of the Enlightenment. Oxford: Clarendon Press, 1999.

Hageman, Elizabeth H. "Women's Poetry in Early Modern Britain." In *Women and Literature in Britain 1500–1700*. Edited by Helen Wilcox. Cambridge: Cambridge University Press, 1996, 190–208.

Hannay, Margaret P. " 'Your vertuous and learned Aunt': the Countess of Pembroke as a Mentor to Mary Wroth." In *Reading Mary Wroth: Representing Alternatives in Early Modern England*. Edited by Naomi J. Miller and Gary Waller. Knoxville: University of Tennessee Press, 1991.

"The Countess of Pembroke as a Spenserian Poet." In *Pilgrimage for Love: Festschrift for Josephine A. Roberts*. Edited by Sigrid M. King. Tempe: RETS/MRTS, 1999, 41–62.

" 'House-confinéd maids': the Presentation of Woman's Role in the *Psalmes* of the Countess of Pembroke." *English Literary Renaissance* 24 (1994): 20–35.

" 'My lute awake': Music and Pembroke's *Psalmes*." Paper read at the annual meeting of the Renaissance Society of America, University of Maryland, March 1998.

" 'O Daughter Heare': Reconstructing the Lives of Aristocratic Englishwomen." In *Attending to Women in the Renaissance*. Edited by Betty Travitsky and Adele Seeff. Newark: University of Delaware Press, 1997, 35–63.

Philip's Phoenix: Mary Sidney, Countess of Pembroke. New York: Oxford University Press, 1990.

" 'So may I with the *Psalmist* truly say': Early Modern Englishwomen's Psalm Discourse." In *Write or Be Written: Early Modern Women Poets and Cultural Constraints*. Edited by Barbara Smith and Ursula Appelt. Aldershot: Ashgate Press, forthcoming.

" 'When riches growes': Class Perspective in Pembroke's *Psalmes*." In *Women, Writing, and the Reproduction of Culture in Tudor and Stuart Britain*. Edited by Mary E. Burke, Jane Donawerth, Linda L. Dove, and Karen Nelson. Syracuse: Syracuse University Press, 2000, 77–97.

Hans, Marlene R. "The Pious Mrs. Rowe." *English Studies* 76 (1995): 34–51.

Harper Smith, T. and A. *Acton People 1200–1700*. Acton: Local History Society, 1989.

St. Mary's Acton: a Guide. Acton: Local History Society, 1985.

Hay, Millicent V. *The Life of Robert Sidney, Earl of Leicester (1563–1620)*. Washington, DC: Folger Shakespeare Library, 1984.

Hay-Halpert, Peter. "Who says it's a Man Ray?" *American Photographer*, 6 (1995): 22–24.

Heale, Elizabeth. "Women and the Courtly Love Lyric: The Devonshire MS (BL Additional 17492)." *Modern Language Review* 90 (1995): 296–313.

Heawood, Edward. *Watermarks, Mainly of the Seventeenth and Eighteenth Centuries.* Hilversum, Holland: Paper Publications Society, 1950.

Hind, Arthur M. *Engraving in England in the Sixteenth and Seventeenth Centuries.* 3 vols. Cambridge: Cambridge University Press, 1952.

Hobbs, Mary. *Early Seventeenth-Century Verse Miscellany Manuscripts.* Aldershot: Scholar Press, 1992.

Hobby, Elaine. *Virtue of Necessity: English Women's Writing 1649–1688.* Ann Arbor: University of Michigan Press, 1989.

Hudelson, Richard W. Letter to the editor. *Perspectives* Feb. 1994: 7.

Hughes, Helen Sard. *The Gentle Hertford: her Life and Letters.* New York: Macmillan, 1940.

"Elizabeth Rowe and the Countess of Hertford." *PMLA* 59 (1944): 726–46.

Hunter, J. Paul. "The Insistent I." *Novel* 13 (1979): 19–37.

Before Novels: The Cultural Contexts of Eighteenth-Century English Fiction. New York: W. W. Norton, 1990.

Ilchester, Earl of. *Lord Hervey and his Friends, 1726–38, Based on Letters from Holland House, Melbury, and Ickworth.* London: John Murray, 1950.

John, Lisle Cecil. "Ben Jonson's 'To Sir William Sidney on His Birthday.'" *Modern Language Review* 52 (1957): 168–76.

Johns, Adrian. *The Nature of the Book: Print and Knowledge in the Making.* Chicago: University of Chicago Press, 1998.

Jones, Ann Rosalind. *The Currency of Eros: Women's Love Lyric in Europe, 1540–1620.* Bloomington: Indiana University Press, 1990.

Kernan, Alvin. *Samuel Johnson and the Impact of Print.* Princeton: Princeton University Press, 1987.

King, Kathryn R. "Galesia, Jane Barker, and a Coming to Authorship." In *Anxious Power: Reading, Writing, and Ambivalence in Narrative by Women.* Edited by Carol J. Singley and Susan Elizabeth Sweeney, 91–104. Albany: State University of New York Press, 1993.

"Jane Barker, *Poetical Recreations*, and the Sociable Text." *ELH* 61 (1994): 551–70.

"The Poems of Jane Barker: the Magdalen Manuscript." *Magdalen College Occasional Paper* 3. Edited by C. Y. Ferdinand. Magdalen College, Oxford, 1998.

"Of Needles and Pens and Women's Work." *Tulsa Studies in Women's Literature* 14 (1996): 77–93.

King, Kathryn R., with Jeslyn Medoff. "Jane Barker (1652–1732) and Her Life: the Documentary Record." *Eighteenth-Century Life* 21 (November 1997): 16–38.

Kinnamon, Noel J. "God's 'Scholler': the Countess of Pembroke's *Psalmes* and Beza's *Psalmorum Davidis . . . Libri Quinque.*" *N&Q* March 1997: 85–88.

Klein, Lisa. "Your Humble Handmaid: Elizabethan Gifts of Needlework." *Renaissance Quarterly* 50 (1997): 459–94.

Klene, Jean. "Recreating the Letters of Lady Anne Southwell." In *New Ways of Looking at Old Texts: Papers of the Renaissance English Text Society, 1985–1991.*

Edited by W. Speed Hill. Binghamton, NY: Renaissance English Text Society, 1993, 239–52.

Kothe, Ana. "Displaying the Muse: Print, Prologue, Poetics, and Early Modern Women Writers Published in England and Spain." Ph.D. thesis, University of Maryland (1996).

Kuin, Roger. "Absent Presence: Sidney and Mornay's Library." Paper read at Medieval Congress, Kalamazoo, Michigan, 8 May 1998.

    Chamber Music: Elizabethan Sonnet Sequences and the Pleasure of Criticism. University of Toronto Press, 1997.

    "The Genesis of *Astrophil and Stella*." Paper read at Medieval Congress, Kalamazoo, Michigan, May 2000.

Lamb, Mary Ellen. *Gender and Authorship in the Sidney Circle*. Madison: University of Wisconsin Press, 1990.

Lee, Stephen J. *The Thirty Years War*. London: Routledge, 1991.

Lewalski, Barbara K. *Protestant Poetics*. Princeton: Princeton University Press, 1979.

Lipking, Joanna. "Fair Originals: Women Poets in Male Commendatory Poems." *Eighteenth-Century Life* 12 (1988): 58–72.

Love, Harold. *Scribal Publication in Seventeenth-Century England*. Oxford: Clarendon Press, 1993.

Lysons, Daniel. *The Environs of London*. London, 1795.

Maddison, Arthur R. *An Account of the Sibthorp Family*. Lincoln, 1896.

Marotti, Arthur. *John Donne: Courtier Poet*. Madison: University of Wisconsin Press, 1986.

    Manuscript, Print, and the English Renaissance Lyric. Ithaca: Cornell University Press, 1995.

May, Steven. The *Elizabethan Courtier Poets: the Poems and their Contexts*. Asheville: Pegasus Press, 1999.

    Sir Walter Ralegh. Twayne English Authors Series. Boston: Twayne, 1989.

    "Tudor Aristocrats and the Mythical 'Stigma of Print'." *Renaissance Papers* 10 (1980), 1–18.

McBride, Kari Boyd. "Remembering Orpheus in the Poems of Aemilia Lanyer." *SEL* 38 (1998): 87–108.

McDowell, Paula. "Consuming Women: The Life of the 'Literary Lady' as Popular Culture in Eighteenth-Century England." *Genre* 26 (1993): 219–52.

McEwen, Gilbert D. *The Oracle of the Coffee House: John Dunton's Athenian Mercury*. San Marino: The Huntington Library, 1972.

McGovern, Barbara. *Anne Finch and Her Poetry: a Critical Biography*. Athens and London: University of Georgia Press, 1992.

Medoff, Jeslyn. "The Daughters of Behn and the Problem of Reputation." In *Women, Writing, History 1640–1740*. Edited by Isobel Grundy and Susan Wiseman. Athens: University of Georgia Press, 1992.

Merton, Charlotte. "The Women Who Served Queen Mary and Queen Elizabeth: Ladies, Gentlewomen, and Maids of the Privy Chamber, 1553–1603." Ph.D. thesis, University of Cambridge (1992).

Messenger, Ann. *His and Hers: Essays in Restoration and Eighteenth-Century Literature.* Lexington: University Press of Kentucky, 1986.

Miller, Naomi J. *Changing the Subject: Mary Wroth and Figurations of Gender in Early Modern England.* Lexington: University Press of Kentucky, 1996.

Neale, J. E. *Elizabeth I and her Parliaments.* New York: St. Martin's Press, 1958.

Norbrook, David. " 'The blushing tribute of a borrowed muse': Robert Overton and his Overturning of the Poetic Canon." *English Manuscript Studies* 4 (1993): 220–266.

Orgel, Stephen, and Roy Strong. *Inigo Jones: the Theatre of the Stuart Court.* London: Sotheby Parke Bernet, 1973.

Orrell, John. "Antimo Galli's Description of *The Masque of Beauty.*" *Huntington Library Quarterly* 43 (1979–80): 13–23.

Otten, Charlotte F. *English Women's Voices, 1540–1700.* Miami: Florida International University Press, 1992.

Parker, Geoffrey. *The Thirty Years' War.* London: Routledge, 1984.

Parks, Stephen. *John Dunton and the English Book Trade: a Study of his Career with a Checklist of his Publications.* New York: Garland Publishing, 1976.

Parry, Graham. "Lady Mary Wroth's *Urania.*" *Proceedings of the Leeds Philosophical and Literary Society* (Literary and Historical Section), 21.4 (1975): 51–60.

Patterson, Annabel. *Censorship and Interpretation: the Conditions of Writing and Reading in Early Modern England.* Madison: University of Wisconsin Press, 1984.

Paul, James Balfour (ed.). *The Scots Peerage Founded on Wood's Edition of Sir Robert Douglas's Peerage of Scotland.* 8 vols. Edinburgh: Douglas, 1908.

Pearson, Jacqueline. "The History of *The History of the Nun.*" In *Rereading Aphra Behn: History, Theory, and Criticism.* Edited by Heidi Hutner. Charlottesville: University Press of Virginia, 1993.

Poinar, George O., Jr. *Life in Amber.* Stanford: Stanford University Press, 1992.

Poort, Marjon. "The Desired and Destined Successor." In *Sir Philip Sidney: 1586 and the Creation of a Legend.* Edited by Jan Van Dorsten, Dominic Baker-Smith, and Arthur F. Kinney. Leiden: J. J. Brill and Leiden University Press, 1986, 25–37.

Prescott, Anne Lake. *French Poets and the English Renaissance: Studies in Fame and Transformation.* New Haven: Yale University Press, 1978.

Pritchard, R. E. " 'I Exscribe Your Sonnets': Jonson and Lady Mary Wroth." *Notes & Queries* 242 (1997): 526–8.

Rathmell, J. C. A. "Jonson, Lord L'Isle and Penshurst." *English Literary Renaissance* 1 (1971): 250–60.

Richetti, John J. *Popular Fiction Before Richardson: Narrative Patterns 1700–1739.* Oxford: Clarendon Press, 1992.

Rienstra, Debra K. "Aspiring to Praise: the Sidney–Pembroke Psalter and the English Renaissance Lyric." Ph.D. thesis, Rutgers University, 1995.

"Singing to the Lord a New Song: the Reformation and the English Religious Lyric." *Perspectives* January 1994: 14–18.

Riggs, David. *Ben Jonson: a Life*. Cambridge: Harvard University Press, 1989.

Roberts, Josephine A. "Lady Mary Wroth." In *Dictionary of Literary Biography. Volume One Hundred and Twenty-One. Seventeenth-Century British Nondramatic Poets. First Series*. Edited by M. Thomas Hester. Detroit and London: Gale Research Inc., 1992.

"The Huntington Library Manuscript of Lady Mary Wroth's Play, *Loves Victorie*." *HLQ* 46 (1983), 156–74.

Rothrock, George A. *The Huguenots: a Biography of a Minority*. Chicago: Nelson Hall, 1979.

Rose, Mark. *Authors and Owners: the Invention of Copyright*. Cambridge: Harvard University Press, 1993.

Rowlands, Penelope. "A Posthumous Recovery." *Art News* 95 (1996): 40.

Sanders, Eve Rachele. *Gender and Literacy on Stage in Early Modern England*. Cambridge: Cambridge University Press, 1998.

Saunders, J. W. "From Manuscript to Print: a Note on the Circulation of Poetic MSS. in the Sixteenth Century." *Proceedings of the Leeds Philosophical and Literary Society* 6 (1951): 507–28.

"The Stigma of Print: a Note on the Social Bases of Tudor Poetry." *Essays in Criticism* 1 (1951): 139–64.

Schleiner, Louise. *Tudor and Stuart Women Writers*. Bloomington: Indiana University Press, 1994.

Seaton, Ethel. *Literary Relations of England and Scandinavia in the Seventeenth Century*. Oxford: Clarendon Press, 1935.

Shaw, William A. *The Knights of England*. 2 vols. London: Sherrat and Hughes, 1906.

Sherman, Sandra. "'Does Your Ladyship Mean an Extempore?': Wit, Leisure, and the Mode of Production in Frances Burney's *The Witlings*." *Centennial Review* 40 (1996): 401–28.

Shevelow, Kathryn. *Women and Print Culture: the Construction of Femininity in the Early Periodical*. London and New York: Routledge, 1989.

Shuger, Debora K. *Sacred Rhetoric: the Christian Grand Style in the English Renaissance*. Princeton: Princeton University Press, 1988.

Simons, Judy. *Fanny Burney*. London: Macmillan, 1987.

Simpson, Evelyn M. "John Donne and Sir Thomas Overbury's 'Characters'." *Modern Language Review* 18 (1923): 410–15.

Smith, Logan Pearsall. *The Life and Letters of Sir Henry Wotton*. 2 vols. Oxford: Clarendon Press, 1907.

Smith, Margaret M. "Prepublication Circulation of Literary Texts: the Case of James Macpherson's Ossianic Verses." *Yale University Library Gazette* 64 (1990): 132–57.

Smith-Rosenberg, Carroll. "The Female World of Love and Ritual: Relations Between Women in Nineteenth-Century America." In *Disorderly Conduct: Visions of Gender in Victorian America*. New York: Knopf, 1985.

Spencer, Jane. *The Rise of the Woman Novelist: from Aphra Behn to Jane Austen*. Oxford: Blackwell, 1986.

Stecher, Henry F. *Elizabeth Singer Rowe, the Poetess of Frome: a Study in Eighteenth-Century English Pietism.* Bern and Frankfurt: Herbert Lang and Peter Lang, 1973.

Stephen, Leslie, and Sidney Lee (eds.). *Dictionary of National Biography.* 22 vols. Oxford: Oxford University Press, 1917.

Stewart, Richard W. "Arms and Expeditions: the Ordnance Office and the Assaults on Cadiz (1625) and the Isle of Rhé (1627)." In *War and Government in Britain, 1598–1650.* Edited by Mark Charles Fissel. Manchester: Manchester University Press, 1991, 115–21.

Stortoni, Laura Anna (ed.). *Women Poets of the Italian Renaissance: Courtly Ladies and Courtesans.* Translated by Laura Anna Stortoni and Mary Prentice Lillie. New York: Italic Press, 1997.

Straub, Kristina. *Divided Fictions: Fanny Burney and Feminine Strategy.* Lexington: University Press of Kentucky, 1987.

Straus, Ralph. *The Unspeakeable Curll.* London: Chapman and Hall, 1927.

Taylor, Dick, Jr. "The Masque and the Lance: the Third Earl of Pembroke in Jacobean Court Entertainments." *Tulane Studies in English* 8 (1958): 21–53.

Todd, Janet. *The Sign of Angellica: Women, Writing, and Fiction, 1660–1800.* London: Virago, 1989.

— *A Dictionary of British and American Women Writers 1660–1800.* London: Methuen, 1987.

Trill, Suzanne. " 'Speaking to God in His Phrase and Word': Women's Use of the Psalms in Early Modern England." In *The Nature of Religious Language: a Colloquium*, Roehampton Institute London Papers. Sheffield: Sheffield Academic Press, 1996, 1:269–83.

— "Spectres and Sisters: Mary Sidney and the 'Perennial Puzzle' of Renaissance Women's Writing." In *Renaissance Configurations: Voices/Bodies/Spaces, 1580–1690.* Edited by Gordon McMullan. London: Macmillan, 1998, 191–211.

Tully, Judd. "The Kahlo Cult." *Art News* 93 (1994): 126–33.

Turner, Cheryl. *Living by the Pen: Women Writers in the Eighteenth Century.* London and New York: Routledge, 1992.

Tytler, Sarah, and J. L. Watson. *The Songstresses of Scotland.* 2 vols. London: Strahan & Co., 1871.

Venn, John, and J. A. Venn. *Alumni Cantabrigienses.* Cambridge: Cambridge University Press, 1922.

Vincent, Helen. "'Divine *Sir Philip*'?: Henry Constable's Dedicatory Sonnets and Henry Olney's edition of the *Apologie for Poetrie.*" Paper read at the Sixteenth-Century Studies Conference, St. Louis, October 1999.

Voss, Paul J. "Books for Sale: Advertising and Patronage in Late Elizabethan England." *Sixteenth Century Journal* 29 (1998): 733–56.

Wall, Wendy. *The Imprint of Gender: Authorship and Publication in the English Renaissance.* Ithaca: Cornell University Press, 1993.

Waller, Gary F. *Mary Sidney, Countess of Pembroke: a Critical Study of Her Writings and Literary Milieu.* Salzburg: Institut für Anglistik und Amerikanistik, 1979.

The Sidney Family Romance: Mary Wroth, William Herbert, and the Early Modern Construction of Gender. Detroit: Wayne State University Press, 1993.

" 'This Matching of Contraries': Calvinism and Courtly Philosophy in the Sidney Psalms." *English Studies* 55 (1974): 22–31.

Warkentin, Germaine. "Patrons and Profiteers: Thomas Newman and the 'Violent Enlargement' of *Astrophil and Stella*." *Book Collector* 34 (1985): 461–87.

Watson, Elizabeth Porges. "Narrative Psychomachia: Rescue and Self-Mastery in *Arcadia*." *Sidney Journal* 15 (1997): 21–36.

Wayne, Don E. "Jonson's Sidney: Legacy and Legitimation in *The Forrest*." In *Sir Philip Sidney and the Interpretation of Renaissance Culture*. Edited by Gary F. Waller and M. D. Moore. London: Croom Helm, 1984.

Williams, Franklin. "Sir John Harington." *TLS*, 4 September 1930: 697.

Woudhuysen, H. R. *Sir Philip Sidney and the Circulation of Manuscripts 1558–1640*. Oxford: Clarendon Press, 1996.

Wright, H. Bunker. "Matthew Prior and Elizabeth Singer." *Philological Quarterly* 24 (1945): 71–82.

Ziegler, Georgianna. "Jewels for the Soul: The Psalm Books of Esther Inglis." Paper read at the 1998 annual meeting of the Renaissance Society of America, University of Maryland, March 1998.

Zim, Rivkah. *English Metrical Psalms: Poetry as Praise and Prayer, 1535–1601*. Cambridge: Cambridge University Press, 1987.

Index

Adams, Bishop (of Limerick), 100
Adams, Dr. Bernard, 98
Alexander, Gavin, 20, 30, 34, 46n.69
Alexander, Sir William, 85
All the French Psalm Tunes with English Words, 38
Amber, 121
America Online, 4
Anne, Queen (of England), 74, 87, 110
Askew, Anne, 23
Astell, Mary, 194
Attridge, Derek, 66
Aubrey, John, 22, 28
Augustine, Saint, 95
Austern, Linda, 38

Ballard, George, 134
Ballaster, Ros, 163
Banks, Mary, 183
Barash, Carol, 176
Barker, Jane, 137–53, 179n.29, 191; and
    Jacobitism, 137, 138, 139–40, 141, 142,
    144–6, 147, 150; and manuscript culture,
    137–40, 142–43, 149–50, 151–52; and
    print publication, 141–42, 147, 152–53;
    and religion, 139, 144–45. Works: "A
    Collection on Poems Refering to the
    Times," 138, 145, 149; "Fidelia alone,"
    145; "Fidelia walking the Lady Abess
    comes to her," 139; *Lining of the Patch-Work
    Screen*, 137, 147–53; *A Patch-Work Screen for
    the Ladies*, 137, 141–49; "Poems on Several
    Occasions in Three Parts," 138, 145,
    155n.9; *Poetical Recreations*, 138, 143, 154n.6
Barthes, Roland, 2
Bath, England, 134
Battiferra, Anne, 23
Baxter, Nathaniel, 19
Beal, Peter, 8, 121, 159
Beaumont, Francis and John Fletcher, 158
Bedford, Lucy Russell, Countess of, 23,
    92n.50, 110

Beer, Anna, 119n.45
Behn, Aphra, 138, 182, 183, 192, 193
Beilin, Elaine, 85
Bentley, Thomas, 23
Bèze, Theodore de, 21, 62, 64, 68, 71n.19
Bingley, Sir Ralph, 99
Biondi, Giovanni Francesco, 191
Bland, Mark, 30
Blount, Lady Anne, 99
Bluestockings, 207–08, 219, 221n.20
Bodenham, John, 32–33
Book of Common Prayer, 38
Bowden, Henry, 168
Bowker, John, 95
Bowyer, Ann, 102
Boyle, Sir Richard, *see* Cork, Earl of
Brennan, Michael, 26, 30, 35, 39, 46n.69
Breton, Nicholas, 22, 30
British Library, 96, 97
Brooke, Frances, 208
Browne, Sir Thomas (cousin of Sir Richard
    Boyle), 97
Buchanan, George, 64
Bulstrode, Cecily, 110
Burnet, Gilbert (Bishop of Salisbury), 184
Burney, Dr. Charles, 204, 205, 208, 210, 220
Burney, Frances, 169–70, 201–20; and
    authorship, 207, 211–12, 220; and
    Bluestockings, 202, 205; and manuscript
    circulation, 201–2; and Elizabeth
    Montagu, 206, 208. Works: *Camilla*, 209,
    210, 219; *Ceclia*, 219; *Evelina*, 201, 207,
    208, 219; *Memoirs of Doctor Burney*, 203;
    The Witlings, 204–20
Burney, Susanna, 204, 208–09, 215
Bute, Mary Wortley Montagu Stuart, Countess
    of, 183–98; rift with mother, 194;
    manuscript writings of, 185, 186, 189–92,
    197; as "Sylvia," 189, 192, 193, 195–96
Butler, Martin, 86
Bysshe, Edward, 214

240